UNDER THE GAZE OF THE FATHER

Visit our web site at
www.albahouse.org
(for orders www.stpauls.us)

or call 1-800-343-2522 (ALBA)
and request current catalog

CONCEPCIÓN CABRERA DE ARMIDA

Under the Gaze of the Father
Conchita's Reflections on a Retreat

Retreat Directed by Archbishop Luis M. Martínez
on the Grace of the Mystical Incarnation
1935

ST PAULS

Original Spanish title *La Encarnación Mística*,
Ejercicios Espirituales 1935, Ediciones Cimiento, México
Presentation and Commentary
Clara Eugenia Labarthe, RCSCJ
Translated, edited and annotated for the English edition by
Sr. Elzbieta Sadowska, RCSCJ and Msgr. Arthur B. Calkins.
Cover: Fr. Eugenio Cárdenas Ramos, Missionary of the Holy Spirit

Library of Congress Cataloging-in-Publication Data

Conchita, 1862-1937.
 [Encarnación mística. English].
 Under the gaze of the Father : retreat directed by Archbishop Luis M. Martínez on the Grace of the Mystical Incarnation, 1935 / Concepción Cabrera de Armida.
   p. cm.
 Translated, edited, and annotated for the English ed. by Elzbieta Sadowska and Arthur B. Calkins.
 Includes bibliographical references.
 ISBN 978-0-8189-1340-2
 1. Spiritual life—Catholic Church. 2. Martínez, Luis M. (Luis Maria), 1881-1956—Sermons. 3. Spiritual retreats. I. Martínez, Louis, 1881-1956. II. Sadowska, Elzbieta. III. Calkins, Arthur Burton. IV. Title.
 BX2350.3.C6513 2005
 269'.6—dc23
                        2011021976

Nihil Obstat
Rafael Ledezma, M.Sp.S.
Jesús María, San Luis Potosí, Mexico
August 4, 1997

Imprimatur
Melecio Picazo, M.Sp.S.
August 4, 1997

Produced and designed in the United States of America by the
Fathers and Brothers of the Society of St. Paul,
2187 Victory Boulevard, Staten Island, New York 10314-6603
as part of their communications apostolate.

ISBN 10: 0-8189-1340-1
ISBN 13: 978-0-8189-1340-2

© *Copyright 2011 by the Society of St. Paul / Alba House*

Printing Information:

Current Printing - first digit	1	2	3	4	5	6	7	8	9	10

Year of Current Printing - first year shown

2011   2012   2013   2014   2015   2016   2017   2018   2019   2020

ACKNOWLEDGMENTS

Our heartfelt gratitude
to Msgr. Arthur B. Calkins for theological consultation,
to James Wierzbicki and all who have collaborated
in the preparation of this book.

TABLE OF CONTENTS

Presentation xi

Biographical Notes xiii

Introduction xix

October 14, 1935 - 1st Day
Meditation of Archbishop Martínez 3
Personal Reflection of Conchita 6

October 15, 1935 - 2nd Day
Meditation of Archbishop Martínez 9
Personal Reflection of Conchita 13

October 16, 1935 - 3rd Day
Meditation of Archbishop Martínez 21
Personal Reflection of Conchita 25

October 17, 1935 - 4th Day
Meditation of Archbishop Martínez 33
Personal Reflection of Conchita 37

October 18, 1935 - 5th Day
Meditation of Archbishop Martínez 38
Personal Reflection of Conchita 40

October 19, 1935 - 6th Day
Meditation of Archbishop Martínez 43
Personal Reflection of Conchita 48

October 20, 1935 - 7th Day
Meditation of Archbishop Martínez 51
Personal Reflection of Conchita 54

October 21, 1935 - 8th Day
Meditation of Archbishop Martínez 59
Personal Reflection of Conchita 63

October 22, 1935 - 9th Day
Meditation of Archbishop Martínez 64
Personal Reflection of Conchita 67

October 23, 1935 - 10th Day
Meditation of Archbishop Martínez 68
Personal Reflection of Conchita 72

October 24, 1935 - 11th Day
Meditation of Archbishop Martínez 75
Personal Reflection of Conchita 78

October 25, 1935 - 12th Day
Meditation of Archbishop Martínez 81
Personal Reflection of Conchita 85

October 26, 1935 - 13th Day
Meditation of Archbishop Martínez 88
Personal Reflection of Conchita 92

October 27, 1935 - 14th Day
Meditation of Archbishop Martínez 92
Personal Reflection of Conchita 96

October 28, 1935 - 15th Day
Meditation of Archbishop Martínez 98
Personal Reflection of Conchita 103

October 29, 1935 - 16th Day
Meditation of Archbishop Martínez 103
Personal Reflection of Conchita 107

October 30, 1935 - 17th Day
Meditation of Archbishop Martínez 110
Personal Reflection of Conchita 112

Table of Contents

October 31, 1935 - 18th Day
Meditation of Archbishop Martínez..................................113
Personal Reflection of Conchita................................117

November 1, 1935 - 19th Day
Meditation of Archbishop Martínez..................................117
Personal Reflection of Conchita................................119

November 2, 1935 - 20th Day
Meditation of Archbishop Martínez..................................120
Personal Reflection of Conchita................................123

November 3, 1935 - 21st Day
Meditation of Archbishop Martínez..................................124
Personal Reflection of Conchita................................127

November 4, 1935 - 22nd Day
Meditation of Archbishop Martínez..................................128
Personal Reflection of Conchita................................132

November 5, 1935 - 23rd Day
Meditation of Archbishop Martínez..................................132
Personal Reflection of Conchita................................136

November 6, 1935 - 24th Day
Meditation of Archbishop Martínez..................................137
Personal Reflection of Conchita................................142

November 7, 1935 - 25th Day
Meditation of Archbishop Martínez..................................143
Personal Reflection of Conchita................................146

November 8, 1935 - 26th Day
Personal Reflection of Conchita................................148

November 9, 1935 - 27th Day
Meditation of Archbishop Martínez..................................149
Personal Reflection of Conchita................................153

November 10, 1935 - 28th Day
Meditation of Archbishop Martínez 154
Personal Reflection of Conchita 157

November 11, 1935 - 29th Day
Personal Reflection of Conchita 160

November 12, 1935 - 30th Day
Meditation of Archbishop Martínez 160
Personal Reflection of Conchita 164

November 13, 1935 - 31st Day
Personal Reflection of Conchita 165

November 14, 1935 - 32nd Day
Meditation of Archbishop Martínez 167
Personal Reflection of Conchita 171

November 15, 1935 - 33rd Day
Meditation of Archbishop Martínez 173
Personal Reflection of Conchita 176

November 16, 1935 - 34th Day
Meditation of Archbishop Martínez 179
Personal Reflection of Conchita 183

November 17, 1935 - 35th Day
Meditation of Archbishop Martínez 183
Personal Reflection of Conchita 187

November 18, 1935 - 36th Day
Meditation of Archbishop Martínez 189
Personal Reflection of Conchita 197

Chart of Retreats of Concepción Cabrera de Armida
with Bishop Luis M. Martínez: 1925-1936 199

Endnotes 201

Works by Archbishop Martínez and
Concepción Cabrera de Armida 217

PRESENTATION

Declared Venerable by His Holiness Pope John Paul II on December 20th 1999, Conchita is a bright star in the firmament of the Church's mystics. She fervently wished to love her Lord in a humble, simple, hidden life as wife, mother of nine children and widow. But the Lord singled her out to be the foundress of the Works of the Cross and He endowed her with all of the graces necessary, crowned her with the extraordinary grace of the mystical incarnation, a grace which is the source of many other graces for the life of the Church. The Almighty's gaze rested upon Conchita's humility and insignificance, and raised her to unimaginable heights in a way reminiscent of what He had done in the Virgin Mary.

The mystical incarnation may be compared to the indwelling of Jesus in Mary from the moment of His conception in her womb. The Lord had raised Mary to a level of holiness never to be equaled by any other human being. Nonetheless, the specific grace granted to Conchita on March 25th 1906, as far as we know, has been granted to only a limited number of souls. The fundamental rule is that, even though God grants extraordinary graces to chosen souls, what He confers on them is eventually intended for the up-building of the entire Body of Christ. Since the mystical incarnation which Conchita experienced is rooted in the sacrament of baptism, this grace also constitutes for all of us an invitation to live our baptismal commitment at an ever deeper level. This is precisely what the Fathers of the Second Vatican Council wanted to emphasize in the fifth chapter of *Lumen Gentium* on the universal call to holiness.

Conchita's existence began to enter into new spiritual dimensions when she received the grace of the mystical incarnation, but, as one can see from reading this retreat notebook, it required her cooperation for the rest of her life. She is for all of us, then, a model and example in total submission to the unique grace which the Lord intends for each one of us.

✠ Bishop Joseph J. Madera, M.Sp.S. (Emeritus)
Archdiocese for Military Services
2330 John Still Dr.
Sacramento, CA 95832
USA

BIOGRAPHICAL NOTES

The Venerable Concepción Cabrera de Armida (December 8, 1862-March 3, 1937), or Conchita, as she was lovingly called, was a lay woman, wife, mother of a family of nine children, a widow, and a spiritual writer.[1] She has come to be recognized by many as one of the greatest Mexican mystics.

In her family environment Conchita received the sacraments which she lived with great consistency and maturity from her earliest years. Convinced that matrimony was her vocation, she married Francisco Armida García on November 8, 1884. Her life as wife and mother was happy and fulfilling, but she nonetheless experienced interior emptiness: "in spite of all the happiness of earth," she was led to give "her heart more and more to God."[2]

The death of her priest uncle, Canon Luis Arias, in 1886 "shook her to the core," and opened her to a mystical experience which made her understand that "it is necessary not to be taken up with the things of this world."[3] To her desire for divine love, Jesus responded by opening His Heart to her. Her yearning to know "how to love God" became a constant and insatiable longing. "How is it possible not to see in You, my Jesus, the object of my yearning if in receiving You in Communion I feel that my affections and desires are satisfied? Yes, yes, I have found the Beloved of my heart; I was wandering around, thinking to find happiness where it does not exist, and I was always unhappy; but now that my Jesus fills my soul, leaving it inebriated with delight, now, and only now I am happy."[4]

In her first retreat in 1889, she came to understand that "her mission was to save souls."[5] Her life opened up to people outside of her family circle. Very soon, her own family was to form part of this great spiritual family which God gave her in the Works of the Cross[6] and of which she was the spiritual mother.

In the midst of a rich human experience, filled with happiness, but also with innumerable sorrows, she lived her prophetic mission in the Church, which always needs the witness of holiness. Following the extraordinary spiritual itinerary traced out for her by the Holy Spirit, she became a guide for the spiritual lives of others right from the very beginning of her spiritual journey. In 1889 she gave a retreat to the women of *Hacienda Jesús María*, her family's country estate in Mexico.

Conchita, a lay woman, is a prophetic sign in the Church today, where we have been reminded that all are called to holiness.[7] The Lord called her to live a spiritual maternity toward souls, in order to teach that her mission goes beyond all the frontiers of natural motherhood. This led her to experience that filial love, spousal love, maternal and fraternal love find their true fullness in God, the source of all love, which all human beings desire.

The seventy-five years of Conchita's life coincided with the most severe persecution of the Church in Mexico: from the victory of the Juarez party (1861) until General Ávila Camacho became president (1940). The peaceful environment of the cities and estates of Mexico was disturbed by the great social changes introduced by the liberal Constitution of 1857 and the religious persecution characterized by the expulsion of bishops, priests and religious. During several of these years, the celebration of all religious services was legally prohibited.

Her Spiritual Guides

In spite of the difficult political and religious situation, the Venerable Concepción Cabrera consistently sought the help of enlightened spiritual directors, who gave her wise counsel. In her spiritual journey, she was guided by Father Alberto Cuscó y Mir,

Biographical Notes

S.J. (1893-1903), Father Felix de Jesús Rougier, Archbishop Ramón Ibarra y González (1912-1917), Bishop Emeterio Valverde (1917-1925) and Archbishop Luis M. Martínez[8] (1925-1937).

Under the direction given her by Archbishop Luis M. Martínez,[9] whom Jesus called "son of light," Conchita reached the highest and final stage of her spiritual journey. He helped her to understand in greater depth all the graces she had received, to open herself to receive new ones and prepared her for her encounter with God (1937).

Conchita used to make a directed retreat (spiritual exercises) every year. During her life she made fifty-four retreats, eleven of these with Archbishop Martínez. In 1923, sickness prevented her from making her customary retreat with then Bishop Martínez on Pentecost (May 20). On November 4, 1923, Conchita wrote in her *Account of Conscience*[10] this brief note: "Today His Excellency Bishop Martínez came. I pleaded with him to give a little help to my soul."

In her letter of November 24, 1923,[11] Conchita wrote to Bishop Martínez: "For a long time, in reading your writings,[12] in hearing you preach, you said what I already knew, what I felt, what God had asked me so many times. Then I asked God to open a path before me which would bring me closer to you. He has done it all. I hope that in your kindness you will continue to help me, out of love for God, that from what you read of my writings, you will show me the way, will give me the right practices, will tighten the screws, so that before I die, at least during my last days, I may fulfill the divine will in everything and may not keep anything in the wardrobe. Please give me a shake, because I am dusty. Tell me clearly my great defects, so that I may correct myself. What moves me the most is gratitude for God's benefits, but how many times I have even forgotten to be grateful! I recognize that I need a more intense interior life, recollection and prayer. I need to center my life on the mystical incarnation."

On November 28, 1923, Bishop Martínez answered her letter, telling her that he would give her the retreat in December or in

Lent of 1924. Several difficulties prevented Conchita from going to Morelia in 1924, where he was then Auxiliary Bishop. Spiritual direction with Bishop Martínez continued by mail.

From reading Conchita's writings, Bishop Martínez was able to orient her, taking into account the spiritual graces which she had already received and explaining to her the further degrees to which she should aspire. In this way, he helped her to attain maturity in what she had received and impelled her to open herself to new graces which God in His goodness was preparing for her. The meditations which Bishop Martínez gave Conchita were based on her writings, which he illuminated with his theological knowledge.

From his first letter to her (November 28, 1923), Bishop Martínez insisted that Conchita "had to believe with absolute firmness in God's graces, especially in the *great grace.*" "Constantly consider that your principal duty and, in a certain way, the only one, is to correspond to the strongest inspiration, to the most ardent desire of the Holy Spirit, which is to make you enter fully into the outstanding grace of the mystical incarnation. This grace, under its varied and very rich aspects, has to be the constant object of your *prayer* when God does not dispose otherwise. Your particular examen should also be about the same grace. Our Lord told you a long time ago that your particular examen should be about the Chain,[13] which is the practical application of the mystical incarnation. Your spiritual reading should ordinarily be on your *Account of Conscience*, preferring whatever refers more closely to the mystical incarnation."

In 1925, Bishop Martínez came to Mexico City for health reasons and gave Conchita the retreat in the house of the Religious of the Cross of the Sacred Heart of Jesus. He led her to meditate on the graces that she had received in order to thank the Lord for them. He exhorted her to abandon herself into God's hands, to follow His inspirations faithfully, to walk without being in a hurry, following God's rhythm, in union with Mary.[14] Conchita drew up an account of the graces which she had received up to that time.[15]

Biographical Notes

The resolution she made during that retreat was to simplify her life, basing herself ever more fully upon the mystical incarnation.

On August 15, 1925, Conchita wrote in her letter to Bishop Martínez: "I feel that I am understood, that you can read me, that I am guided. I really see that God has been preparing you for me. I had begged for a director for so long! I can assure you that the name that the Lord gave you is a thousand times wonderful. How much light, and how it radiates and penetrates into my poor and dark soul."

But the relationship and the spiritual influence between the two reached a more profound stage of intimacy from the retreat of 1926 on the theme of "Loving with the Holy Spirit." In the retreats of the following years, Conchita continued to study in depth the great mysteries that Jesus had revealed to her from the beginning of her spiritual journey. Although often touched upon previously, the moment that Providence decreed she should analyze her central grace – the mystical incarnation – came about more thoroughly in 1935, a short time before her death in 1937.

INTRODUCTION

What is the Mystical Incarnation?

The experience of the "mystical incarnation" lived by Concepción Cabrera de Armida offers us a special insight into the unique mystery of the Incarnation of the Son of God "by the power of the Holy Spirit" in the womb of Mary. All the baptized, called to live their union and transformation into Jesus, like Mary and with Mary, can unite themselves to Jesus in His Incarnation, in His redeeming Passion and in His glorious Resurrection. By baptism, the Christian is assimilated and incorporated into Jesus Christ in an intimate and vital union, like that existing between the branches and the vine. That is why it is possible to affirm that "through baptism, we have already been united with Christ."[16]

"The mystical incarnation is the intimate and perfect transformation of the soul, that united to the Holy Spirit through the purest and most profound love, receives from Him the fruitfulness of the Father, and becomes Jesus in order to share in an ineffable way in His intimate priesthood, exercising this priesthood fruitfully on behalf of souls, especially on behalf of priests,"[17] according to the words of Archbishop Martínez. Christ becomes incarnate in the heart of the believer: possessing, invading him in order to attract him, to involve him and to associate him in His work of Redemption, according to the words of St. Paul, "in my flesh, I am filling up what is lacking in the afflictions of Christ on behalf of His Body, which is the Church" (Col 1:24).

In the spiritual itinerary of Concepción Cabrera de Armida,

the centrality of the grace of the mystical incarnation stands out because it is fundamental for the development of her mission – the salvation of souls in union with Jesus.

In this way, a continuous relation with the Holy Trinity was established in Conchita, because she possessed Christ and had put on His sentiments, constantly offering Him to the Father and offering herself in union with Him, with the same personal love of the Son, that is to say, with the Holy Spirit. She lived, breathed and acted in union with the Three Divine Persons, in a connatural intimacy with the Holy Trinity.

This grace which characterized the life of Conchita is a mystical grace of divine and real[18] union with the Word, but this should not be understood materially, as if the Word became incarnate in her body, as He did in Mary. One must never take this expression literally. The symbolic language of the mystics is different from the speculative language of theologians.

It is a particular grace, but not foreign to the development of Christian life, since the mystery of the Incarnation is present in the entire economy of the Church, which acts efficaciously through its sacraments. The Incarnation of the Word is mystically renewed in each sacrament, especially in the Eucharist. In each Mass and Communion, the Word descends and unites Himself with the believer and a sort of mystical incarnation is realized. The Church is the image of Mary because of her virginal fruitfulness by the power of the Holy Spirit, the Author and Divine Source. By grace, the Holy Spirit makes the Word become incarnate in souls, mystically perpetuating in the Church the Incarnation which took place in Mary. The Christian receives this grace in a special way in the sacraments.[19]

The mystical incarnation was a *pre-existing grace* in the loving design of God for Conchita, which originated in the grace of baptism, and which developed gradually and progressively throughout her whole spiritual journey.[20]

The grace of the mystical incarnation was not a static grace, limited to the day of its reception, March 25, 1906. The whole

Introduction

dynamism of mutual compenetration, of transformation, of progressive degrees of union with God, which are countless, "began" on that day. But God's gifts are measureless and the correspondence of the soul to grace never reaches its fullness in this life.[21]

Jesus spoke of it in this way on July 8, 1925: "The Word made flesh takes intimate possession of the heart of the creature, as if taking life from it because of the transforming union, even though He is always giving life to it, that life of assimilating grace, especially through immolation. Jesus becomes incarnate, is born, grows and lives in the soul, not in the material sense, but through sanctifying, unitive and transforming grace. The mystical incarnation is basically a very powerful transforming grace which simplifies and unites, by means of purity and immolation in union with Jesus, which makes the soul and the whole creature, as far as possible, similar to Him."[22]

The Theology of the Heart

The expression "mystical incarnation" appeared for the first time in the work of the French Jesuit Roger Nicolas (1602-1679): "*Incarnatio mystica sive Christi formitas...*" in 1649. This exact expression does not appear in the works of other theologians, but its equivalent can be found in other theologians and, above all, in many mystics.[23]

The theme of the birth of God in the heart of the believer is fundamental in the ecclesiology of the Fathers of the Church. Through the grace of baptism, Christ comes to dwell in our hearts and to transform them. The Fathers of the Church taught that the Church prolongs the virginal maternity of Mary in the sacrament of baptism.

It suffices to mention the names of Clement of Alexandria (born about the middle of the 2nd century, and died between 211 and 216), Irenaeus (died as a martyr in 204), Origen (185-254) and his disciple Hippolytus of Rome (died as a martyr in Sardinia, in 235). We should not forget the contribution of the great

Greek Fathers: Gregory of Nyssa (ca. 335-after 394), Gregory Nazianzen (329-389), Cyril of Alexandria (375-444). We find this doctrine of the indwelling of Christ through baptism further developed by Procopius of Gaza (465-528) and Anastasius of Sinai (7th century). This theology of man's divinization finds a great interpreter in Maximus the Confessor (580-662). In St. Augustine (354-430), it is especially the mystery of the birth of Christ which allows him to speak about the birth of God in the heart. In the Middle Ages, Gregory the Great (540-604), Rabanus Maurus (780-856), Richard of St. Victor (died 1173), Bernard of Clairvaux (1090-1153), the Cistercian Isaac of Stella (1100-1169, France), Bonaventure (1221-1273), Meister Eckhart (1260-1328), John Tauler (1300-1361) all contribute their own insights into this reality. The unique contribution of women is not lacking on the subject of the transforming union with Christ. I shall mention just one of the Helfta mystics, Gertrude the Great (1256-1302) and an Italian mystic, the Foundress of the Congregation of the Holy Redeemer, Maria Celeste Crostarosa (1696-1755). In this brief paragraph, it is impossible to highlight all of the figures who have enriched our understanding of this doctrine in theology and Christian mysticism up to the present.

The Preparation

Already from the beginning of Conchita's spiritual itinerary (the retreat of 1889), she understood that "her mission was to save souls." In 1894, urged by the ardent desire of externalizing her yearning to belong totally to God, she branded the *monogram* (*JHS*) on her chest.[24] Once she had done this, a supernatural force made her ask, ardently, with an all consuming zeal, for the salvation of souls: "Jesus, Savior of men, save them!" This was the program of her whole life.

On January 23, 1894, Conchita received the grace of spiritual betrothal. This "union of her will with Jesus"[25] gave her "incomparable" happiness. This profound experience of living the Paschal

Introduction

Mystery brought her to mystical death and then to mystical rebirth. In this period she experienced passive purifying graces and desolations, but also graces of experiential knowledge of Jesus' humanity and divinity. The promises received in betrothal were ratified in spiritual marriage on February 9, 1897. This new stage of the graces of union and of transformation in the Beloved constituted a period of new insights on God, who is love, on the Trinity, the generation of the Word, the Incarnation, the Holy Spirit, the Eucharist, the interior sorrows of Jesus and the Church.

Shortly after, February 17, 1897, the Lord promised her the grace of the mystical incarnation. "Prepare yourself for the day on which the Church celebrates the Incarnation of the Divine Word; on that day, I descended to unite Myself with Mary, taking flesh in her most pure womb, to save the world. On that day, I want to unite Myself spiritually with your soul and give you a new life, a divine and immortal life, in time and in eternity."[26] On March 9, Jesus explained to her that "He descended to the most pure womb of Mary to suffer for her [Conchita] and He will descend into Conchita's heart so that she can suffer for Him."[27]

Conchita lived these years of the transforming union, nourishing herself on the nuptial character of ecclesial grace. The Spouse revealed to her soul marvelous secrets, as St. John of the Cross expressed it in his *Spiritual Canticle* (stanza 23).

The Historical Fact

The preparation for this outstanding grace, which was to be the central grace of her life, lasted nine years. Conchita narrated as follows the moment when she received the grace of the mystical incarnation on March 25, 1906.[28]

"Before Mass, kneeling in front of the Tabernacle, I humbled myself as much as I could, before my Jesus; I asked pardon, renewed my vows:[29] I promised Him not to fill my heart with earthly things as I had done until now and in this way, empty, I received Him in Communion.[30]

"I wanted to tell my Jesus many things at the 'Incarnatus'[31] and then I did not even know when it was.

"So then in the first 'memento'[32] of the Mass, I felt the presence of my Jesus beside me, and heard His divine voice telling me: 'I am here' (the Lord told me), 'I want to become mystically incarnate in your heart. I fulfill what I offer; I have been preparing you in a thousand ways, and the moment has come to fulfill My promise, RECEIVE ME.' I felt joy mixed with an indescribable shame. I thought that I had already received Him in Communion, but He, as if guessing my thoughts, continued.

"'It is not like that; besides, today you have received Me in another way. I take possession of your heart; I become mystically incarnate in it, so as never to be separated. This is a very great grace which My goodness has been preparing for you; humble yourself and be grateful for it.'"

Because the grace of the mystical incarnation is a kind of "reproduction" of the Incarnation of the Word which took place in Mary, this was realized expressly on March 25. Conchita received it during Mass because the grace is linked intrinsically to the Eucharistic mystery, the sacrament of the Incarnation of the Word. It will be a sort of continuation of the Eucharistic presence in the soul and its effects will be similar to those which Eucharistic communion leaves,[33] but more intense; it is a living and palpitating union with the soul.[34] Conchita was already living in an attitude of poverty, purity, humility, light, transparency, openness, passivity, and spiritual modesty before God. The intensity of the "divine invasion" left her exhausted, with her body worn out, but filled with a holy joy, peace and indescribable well-being.[35]

This new presence of Jesus in her soul absorbed all her energy and her life in such a way that she wanted only to speak of Him, think of Him, aspire to Him, embrace Him, drink Him in, feel Him, breathe Him... in other words, she was attracted, drawn and absorbed in God.[36]

Introduction

Under the gaze of the Father

"God, the Father of our Lord Jesus Christ" (Rm 15:6; 2 Cor 1:2) took the initiative for the redemptive Incarnation of the Word: "When the fullness of time arrived, God sent His Son" (Gal 4:4). Christ is the One sent by the Father (cf. Mt 10:40; Jn 4:34) to fulfill the work of the Father in the world (cf. Jn 5:17, 19ff). The free and gratuitous initiative (Eph 1:4-11; Rm 11:32) of the Father is a commitment of love and comes from God who is love: "Because God so loved the world as to give His only begotten Son, so that all who believe in Him will not perish but will have eternal life" (Jn 3:16).

When the Father gazes, He engenders the Word out of Love, and this is the origin of the mystical incarnation. There where the Father contemplates His Word in the soul, communicated by the Holy Spirit, there He rests His gaze, He empties Himself and rejoices in Himself, along with the Divine Persons who are joined to Him; that is to say, in His Divine Son and in the Holy Spirit. The Father only sees His Word, through the eyes of Love, and in His Word He sees all things.[37]

During the Retreat of 1935, Archbishop Martínez reminded Conchita: "St. Paul says that 'every fatherhood takes its name from the Father in heaven and on earth.' Consequently, the mystical incarnation originates in the heavenly Father, whose reflection it is."[38]

Conchita first perceived the grace of the Father's gaze in 1894, when, after receiving Communion in the Church of Our Lady of Mount Carmel in San Luis Potosí, she suddenly heard the Lord say to her, "The Father is gazing upon you." As she recounted later, those words made her tremble with awe and filled her with love, though she told nobody at the time about it, and did not even know that it was Jesus who had spoken those words and caused her to understand that this divine gaze communicated to her the germ of the grace of the mystical incarnation. Again, in 1935, toward the end of Conchita's life, during the retreat on the general theme of the mystical incarnation, Conchita meditated on that inexhaustible mystery of the Father's gaze, as she had done so fruitfully since that grace had been imparted.[39]

On June 8, 1901, Conchita recorded in her *Account of Conscience* (17, 42-44) "Hours of silence at the foot of the Tabernacle," because "there the One I love the most on earth is locked up... Jesus as Host, sacrificed for me, hidden... silent... obedient... waiting..." "Oh, and how much one can learn at the foot of the Tabernacle!" she would exclaim. Conchita went there to tell Him about her love, her distress over her ingratitude, to ask for graces, to contemplate Him. That day she heard again: "The Father is here looking at you... the Son, offering you His Blood... and the Holy Spirit beating His wings to come to your soul. The Three Divine Persons desire to enter your heart, and to form in it their throne... their cross... their nest... This I heard, and I remained confused... overwhelmed... inflamed before such condescension. He made me see His greatness... power... immensity... Wisdom... and Love... and I (...) placed my forehead on the ground, and I opened the doors of my soul to that most Blessed Trinity, which is real... imprisoned... locked... in a host."

At different moments of her life, Conchita recalled the experience of the Father's gaze. Archbishop Martínez frequently reminded her of the various aspects of that gaze during the retreats that she made with him.

She became ever more aware of the gaze of the Father as a fundamental dynamism in her life. Since "to live under the gaze of the Father is to receive His gift constantly; it is to possess Jesus, the end and precious fruit of this gaze"; it is to live a fruitful life in divine light and eternal love. This gaze is constant even if it is not always perceived by the recipient in a conscious way. "The transformation into Jesus and the gaze of the Father are two aspects of the same incomparable grace." The gaze of God becomes "the outpouring of divine love." "It is not a simple gaze of love, but a gaze which transforms and divinizes, which fuses the soul with God."[40] It is not sufficient to receive the Father's gaze in a merely passive

Introduction

way; rather, one must be open to the divine gaze, which has the power to "inflame in our eyes the fire of our intimate gaze." "Both gazes, the one that comes from heaven and the other that ascends from earth meet, join and are fused."[41] The fruitful gaze of the Father introduces the soul into the bosom of the Trinity. The soul receives the capacity of looking at the Father as Jesus looks at Him and looks at Jesus as the Father looks at Him. The soul acquires a priestly gaze like that of Jesus: "the gaze of the One who loves and offers Himself for the glory of the Father, of the One who implores graces for souls." Jesus grants His powerful gaze to the soul in order to disperse the shadows which envelop souls and purify them so that the Father's image can be found in them.[42]

Development of the grace

The grace of the mystical incarnation implies an itinerary. This is how Jesus explained it to Conchita on May 31, 1927: "On placing the seal of the Holy Spirit in your soul on the day of your baptism, I gave it the gift of the mystical incarnation and this grace continued developing, without your understanding it, until it achieved its goal. This was accomplished by your reliving My life, your coming to understand the ideal that I had for your soul, and your being transformed into Me and thus divinized."[43]

In the development of this grace we can distinguish three different stages: (1) her entry into the mystery of being priest and victim with Christ, (2) her deeper penetration into the mystery of the Eucharist and (3) her deeper awareness of Mary's role in her life. In some way, all these aspects are present from the beginning, but pedagogically, Conchita experienced different aspects with greater intensity and understanding at determinate stages in her spiritual journey.

1. *The aspect of being priest and victim.* In this first stage Conchita understood that the mystical incarnation of Jesus in her has an oblational element. She learned to offer the Word to the Father and to offer herself in union with Him for the same redemptive

purpose. Conchita's intercession acquired a fundamental value by her possessing within her the Divine Victim of Calvary and of the Eucharist. By herself she could do nothing, but having Jesus, she had everything. Jesus in her would do all, thus quenching His thirst to save souls.[44]

This is how Jesus explained it: "Look, My daughter, the first thing that I told you about the mystical incarnation was that you should offer Me on the altar of your heart to My Eternal Father as a holy victim for the world, in atonement for sins, and that you should offer yourself in union with Me."[45]

Conchita was to imitate the Father's love since this is the most perfect love. She was to imitate Mary in uniting her will with the Father's,[46] in offering Jesus on the altar of her soul for the good and the bad.[47]

This is the fundamental mission of priests and it was the co-redeeming mission of Conchita: to sacrifice Jesus for all. In this way, the grace of the mystical incarnation places her in the center of the economy of the Redemption: only the Word became flesh for our salvation and becomes mystically incarnate to be crucified in souls for the world.[48]

The personal mission of Conchita to save souls was identified with the mission of the priest. She would not hold Jesus in her hands like the priest, but she would have Him in her heart, where she could offer the sacrifice pleasing to the Father, and she could identify herself with the Divine Victim by immolating herself in union with Him. Conchita in her heart was at the same time altar and victim,[49] and could render to God the true worship "in spirit and in truth" (Jn 4:23) inaugurated in the new economy of salvation.

Conchita, by virtue of the mystical incarnation, would exercise her baptismal priesthood, not only offering the Incarnate Word, but offering herself in union with Him, that is, by living fully the dynamism of priest and victim.[50] This mission was neatly synthesized by the Lord's oft-repeated words to her: "offer Me and offer yourself," this at every instant, with the purpose of saving souls and of giving glory to the Father.

2. *The Eucharistic aspect.* The Eucharist is the summit and the source of the exercise of the Christian priesthood.[51] It is there that Christ associates His Church in the most eminent way with the offering of His redeeming sacrifice. The faithful, in virtue of their baptismal priesthood, join in the offering of the Eucharist. It is through the sacraments and the exercise of the virtues that the sacred nature and organic structure of the priestly community is brought into operation. The Church, in union with Christ, fulfills the office of priest and victim by offering Him to the Father and offering herself together with Him.[52]

Jesus continued guiding Conchita: "Afterwards I told you to confirm that offering through union and fusion with Me, saying in union with Me: 'This is My Body, this is My Blood,' offering Me and offering yourself to the Eternal Father for the world and in order to obtain graces."[53]

The grace of the mystical incarnation would lead Conchita to live the life of Jesus in such a way that her body was like Jesus' Body and her blood like His Blood, because Jesus, incarnate in her heart, was transforming and uniting her in one and the same immolation. Such an intimate relationship between the Son and Conchita had a redemptive and universal scope: the glory of the Father and the salvation of the world.

In fact, the aspect of oblation acquires an intrinsically Eucharistic connotation; in offering herself, Conchita would not only be assimilated to the Incarnate Word, but would be transformed into Him by means of compenetration and union with the Divine Essence, in order to be one with Christ (cf. Jn 17:20-21). That is why, by the realization of a sort of transubstantiation into Jesus, Conchita could truly say: "this is My Body, this is My Blood,"[54] because she no longer lived her own life, but the life of Christ, who lived in her (cf. Gal 2:20).

Conchita would live this transformation through the exercise of the "Chain of Love."[55] The fruit of the grace of the mystical incarnation is wonderful: "the fruitfulness of the Father is an amazing fruitfulness, because He not only incarnates the Word, but all the virtues as well, so to speak, in the heart, through the Holy Spirit."[56] By the practice of the "Chain," Jesus invited Conchita to the assiduous practice of the virtues and to the offering of Christ and of herself with Him to the Father at every moment of her life.

The *Catechism of the Catholic Church* (n. 1803) teaches us that "a virtue is an habitual and firm disposition to do the good. (...) The goal of a virtuous life is to become like God." Therefore, the practice of the virtues would lead Conchita to be transformed into Christ, "which depends much upon the correspondence of the soul in the practice of the virtues."[57] Conchita was aware that in order to make this offering effective, she would have to become "like the human nature of the Word, with an inseparable, compenetrated divine union, sharing in the divine nature...." Jesus did not possess the virtues in degrees, but rather, He "was the substance of them."[58]

Conchita would live the Mass in a mystically continuous way, prolonging in her heart and in her life the *offertory* and the *consecration*. In this way she would fully live her baptismal priesthood, being a guide and model for the Church and for her spiritual descendants.

On October 20, 1925, Jesus told her: "Your role is that of living a mystically continuous Mass... continuing the offertory, offering Me to the Father and offering yourself with Me, arriving at the consecration repeating in union with Me and My infinite merits: 'This is My Body, this is My Blood.'"[59]

3. *The Marian aspect*. In this third stage, Conchita would live the mystery of the Eucharistic offering in union with Mary. In 1917, Jesus underlined the third stage through which the mystical incarnation passes: "And now I tell you to do all this in union with Mary and with her very heart."[60]

Through the mystical incarnation, Conchita had been associated with the redemptive power of Jesus, and she had to contemplate Mary as a model of this redeeming and universal dynamism. Mary, the Co-redemptrix par excellence, would teach her how to

Introduction

conform her heart to the Heart of Jesus. Mary would teach her to live the priestly and Eucharistic dynamism with a truly motherly heart.

This stage, in which Mary lived her maternal priesthood on behalf of the nascent Church, was the most fruitful in her life, because she continued to offer her Son to the Father and to offer herself in union with Him in order to obtain graces for her new sons. Conchita was to reflect the life of Mary and be a faithful echo of her maternal heart with the same redeeming and glorifying end: the salvation of souls.[61]

Conchita, like Mary, was to be not only mother of Jesus by virtue of the mystical incarnation, but also mother of His Mystical Body, the Church. The participation in the redeeming offering of Jesus would acquire the nuance of ecclesial maternity. Mary would teach her to live her priesthood in a maternal manner.[62]

Conchita would call this stage in the life of Mary, Mother of the Church, "the stage of the solitude of Mary,"[63] which thus expressed Our Lady's intimate and profound sorrow at the absence of her Son.

During these years of solitude, Mary lived her maternal priesthood with perfect joy, with her gaze fixed on her absent Son. Her heart, filled with love and sorrow, longed for full union with the Trinity, while living in faith and hope.

Conchita tried to live this same experience: being the echo of the Heart of Mary, accepting maternally the martyrdom of love for others.[64]

The pneumatological aspect

The pneumatological aspect of the grace of the mystical incarnation is evidently fundamental. The Holy Spirit brought about the mystical incarnation of the Word in Conchita's soul and accompanied the development of this grace, making it bear fruit.

The mystery of the Incarnation and the mystery of the Trinity are intimately and reciprocally related. The Incarnation has its source in the Trinity and the Trinity finds its expression and prolongation *ad extra* in the Incarnation. The fruitfulness of God outside of Himself has its free and gratuitous manifestation not only in creation, but also in the Redemption and in the mission of the Son, who extends participation in the Divine Life to the entire human race.

The Divine Persons act in perfect harmony and synergy among themselves; for instance, the Father acts for and with the Son and in the Holy Spirit. The Incarnation manifests this union of love and activity, in which all three Divine Persons are involved. There is no Incarnation without Trinitarian involvement.

Therefore, since we say that the grace of the mystical incarnation is an extension of the Incarnation in Mary, we can affirm that it is a fundamentally Trinitarian grace which results from the tenderness of the Father, the obedience of the Son and the intense love of the Holy Spirit.[65]

Along with this fundamental Trinitarian aspect, the mystery of the Incarnation of the Son is the work of the Holy Spirit in a specific way. "The fruitfulness of the Father is at work, but the graces are poured out with the cooperation of the Holy Spirit, since He is the Giver of all graces and the one who makes fruitful with His shadow, with His breath, everything that He touches in the order of grace."[66]

On July 3, 1925, Jesus continued to explain to Conchita: "the mystical incarnation of the Word attracts the Holy Spirit, who brought it about in the soul by means of the eternal fruitfulness of the Father and does not separate Himself from it, nurturing it, and overshadowing the Divine Word, Jesus, whose Spirit is the same Holy Spirit."[67]

"Therefore, when the transformation into Jesus is accomplished in the soul, (the mystical incarnation is the grace which helps to bring this about), the Holy Spirit also comes to be the spirit of the creature, to a greater or lesser extent, according to the intensity and degree of transformation, which depends on how the soul corresponds with the virtues. Then, the Holy Spirit, absorbing the spirit of the creature being transformed, fills it with that most pure love which He is. And then with the same love, the creature loves the Divine Word, with the same love with which the Father loves Him and the Father is loved, that is to say, with the perfection of love."[68]

In fact, Conchita would learn to love with the same Spirit of Jesus, that is to say, with the Holy Spirit. She would learn to love Jesus and the Father with the Holy Spirit. In the same way, her love for souls was to be the Holy Spirit Himself.[69] Conchita was unified in love so as "to love with the Holy Spirit." This would have been impossible if her love had not been a participation in God's own love. It was God who allowed her to be able to love with His own inter-Trinitarian love, because, in fact, "the love of God has been poured out into our hearts through the Holy Spirit that has been given to us" (Rm 5:5).

The attainment of "loving with the Holy Spirit" would broaden the dimensions of Conchita's heart, not physically, but in her capacity to love more, in the profundity of love which is never satisfied and which eventually became a martyrdom of love.

Another important aspect of the action of the Holy Spirit in Christ is that He offered Himself to His Father through the Holy Spirit from the moment of the Incarnation until the Cross. This is how the text of the Hebrews 9:14 speaks of Christ: "who through the eternal Spirit offered Himself unblemished to God." The offering of Christ and one's own immolation in union with Him is realized always under the sanctifying action of the Holy Spirit.[70]

The transformation into Christ and the divinization

Transformation into Christ is one of the fundamental aspects of the grace of the mystical incarnation. Through baptism we come to share in the Divine Nature (cf. 2 P 1:4). The Divinity possesses, absorbs and divinizes the creature. This transformation is progressive; it comprises innumerable degrees until it culminates in what St. Paul's words express so well, "yet I live, no longer I, but Christ lives in me" (Gal 2:20), and it requires faithful collaboration on the part of the human being. The creature is not destroyed, but "this grace is so sublime, great and powerful, in this degree of transformation, that the germ of evil remains so weakened that grace dominates it; and then the creature, lost in the Creator, absorbed in God and profoundly penetrated by Him, loves, feels, thinks, acts, desires and wants like the Beloved; both in the most intimate, spiritual and divine part, as in the physical and human part. The Holy Spirit is the only one who can bring about this degree [of transformation], since He becomes the soul of that soul, and the life of that body."[71]

Despite her fears, Conchita progressively came to understand the grace bestowed on her. The words of Jesus, however, made her tremble: "From the time of the mystical incarnation, your body is like My Body – Oh my God, what an embarrassment! – and your blood like My Blood, because I have the power to transform.... I live in you by a sort of hypostatic union, My poor creature; then, allow Me to live My own life in you, giving yourself to souls as I gave Myself, for the same cause and with the same purpose, that is, the glory of My Father and the salvation of the world."[72]

The soul receives new life in the Risen Christ and is then able to love with the Holy Spirit even though the fullness of this love can only be attained in heaven. This new relationship with the Trinity made Conchita experience the divine "as inundating the human part of her being, like an overflowing of the divine which permeated her soul." She felt herself "as if deified, as if she could not separate herself from the divine."[73] Divinization is not an end in itself, but rather a means so that the divinized person becomes ever more oriented to glorify the Trinity and to cooperate with Jesus Christ for the salvation of the world.

Ecclesial Fruitfulness

The grace of the mystical incarnation was multiple in its effects for others and confirmed Conchita in her mission as spiritual

Introduction

mother. Archbishop Luis M. Martínez often stressed the aspect of the maternal fruitfulness which this grace implies.

"The grace of the mystical incarnation is a precious reflection of the Father's fruitfulness, which the Holy Spirit has put in your soul, so that you can cooperate in the mystical formation of Jesus in your own soul and in that of others. It is a grace of divine fruitfulness, the goal of which is Jesus. But the essential purpose of this precious grace is to produce Jesus mystically in souls; it is essentially a grace of fruitfulness,"[74] especially on behalf of priests.

Archbishop Martínez wrote on October 23, 1935: "Upon pouring Himself out in the soul through the mystical incarnation, the Holy Spirit not only makes it Jesus, but also communicates spiritual fruitfulness to it so that the soul may give Jesus to other souls. One's motherhood of Jesus has as its logical consequence one's motherhood of souls, for the whole Jesus, so to speak, also includes His Mystical Body."[75] It is a special gift to give Jesus, to be mystically a mother of other souls.

Conchita had begun this new stage of "priestly" maternity already in 1927. The fruitfulness of the grace of the mystical incarnation "extended" itself to the "Jesus" represented on earth by His priests. This new priestly maternity made her heart beat in unison with the Heart of Jesus. Conchita's heart became the echo of all His joys and sorrows. A covenant was thus established between the Heart of the Son and that of the mother.[76] Conchita participated intimately in Jesus' love and sorrows for His priests. From 1927 to 1932, she received profound confidences on Jesus' love for His priests.[77]

The vocation and mission of Conchita to live her maternal priesthood[78] took the decided orientation of motherhood towards priests. Conchita became aware that she belonged to the Church and that she belonged to priests in a particular way. On receiving the Incarnate Word mystically in her heart, along with Jesus, the Eternal Priest, she received all priests.[79]

In her spiritual maternity all had a place: the pope, with the burdens of the entire Church, cardinals, archbishops, bishops, parish priests, priests and finally, seminarians with their hesitations and vocational struggles.[80]

Conchita's desire to "save souls" found a specific outlet in obtaining from Christ the graces of transformation for priests, so that they would become truly holy priests.

Jesus explained it to her in this way: "If you want to save souls, we have arrived at the powerful and only means: holy priests. And they will be holy in the measure that you sanctify yourself; and they will be pure, in the measure of your purity; and they will be sanctified in the measure of your sacrifices. But all of this will happen, not because of what you are, but because of what you have in you, because of your union with the Word by means of the mystical incarnation, because of My infinite merits, which you have in your hands by having Me in your heart."[81]

The Glory of the Father

The glory of the Father is the crowning grace of the mystical incarnation. In this last stage (1935-1937) of her spiritual life, Conchita consciously simplified and oriented her entire life to seeking only the glory of the Father. This characteristic is the final development of the mystical incarnation. She lived her baptismal priesthood for the Church and especially for priests, with the ultimate purpose of glorifying the Father.

On November 16, 1935, Archbishop Martínez wrote: "As the mystical incarnation has its source in the bosom of the Father, so it also finds its consummation in this loving bosom."[82]

Conchita identified herself with Jesus and with His sentiments, to the extent that she became the echo of His love and His sorrows. By her transformation into Jesus, she would also become assimilated in love to the Father's saving designs and would thus glorify Him.[83]

"When the soul occupies itself only in giving glory to the Father, in consuming all its energies, desires and loves in the one desire and love, ... offering itself in union with the Word to the

Introduction

Father as a victim of eternal expiation, ... only to give Him glory, then she lives the perfect interior life, that is the crowning of the mystical incarnation," according to the wise comments of Archbishop Martínez.[84]

Doing everything for the glory of God is the full development of the mystical incarnation. The Divine Word is the center, the channel by which we give glory to the Father and by which His grace descends, converted in charisms of the highest value. The Divine Word pours Himself out in other souls because of the soul that gives Him glory. Everything that goes from the earth to heaven in union with Jesus returns from heaven to earth, through Jesus, enriched with graces.[85]

The fact that Conchita oriented her entire person to the glory of the Father is obviously not in opposition to her exercise of her maternal priesthood for the Church and for priests. She would not leave aside all her previous spiritual experiences and orientations, but this final aspect is the complement and the crowning of all of God's work in her.[86]

Archbishop Martínez concluded the retreat by inviting Conchita to "live under the gaze of the Father and to correspond to this intimate gaze by which 'God should be all in all' for her." He exhorted her, saying: "You must live the grace of the mystical incarnation intensely and cooperate with all your strength in its full development and happy consummation."[87]

Our baptism is a wonderful gift which has to be lived in fullness. The Word became flesh to make us "partakers of the Divine Nature." "The only begotten Son of God, wanting to make us sharers in His divinity, assumed our nature, so that He, made man, might make men gods."[88]

Sr. Elzbieta Sadowska, RCSCJ
Msgr. Arthur Burton Calkins

Biblical Abbreviations

OLD TESTAMENT

Genesis	Gn	Nehemiah	Ne	Baruch	Ba
Exodus	Ex	Tobit	Tb	Ezekiel	Ezk
Leviticus	Lv	Judith	Jdt	Daniel	Dn
Numbers	Nb	Esther	Est	Hosea	Ho
Deuteronomy	Dt	1 Maccabees	1 M	Joel	Jl
Joshua	Jos	2 Maccabees	2 M	Amos	Am
Judges	Jg	Job	Jb	Obadiah	Ob
Ruth	Rt	Psalms	Ps	Jonah	Jon
1 Samuel	1 S	Proverbs	Pr	Micah	Mi
2 Samuel	2 S	Ecclesiastes	Ec	Nahum	Na
1 Kings	1 K	Song of Songs	Sg	Habakkuk	Hab
2 Kings	2 K	Wisdom	Ws	Zephaniah	Zp
1 Chronicles	1 Ch	Sirach	Si	Haggai	Hg
2 Chronicles	2 Ch	Isaiah	Is	Malachi	Ml
Ezra	Ezr	Jeremiah	Jr	Zechariah	Zc
		Lamentations	Lm		

NEW TESTAMENT

Matthew	Mt	Ephesians	Eph	Hebrews	Heb
Mark	Mk	Philippians	Ph	James	Jm
Luke	Lk	Colossians	Col	1 Peter	1 P
John	Jn	1 Thessalonians	1 Th	2 Peter	2 P
Acts	Ac	2 Thessalonians	2 Th	1 John	1 Jn
Romans	Rm	1 Timothy	1 Tm	2 John	2 Jn
1 Corinthians	1 Cor	2 Timothy	2 Tm	3 John	3 Jn
2 Corinthians	2 Cor	Titus	Tt	Jude	Jude
Galatians	Gal	Philemon	Phm	Revelation	Rv

Retreat Directed by
Archbishop Luis M. Martínez
Morelia, Mexico, 1935

October 14, 1935 [89]

FIRST DAY

Meditation of Archbishop Martínez

As in the previous retreats,[90] the preparation should consist in placing the soul in a state of full and loving docility to the divine action. This disposition requires a threefold self-emptying, and a threefold self-offering.

First, to empty oneself so as not to oppose the motion of the Holy Spirit, and to offer oneself without reserve to His love and action.

Second, to empty oneself so that Jesus may live in one's soul, and to offer oneself to Him in full loving self-giving so that the mystery of unity may be accomplished.

Third, to empty oneself before the heavenly Father so that one's own will may disappear, offering it in holocaust so that the divine will may be done on earth as it is in heaven.

With regard to the Holy Spirit

St. Paul says that we do not know how to pray as we ought, but that the Holy Spirit Himself intercedes for us with inexpressible groaning.[91] How could we know the intimate ways to get to where God is calling us, and how could we discover His loving designs for us, if the loving and effective action of the Divine Spirit did not guide us?

Neither I nor you will direct this retreat, but He who does what He pleases, as He has done throughout your life, as an owner disposes of what is His, as an artist who completes His work, as a spouse who treats His bride lovingly.

Were we to direct this retreat, we would choose the goal we would like to reach. We would try to discover the best paths to reach our goal. We would try to prepare a spiritual program for these days.

But in a very special way these are God's days, not like all the other days of your life, because He will dispose of your soul, which belongs to Him without external attachments, and will take His pleasure in it with an ineffable intimacy of love. The Holy Spirit is your Lord, for He is God, for He is your Spouse and your Lord, because you have offered yourself to Him totally a thousand times, and the Holy Spirit will act in these days as He pleases. It is for you to empty yourself before His Majesty, surrendering in full docility to His love and action.

In these days you will efface yourself, looking to Him alone, who is *All*, for everything; the handmaid of the Lord who, with the eyes of your soul fixed on Him, desires nothing other than that all should be done in you according to the Divine Word; the enamored bride who, with ardor and total love, offers herself to the Divine Spouse to please Him.

Without any program, without your own initiative, without any yearning except that of letting the Holy Spirit guide you, you will cast yourself into this ocean of infinite love, forgetful of everything, even of yourself, letting yourself be enveloped by its huge waves, as you float on its depths.

What will the Holy Spirit do with you?

Where will He guide you?

What paths will He make you traverse?

What sentiments will He inspire in your soul?

What abyss will He show you?

Will He fill you with heavenly consolation or with unspeakable bitterness?

Only He knows. All we know is that, for you, these days will be full of intense love, divine intimacy, and of entire possession by the Holy Spirit.

With divine, loving liberty, the Holy Spirit will dispose of His bride, and will lead her into the bosom of love, accomplishing in her His ineffable designs.

Whatever He may do, you will be happy, because you are pleasing to Him, because you let Him have His way in you, because

Conchita's Reflections on a Retreat

whatever He does is wisdom, love and happiness.

Is it not true that you accept beforehand these exercises, as He wishes?

But to accept would mean too little. You should offer yourself, surrender to Him, disappear in Him. I don't know how to explain to you how absolute, full and sweet this offering to the Holy Spirit should be.

It is not enough to tell you that your soul should be like those tiny feathers carried effortlessly by the wind, which makes them whirl around playfully, now lifting them up very high, now carrying them far away. It is still not enough to tell you to be like resonant instruments, which vibrate at the musician's slightest touch, responding to his interior inspiration, becoming an extension of his genius.

It is better for me to tell you to be an ideal, faithful bride of the Holy Spirit, united to Him by the ineffable bond of love, whose longing and happiness is to please your Spouse, anticipating His thoughts and echoing His intimate desire.

Maybe you have not thought deeply enough that you are the bride of the Holy Spirit.[92] For many years, He has been united with your soul in ineffable love, and has communicated to you the fruitfulness of the Father, so that Jesus may live in your soul.

The bride must love the Spouse with perfect fidelity; must please Him with an exquisite solicitude; and must offer herself to Him with perfect self-forgetfulness and total self-donation.

During these days, you should be the faithful and loving bride of the Holy Spirit. Let Him possess you without obstacles or reserve, with perfect self-abandonment and love.

Let the Holy Spirit do with you as He wills. Let Him envelop you in silence, or lull you with heavenly harmony. Let Him console or immolate you. Let Him penetrate you to the inmost recesses of your soul. Let Him fashion you as He pleases, and shake you with His powerful action, and permeate you with His victorious love.[93]

This period of your preparation could be expressed through

an incomparable verse of St. John of the Cross:

> *"I abandoned and forgot myself,*
> *laying my face on my Beloved;*
> *all things ceased; I went out from myself,*
> *leaving my cares*
> *forgotten among the lilies."*[94]

The first verse indicates the forgetfulness of self and the profound self-annihilation with which you should start in these holy days. Lay your head trustingly on your Beloved, with sweet abandonment. How great a need of rest you have after this exhausting and hard year. The Beloved invites you to peace and quiet. He wants you to lay your face on Him.

"All things ceased": the noise of worldly things, the thundering of storms, the cries of fear and longing; in the divine silence of love you will rest in the peace of the Holy Spirit.

"I went out from myself," means not only to abandon all one's cares, but also to offer oneself to the sweet will, to the supreme action of the Beloved.

May the fragrance of the purity, the atmosphere which the Beloved breathes, envelop your soul; and by the triumphant virtue of the purity of your love, of your total unselfishness, may you forget everything:

"As if leaving your cares forgotten among the lilies."

Personal Reflection of Conchita [95]

FIRST DAY

I am dedicating this retreat to the Holy Trinity through the immaculate hands of Our Lady of Guadalupe.

Last night, I made an unconditional offering to my Jesus in the little oratory where He is now, for whatever He wishes of me.

Conchita's Reflections on a Retreat

Today, during communion, I renewed my *unconditional* offering, so that He might make and unmake me as He pleases.

As soon as I focus on Him, tears come to my eyes. Why? I feel devastated, deeply saddened, but *I want to console Him.*

Before Jesus, I am ashamed of my bad behavior, but in spite of my feeling miserable, *He loves me* and His gifts are without repentance.

It is true that I have undergone a very painful and bitter year, without consolation, after having offered *all* my prayers on behalf of priests; with so many worries, humiliations and afflictions of every kind in the Works of the Cross... Many times Satan managed to keep me away from prayer, but even as I was struggling in the dark, I never stopped loving Jesus deep down in my heart, although I felt cold and sorrowful.

Is it not true, Lord of my soul?

Here we are alone at last, Heart to heart, and I am going to spend these days in the shadow of the Holy Spirit, in intimate union with the adorable Trinity.

With all earthly things far from me, I will abase myself to the bottomless bottom of my nothingness before each Divine Person, unburdening myself of all that made me feel ashamed whenever I thought about it, so that my soul may be the bride of the Holy Spirit.

Reflecting on the Archbishop's preparatory text, I prayed the Lord to grant me self-forgetfulness.

Lord, grant me the grace to place my soul at Your feet in full and loving docility to Your divine action, and to act only under the motion of the Holy Spirit, giving myself without resistance to Your love.

I desire to sacrifice my own will to the Father in order to live only by His will.

These are *God's days*, and self-annihilated, I will offer myself to Him.

I will be a *nothing* that expects everything from the *All.*

What will the Holy Spirit do with me? Where will He lead

me? (Archbishop's point.) Along what paths will He take me? What sentiments will He inspire in my soul? What abyss will He open up before me? Will He fill me with heavenly consolation, or with unspeakable bitterness? Only He knows! But these days will be full of love, divine intimacy, and total possession by the Holy Spirit.

May He deal with me freely. I will be happy with whatever He does, accepting this retreat in advance to please Him. May He talk to me or be silent, immolate me or give me consolation; everything will be of value to me and a token of His tenderness.

I am trying to attain:

1. Self-forgetfulness and profound self-annihilation.
2. I will "lay my face on my Beloved" in sweet abandonment.
3. I will not listen to the noise of worldly things, the roaring of the storms of the soul, its cries of fear and desire, but try to live in the silence of love.
4. I will give myself a thousand times to the sweet and almighty will of God.
5. I will leave behind me my fears, concerns and preoccupations.
6. May the purity which Jesus breathes surround me. I am leaving to Him all my cares.

I shall do all this with the help of my heavenly Mother.

Oh, my Jesus, accept my resolutions, and help me to carry them out.

Conchita's Reflections on a Retreat

October 15, 1935
SECOND DAY

Meditation of Archbishop Martínez

With regard to Jesus

It is already a long time that Jesus dwells in you, and He renews in you His intimate immolation. Every day He seems to be more at home in your soul, and you feel as if He is expanding His interior suffering in your soul. That is why your life seems to be more sorrowful every year, and the bitterness in your heart more intense. But if this is so, Jesus will be more united with your soul each day, and the more you disappear, the more perfectly Jesus dwells in you.

Each year, during these heavenly days, for they are Jesus' days, He takes fuller possession of your heart by the expansion of love and suffering. Each year as you efface yourself more and more, the more fully He dwells in His chosen soul. That is why your retreats have two profound meanings:

First, they are days when Jesus takes your soul exclusively for Himself, and during which time He belongs entirely to His mother.[96] During the year, how many people and how many activities have contested the right to your soul with Jesus! No doubt that in all these occupations He is all yours, and you are all His. But love aspires to exclusive moments devoted to love, not to transform work into love, but for the full absorption that love works in the life of those in love. This is so not only because our activities cannot be transformed in love, but because love wants to realize itself in full absorption in the lives of those in love; moments in which love fulfils all its demands and turns the soul away from what is earthly, to sink into its boundless womb; moments in which Jesus totally disposes of the soul without limitations or obstacles, and the soul offers itself fully to Jesus and enjoys Him entirely.

Your retreats are days in which Jesus fully disposes of your soul as it pleases Him; they are days in which you fully dispose of Jesus and enjoy Him.

For this reason, these days have a second, very profound meaning. In them, Jesus is preparing His mother's heart so as to accomplish, ever more effectively, His loving design in it. Do you remember that during one of your retreats Jesus explained to you everything He had been accomplishing? In fact, what He is doing in each retreat is to enlarge your heart and the more it is expanded, the more abundant and exquisite is the wine of love which He can pour into it, particularly, the royal absinthe[97] of His intimate sorrows.

A poor human heart could not endure to receive at one time the entire mystery of Jesus' love and the treasure of His suffering that He seeks to deposit in it. In order to show Jesus tenderness and to console Him, it would be good if He could alleviate His heart by pouring it out into your motherly heart, but He must accept the fragility of the creature and the laws that He established. So He accomplishes the loving operation slowly.

Every year, especially during your retreat, He expands your soul and suffuses it with more love and suffering. When the soul expands and the creature disappears, one is further transformed into Jesus. The soul dies to itself and lets Jesus live in it.

You are aware of the divine action, but you are unaware of the magnitude of its effects. You know that God has visited you, that His glory[98] passed near you, as Moses felt it pass by him on the top of the mountain. You hear His words of life, and feel His ineffable outpourings. You know that the fire descended from heaven, because your heart burns and seems to break due to the crackling flames of divine love. Yet you seem to be unaware that your soul has been expanded, your spirit transformed, and your heart enveloped in flames.

The only effect that you recognize is the fact that the ocean of bitterness you carry within you has grown, but you hardly understand the divine effects, because the quality of this divine bitterness, its profound meaning and divine essence, escape you.

Conchita's Reflections on a Retreat

There is love deep down in this bitterness which grows each year. It is Jesus who unites Himself to you more closely in every retreat, and dwells in you in a more ineffable way. It is the heart of your Son who gives Himself to you more perfectly in every divine operation, and communicates to you more intensely His intimate and ineffable mystery.

How much will Jesus expand your heart in these days? What new fire of love will His tenderness communicate to you? What new treasure of exquisite, fruitful, unspeakable suffering will Jesus deposit in your heart, pouring into it His infinite Heart? Only He knows. It is for you to prepare yourself for the divine outpouring: to open your soul so that Jesus may make it immense, to offer yourself to Him so that He can fill you with His life.

The rule is this: *self-emptying, self-offering.*

The self-emptying of your soul before Jesus consists in the disappearance of your life in order to receive the divine life. It consists in the self-emptying of what is earthly, especially of the ego, in order to receive Jesus with His triumphal progress, with His loving and divine expansion.

Do you not understand what it means? *Shyness* is clearly a human characteristic, whereas *boldness* is an unmistakable mark of the divine. Scripture says that our thoughts are timid. So are our affections, projects, desires and expectations, because the limitation of our being and activity colors everything that is human with shyness.

When we think about ourselves, when we rely on our own resources, we are necessarily shy if we do not want to be stupid and foolishly bold. When our old self disappears and God fills us with His light, love and strength, we experience the divine boldness and exclaim with the Apostle: *"I have the strength for everything through Him who empowers me."*[99]

In your person shyness has different aspects which show signs of the presence of "self." You do not want to approach Jesus, or rather, you feel awkward in His presence. Why? You think about yourself, about your unworthiness, your limitations and your misery. You feel the vague attraction of all the things which pull you away from Jesus, which impede your bold confidence that breaks the veil of the third love.[100]

Forget yourself and think about Jesus, about your beloved Son whose benevolent Heart forgives everything, whose never-failing faithfulness assures you that His gifts are bestowed without repentance, whose victorious love triumphs over our misery.

Your long life is a proof of the love, fidelity and constant generosity of the divine Heart.

Do not expect Him to force you by His goodness to be confident, to cast yourself into His arms, into His Heart, to be lovingly bold. Pay Him homage, anticipating His goodness, His tenderness, with the boldness of the third love.

To act like this is to pay homage to Jesus, because it means to proclaim that He is *infinitely good, unspeakably faithful and delightfully loving.*

The other aspect of the shyness which appears sometimes in your soul consists in not looking directly at the graces which God has bestowed upon you, not acknowledging them and, in some cases, even doubting them. When will you have the boldness to sing your "magnificat," even if modest and limited, as Mary sang hers, triumphant and magnificent?

When will you totally forget yourself? When will you disappear completely? When will you surrender yourself before the majesty of love and the goodness of Jesus?

No grace should frighten us, except when we compare it with our smallness. For in relation to divine love, even the most wonderful grace is not excessive. What is admirable, incomprehensible, overwhelming is that God loves us, but once this love is accepted, nothing seems rare, prodigious or exorbitant.

Consider any of God's graces, compare the one which seems to you the greatest and most incredible with His infinite love, and tell me if it is excessive.[101]

The only shyness you do not have in your soul is shyness before suffering, for God made you strong and bold in suffering, especially interior suffering, given that interior suffering is especially for Him. The intimacy of joy or suffering, of light or darkness, is of little importance, since it will always be love and, in any case, it is intimacy with Jesus who is your Lord, Love and All.

Tell Jesus you do not know what intimate operation He will accomplish in your soul during this retreat, but that you give Him full liberty to act, because you love Him beyond measure, and accept the sovereignty of His power and love.

If upon expanding your soul, He kills you, tell Him that you will be happy; and if He makes your existence more bitter and cruel, you will be even happier, because you will receive the sweet Son with His Heart enveloped in flames and permeated with divine suffering in your soul; and this Son and this Heart are your treasure, in time and in eternity.

Personal Reflection of Conchita
SECOND DAY

Effacement and self-emptying. Profound humility and total self-giving.

I should forget what I am and trust; I should stop thinking about my wretchedness and think only about Jesus' mercy.

I should anticipate Jesus' goodness with the boldness of the third love.

Has Jesus ever failed me during all these years and circumstances of life?

Has He not forgiven me, glossing over my faults and lack of generosity?

So I should do away with my shyness forever, being conscious that I am nothing, and lose myself in Him who is All, as the drop of bile disappears in the syrup, as garbage which is cast into the fire.[102] No more dwelling on myself, no more hesitation, my Jesus.

Who would believe that I am an obstacle to myself, that with foolish humility (I can see it clearly), I cut my wings which would carry me to You? Why am I like this, Jesus of my soul? I do not want to die without giving You the measure You marked out for me, without fulfilling Your plans on earth.

Lord, during this retreat You will give me a big push, You will cut the threads of my *ego* which keep me from moving toward You with the swiftness I need, won't You? Why am I so terrible? Why do people consider me good? What an irony! To think that I put up with this opinion!

My dear Jesus, remove everything that is an obstacle to uniting myself with You. You who are, as the meditation says, "*infinitely good, unspeakably faithful, delicately loving.*" What prevents me from knowing You? During this retreat, I want You to show my soul what *You are like*.

Though wretched and vile, when will I sing my "magnificat" fearlessly, without limitations, looking *directly* at the graces of God?[103]

Give me, Lord, the boldness of the third love, to love more and to suffer more. Why should I fear the heights, or the suffering, if I have You?

I will empty myself: first, by examining my limitations, and then by forgetting my wretchedness, in order to feel the delights of Your love and praise its wonders in my poor soul. I will also empty myself by forgetting my weakness, being ready to suffer all sorrows while leaning on You. Why should I be surprised at the magnitude of God's goodness and grace?

The Archbishop's meditation reads: "No grace should frighten us, except when we compare it with our smallness. For in relation to divine love, even the most wonderful grace is not excessive. What is admirable, incomprehensible, overwhelming, is that God loves us, but once this love is accepted, nothing seems rare, prodigious or exorbitant. Consider any of God's graces, compare the one which may seem to you the greatest and most incredible with His infinite love and tell me if it is excessive."[104]

How beautiful! How consoling! What an abyss of light one can discover in it!

Conchita's Reflections on a Retreat

Jesus has always been *mine*. That is true! He gave me *everything*: His Word, His life, His secrets, His Heart, His love, His interior suffering, His Works of the Cross, and His priests. My God! He gave me a family so that *my own blood* could love Him. Two consecrated children![105]

What have I given Him back? Though full of imperfections, I offered Him what I am and what I have, and what I could have. My body with all its suffering; my soul with all its love and bitterness; my life, along with the lives of my children;[106] all my hours consecrated to Him, my tears; so much! My martyrdom for His glory – often caused by the Works of the Cross! – my joys, hopes, expectations, my time and eternity....

Though I am worth nothing, in this retreat I will offer myself to Him with the full and exclusive intimacy He wishes; with the adjustments He wants in order to expand my soul, as happens every time I make a retreat, so that He may pour His love and sorrows into my soul. *More love, more suffering*! I will offer myself a thousand times in order to arrive at the perfect union, to the mysterious required changes.

Oh Jesus, my Jesus! During these days, unite me deeply to You in the intimacy of joy or suffering, of light or darkness; it does not matter, because in any of these phases, Your love will shine.

I am unaware of Your intimate workings in my soul, as I trust You realize, but You work with absolute liberty, and I know You will do all out of love. If in expanding my soul You *kill me*, it will be a blessed death! I will feel happy dying in Your hands.

If You want me to live a bitter and more cruel life, without Your consolation, Your words, Your tangible presence, I will live in faith, hope and love, *serenely* doing Your will.

Here, before this little altar where You are, I give You my soul to be absorbed by Yours, my life so that You may fill it with Your life, making it immense. I want only Your divine life. Empty my heart of what is created, so that You may fit into it with Your ever-expanding love.

My spiritual director says that in my retreat I feel the divine workings in my soul, but I am unaware of the magnitude of its effect, without knowing that Jesus expands, transforms, and envelops it in the flames of His love.

I must believe that at the bottom of my bitterness there is love, love which grows each year, and that Jesus unites Himself with my soul in ever closer union.

He says that I cannot perceive these operations, this gradual expansion and that I do not understand the divine effect of my suffering, nor do I understand the quality of my bitterness, nor its deep meaning, nor its divine essence.

As long as my director understands it, that is enough for me! It is true that each year after my retreat I feel more sorrowful and the ocean of bitterness grows in my soul.

The *expansion* that God works in my spirit tends to make the creature disappear, to transform it more into Jesus, so that it may die to itself, and Jesus may live in it.

Jesus is silent, moving as birds in certain seasons, and I am letting Him. I hope He will feel sorry for me. To come from so far, only to be enveloped in His silence! Obviously, I only desire what pleases Him, but I wish that He would speak to me.

I am calm and happy with Jesus' silence. I am amazed at the peace He gave me, and at my loving and sincere acceptance of His will, even though I spent the whole time of the retreat gazing on Him… contemplating Him silently, with the mute language of loving abandonment, with the self-giving which encompasses all the offerings of my life.

He, only He, without any self-interest, conditions, abandoned as a child on His loving bosom.

If it pleases Him, I only want to move at the breath of His divine will, which is also mine.

Yesterday, I wanted to listen to His voice, to enjoy that divine tone of His voice that pierces all the fibers of my soul, but today, I do not.

If He does not want it, if He does not want to communicate Himself as He used to, I will be tranquil and happy to accept His will.

Conchita's Reflections on a Retreat

Today, as soon as I placed myself in the presence of God, I experienced the interior light which is at the same time a word, a sound, like a cascade of concepts. It is an understanding, it is His voice. It is Jesus![107]

The Gaze as a Germ of the Mystical Incarnation[108]

As soon as I placed myself in God's presence, Jesus spoke the following: "From that very moment, after having received communion, when you had heard that voice in your soul which was telling you 'The Father is gazing on you,' as I have already told you, from that very moment, Jesus germinated in your heart by the power of the Father's fruitfulness, which was in that gaze.[109]

"Everything in the Father is fruitfulness; He cannot move, so to speak, without reproducing Himself in all things, and even in the Word Himself, whom He generates always, giving Him His own substance and life; as fruit of this mutual and holy communication, the Holy Spirit receives His vitality, produced by the infinite love between the Father and the Word.

"God is an abyss of light, and the light is fruitfulness, as all His attributes are."

"But my Jesus, tell me, for example, is justice fruitful? In what way?"

"The divine will operates in it; that divine will which is justice, rectitude and power: that is love!

"The Father is the will and so He acts through His attributes: in His goodness attracting, in His mercy forgiving, in His omnipotence creating and so on, giving Himself to souls, together with the Word and the Holy Spirit, who constitute with Him one God.

"The Father, though a distinct Person, possesses one substance, one essence with the Son and the Holy Spirit. All act together in unity; all Three Persons are totally united."[110]

"Tell me Jesus, does the Word have fruitfulness? I thought that only the Father and the Holy Spirit have it, as in the Incarnation."

"The Word is inseparable in His divinity from the Father and the Holy Spirit, and the Three Divine Persons act conjointly. They cannot be separated or divided. They are, have been, and will be but one God. They are, as I have told you, totally united. They are Three Persons in one Divinity, power, will, and attributes.

"The Word took flesh from Mary; He clothed Himself in humanity out of love for the Father and humankind in order to realize *one will of love* on earth.

"The Holy Spirit brings about the mystical incarnation through the Father's fruitfulness, giving His Word made man out of love for the sake of many. But the Three Divine Persons concur in this mystery of love because they are one sole Divinity, will and charity."

"Lord, You told me that the mystical incarnation was accomplished by the Father's gaze on my soul, so why have so many years passed in order for it to be realized and for me to know it?"

"For God years do not exist. He acts, and in due time, when it pleases Him, and when He sees the conditions fulfilled, He reveals His work, He lets it be known; but the work is accomplished in His mind, for in His foreknowledge of things they are already accomplished. For so it is with God.

"In the soul the *will* is the mover which directs it to heaven or hell. In the will, a power of the soul, God is reflected, and the germ of the divine exists in it. If man in his perversion misuses his free will, God is not guilty, but this holy, precious will suffices for man to be saved. This *will*, united to the divine will, glorifies God and brings about eternal happiness."

He didn't tell me more, but within me I understood bottomless abysses.

Father,[111] why does God permeate me with the most radiant light as soon as the Holy Trinity is mentioned? What I managed to express by His inspiration is only a shadow, but the ocean remains within me.[112]

Oh my Jesus! I am grateful that You communicated Yourself to me, but remember that I offered You the act of willing only what

Conchita's Reflections on a Retreat

You will, whether You are communicative or silent.

I am going to read and reflect on the meditation text.

My dear Mother, I want to pass these delightful hours close to you, for they are Jesus' hours, and they will not come back. Take care of the Works of the Cross and of my children.

What a wonderful meditation has fallen to me today (very appropriate, even without my director's knowing it) on the close relation I should have with the Eternal Father who in His infinite tenderness, communicates to me His divine fruitfulness in a singular way.[113]

My God, how is it possible that I can call Jesus my Son, just as the Father does, and not die of shame?

What profound gratitude and loving adoration should I have toward the Father!

If we should all annihilate ourselves before His infinite majesty, how much more should I annihilate myself, since my soul has received Jesus Himself as *Gift*?[114]

To what extent should I annihilate myself?

I have received Jesus as *Gift* from the Father's tenderness, and by the grace of the mystical incarnation the divine mystery is renewed in the silence of the soul. My God!

The Father generates Jesus in our heart and by ineffable condescension enables us to repeat deep in our souls the mysterious expression: *"You are My Son; today I have begotten You."*[115]

"Should one not die of gratitude and love, and lose oneself delightfully in the depths of incomprehensible annihilation?" I read in the meditation.

This should be the basis of my relation with the Father. This should be my attitude: the self-annihilation of supreme adoration and most profound love.

What can be left for the creature in this loving annihilation? What initiative, will, desire can be left for us when one is aware of this mystery?

Above all, during these days of retreat, my soul should expand immeasurably, if possible.

I read in the meditation: "Since the Father has given you Jesus, communicated His fruitfulness to you, put His divine word in your creaturely mouth, (my God!), what else could you do but annihilate yourself before the Father, without your own will and desire; or rather, annihilate yourself to pay Him the homage of adoration, gratitude and love, without any other will but the divine one, without any other desire but the glory of God?

From the depths of this self-annihilation should emerge a vigorous, ardent, full offering of justice and love to the will of the Father and to His divine design."[116]

I have offered myself for the hundredth time to my beloved Father, and I have deeply abased myself in the ashes, while admitting His infinite gentleness for me. I never want to have my own will any more and every day, at each moment, I will lose myself in His adorable will and love it.

To love the divine will is to love Jesus, to be united to Him, to enter His Heart, to live His life.

What else did Jesus accomplish on earth if not His Father's will, loving until death on the Cross? Was not His dominant passion to please His beloved Father?

In this retreat my supreme desire is to let Him do with me as He pleases. It is to offer myself lovingly, with confidence, ardently to His will so that the divine design may be accomplished in me. My only purpose is to please Him! My only hope is to be refashioned by this divine Artisan. My only desire is that the divine will be done in me, in the Works of the Cross, in my children, and in everything, even though this will may crush, crucify, and kill me!

O holy Father, my Father, dear Father! I give You thanks for all Your benefits and loving concern! But most of all, I thank You for having given me Jesus, even though He must be offered and crucified. Even though I must do without His consolation for the sake of His beloved priests.

Conchita's Reflections on a Retreat

October 16, 1935
THIRD DAY

Meditation of Archbishop Martínez

With regard to the Father

You have very close relations with the Father, who in His infinite tenderness bestowed His divine fruitfulness on you in a singular way. If you only knew the gift of God! It is because of this ineffable fruitfulness that the Son of the Father is your Son in a mystical way, and you can call Him your Son in the same way that the Father does, and Jesus is yours, ineffably yours.

If the only reason you had to love the Father were the gift of His Son, you should live and die for Him out of love.

This reason is enough for you to annihilate yourself profoundly and to give yourself to Him without reserve. Undoubtedly, before the majesty of the Father every creature should empty itself to the greatest extent possible. Before God, the basic attitude of every creature is the self-annihilation of adoration.

Jesus' soul lived like this on earth, in total surrender to the Father, and even in the splendor of glory, it hands everything over to the Father in delightful and beatific self-surrender.

I think that one of the delights of heaven must be a feeling of one's nothingness before the majesty of God, as a beautiful contrast, as homage of adoration, as a source of bliss.

How happy must the blessed be in knowing that God is all and that they are nothing, savoring the divine statement of St. Paul: *"In Him all things hold together."*[117] Yet the self-annihilation of adoration effectively expands through the surrender of self in love and gratitude.

Love annihilates, because the lover loses himself in the Beloved. Who can believe it! Annihilation is one of the most delightful charms of love.

When the soul thinks that it is nothing, and yet knows that

it is loved, it delights in self-surrender, in offering this nothingness as a pedestal of love; the more profound our nothingness, the greater our love.

I think that this self-surrender is so delightful that if we were not already nothing we would wish to be so.

Since God is the fullness of love, there is nothing that could be compared with nothingness or carrying the treasure of infinite love in the womb of this nothingness.

But when the soul receives Jesus, the Gift of love, the incomparable, sweet, divine Jesus, I dare say this loving self-surrender takes on almost infinite proportions.

Alas! When we consider that the Father gave us Jesus in an outburst of His infinite tenderness; when we immerse ourselves in the unfathomable statement of Scripture: *"For God so loved the world that He gave His only Son,"*[118] our heart melts with gratitude and love; and we are happily immersed in an abyss of loving self-surrender.

Even sweeter, more wonderful than receiving Jesus as a Gift of divine tenderness, is receiving the Father's fruitfulness, which renews the divine mystery in the silence of the soul.

Since the Father begets Jesus in our heart, through His ineffable condescension, we can repeat in the depths of our souls the mysterious expression: *"You are My Son; today I have begotten You."* Should one not die of gratitude and love, and lose oneself delightfully in the depth of incomprehensible annihilation?

This should be your attitude. This should be the foundation of your life in relation to the Father: the self-annihilation that is supreme adoration and most profound love.

What remains of the creature in this loving surrender? How can we not forget ourselves when we have received the unspeakable gift? Can our own initiative, will, or desire remain in us when we are aware of this mystery?

If your whole life is to be a continuous self-surrender, then during these retreat days in which you enter into God's bosom, drawing ever closer to the infinite majesty and eternal love, your soul's self-surrender should simplify notably.

Since the Father has given you Jesus, communicated His fruitfulness to you, put His divine word in your creaturely mouth, what else could you do but annihilate yourself before the Father, without your own will and desire; or rather, annihilate yourself to pay Him the homage of adoration, gratitude and love, without any other will but the divine one, without any other desire but the glory of God?

From the depths of this self-annihilation should emerge a vigorous, ardent, full offering of justice and love to the will of the Father and to His divine designs.

Have you thought deeply what the will of the Father means? This will is wisdom, beauty and love. If we understood it, we would never want anything else.

For the blessed, doing God's will means happiness always and everywhere. They offer themselves to it in an ecstasy of love, wonder and pleasure.

During His earthly life, it was Jesus' delight to accomplish His Father's will. "*I always do what is pleasing to Him,*"[119] Jesus said with profound satisfaction.

The essence of holiness, love and wisdom is to offer oneself to the divine will; to become holy means to live and die surrendered – without resistance, with firm commitment, loving self-giving – to this adorable will; to love is to lose one's own will and to project oneself into the will of the Beloved.

To be wise is to submit oneself consciously to this supreme norm; to be blessed means taking intimate delight in accomplishing His will. If we proceeded into the depths of the mystery, we would understand that the supreme art – the most exquisite esthetic emotion – would be experiencing the fullness of the beauty, the unspeakable harmony of God's will being done in the universe.

For each soul, all these things: love, wisdom, holiness, art and blessedness, consist in accomplishing God's will. May the soul live to do it! May the loving designs of God be *fully, suitably* and *lovingly* realized in it.

Each day, at every moment, at every stage of our spiritual journey, we should renew and perfect our resolution to do God's will.

So, in a singular way, during these holy days when your intimacy with God is ever more perfected, and your soul is adjusting to the divine effusion and activity, you should set out with new and loving self-abandonment to God's will.

This self-abandonment means being attuned to the soul of Jesus; it means giving thanks to the Father for His unspeakably precious gift; it means being in harmony with the fruitfulness you received from the divine bosom.

If the mystical incarnation is the sharing in the fruitfulness of the Father, then the putting into practice and development of this outstanding grace should be losing oneself in His adorable will.

After all, Jesus is God's will and Jesus Crucified, as the Apostle Paul teaches. Creation, history and the Church have a center, a key and a meaning: Jesus Crucified.

To love God's will is to love Jesus, to be united to Him, to enter into the depths of His mystery.

From this profound perspective, the Works of the Cross have as their goal to do God's will, giving Jesus to the world and spreading everywhere the efficacy and glory of the Cross.[120]

Therefore, your greatest desire during this retreat should be the accomplishment of the divine design in you, and the best preparation would be your loving self-offering to the divine will.

Whatever the divine will may dispose for you, will be most beautiful, holy and blessed. Words or silence, consolation or bitterness, light or darkness. Isn't it true that you do not prefer any one of these things, but you desire only what the Father wants from you?

We do not know what He will choose from among the things I have enumerated, but we surely know that He will choose Jesus and Jesus Crucified; that He will give Him to you and that you will be able to receive Him in your soul through the prodigious virtue of the divine fruitfulness.

Conchita's Reflections on a Retreat

So empty yourself before the Heavenly Father, and give yourself fully to His divine will, saying with Jesus: "*I always do what is pleasing to Him.*" And then again: "*Yet not My will, but Yours be done.*"[121]

Personal Reflection of Conchita
THIRD DAY

Today my spiritual director says that my retreat begins and that the previous meditations were just preparation.

Before Mass, upon entering the oratory (the delightful Little Cave,[122] as I call it), I heard Jesus saying: "Tell your spiritual director that I am pleased with the subject he has chosen for the retreat, because you need it, and I inspired him with this idea because I wanted it. Tell him that I will help him."

I was impressed by today's meditation on the mystical incarnation. The immense, almost infinite weight of this grace, I would say, crushes me and overwhelms me, but at the same time raises me up, elevates my soul to heaven.

I recall with emotion the stages of my life with its sweet memories, with its doubts, struggles and nameless forms of martyrdoms.

My life was always full of love and suffering, of a thousand kinds of grace, and heart-rending tears.

Here I will outline what refers to the mystical incarnation.

"The Father is gazing upon you," words which vibrated in my soul, making me tremble with awe and filling me with love that day in San Luis Potosí in the Church of Our Lady of Mount Carmel, in the corner on the right, in the Chapel of the Blessed Sacrament, which is on the left. (I went to visit that place when I was in San Luis, recalling what I had experienced in my soul at that time and giving thanks).[123]

After receiving communion, I unexpectedly heard those divine words, which filled me with love and I told nobody at the time about it. I did not even know that it was Jesus who spoke.

Now He tells me that in that gaze of the divine Father, the germ of the mystical incarnation was communicated to me. How could one imagine such a thing? I used to wonder: "Why is the Father gazing upon me?"

Now I remember a humorous situation that happened to me in that church. My heart was burning with love for Jesus, and looking toward the tabernacle at the main altar, I was speaking to Him and laughing.

I did not notice the sacristan arranging things on the altar. After many gestures, smiling and gazing at Jesus, the sacristan thought I was gesturing to him, and he very kindly approached me and asked whether I was calling him. I understood my blunder, and blushed. Not knowing what to say, it occurred to me to ask about the flowers. But I was just overflowing with love for my Jesus in the tabernacle.

Some time passed and I noticed a special trembling in my soul when priests pronounced the divine word at the moment of "Et Incarnatus est," and in the last Gospel of St. John at the end of Mass. My heart would fill with singular love and it seemed to me that I was understanding and *experiencing* that sublime Gospel.[124]

Later on, in Mexico City, I often heard those words when I was recollecting myself, and I used to tremble, feeling the irresistible attraction to the Holy Trinity. The words were: *"The Divine Word is pursuing you."*[125]

Why is He pursuing me? I used to repeat to myself, no matter how insistently I heard them. (I referred this to Fr. Mir, who was my spiritual director at that time.)

I can call to mind another experience that happened at that time in the church called the "Tabernacle," situated near the cathedral.

After receiving communion I felt as if I had received the sun, with a thousand rays of light, and I felt them passing through my body as if crossing it. As I felt enveloped in light so I covered my face and I wished that I had a thousand shawls to cover me.

Feeling embarrassed and frightened that others would look at me, I went to hide myself in the corner near the confessional; then I heard a mysterious and sweet voice saying to me: "This is the purification of matter."[126]

Then I thought (I cannot remember if I spoke aloud), "I took a bath yesterday." Then the same voice answered: "It is not this; it is not this kind of cleanliness I am talking about. I confirm you in purity and humility."

I felt ashamed and pleased, and I went home happy.

Certainly, it proved to be true, because I never knew what impurity was, and it never occurred to me that I was useful for something. But I understood that Jesus needed to establish these bases very deep in my soul.

All comes from Him! All graces! Now, after so many years, I realize that all these things were a preparation for the great grace of the mystical incarnation.

Some time later, but not too much later, Jesus spoke to me about the Divine Word, and I noted it in my account of conscience.

One day Jesus said to me: "Prepare yourself for the day of the Incarnation,[127] because I am going to give you a great grace."

"Am I going to die?" I asked.

"No, on the contrary, you will receive a new life, an immense grace," Jesus replied. "Prepare yourself."[128]

It was February. I told my director, Fr. Mir, about it and he advised me to make a month-long retreat in the best way I could in my home in order to prepare my soul. (My son Salvador was a baby.)

I increased my penances and prayer; my nights were more devoted to Jesus. The obligations of the house, my husband Francisco and my children did not interfere with it.

During those nights of many purifications, I can remember one night being on the "roses,"[129] when I heard Jesus telling me: "The Holy Trinity is here."

I was filled with shame before the infinite majesty, and then

Jesus told me that the spiritual marriage[130] took place at that time.

The effects of that grace in my soul were delightful peace, increasing love, and I wanted to hide and humble myself.

I was waiting anxiously, thinking myself so well prepared for the great day of the Incarnation of 1897.

I didn't know what I was waiting for. I received communion with untold fervor, and my soul was burning with divine love. The day passed and Jesus did not say even a word to me.

I remained hurt and ashamed, full of doubts, weeping, and Jesus acted as if we had never known each other.

Many days later, He began to speak with me, and I did not want to listen to Him at all. I played the fool, and did not pay attention to Him for three reasons. I felt hurt, ashamed and afraid of deception.

Then with His charming and tender voice, which could melt stones, He asked me: "Did I by any chance tell you the year of the great grace I promised you when I had told you to prepare yourself for the day of the Incarnation?"

I surrendered myself, and felt pleased and continued to pay attention to Him, and the Lord kept communicating Himself to me as He pleased.

In that period, Jesus spoke a lot about the Holy Trinity.

Now I remember gaining the Portiuncula Jubilee indulgence[131] in the Chapel of the "Tabernacle," near the cathedral, He told me: "The Works of the Cross in the future will have a day of jubilee like this, approved by the Church."

When will it be?

Eight years passed, and each year on the feast of the Annunciation, ashamed, I remembered that *promise*, even though I didn't know what it would be; the only thing I knew was that it would be a great grace which would bring me a new life.

I used to greet my Jesus, to get up at night to greet Him on His great day and humiliated, I let the hours pass without expecting anything, thinking it might be an illusion on my part.

Conchita's Reflections on a Retreat

How could I know? Yesterday, Jesus told me that the germ of the mystical incarnation had already been growing in my soul due to the fruitful gaze of the Father.

Mysteries of God!

How many forms of martyrdom, ups and downs in the Works of the Cross, suffering, thorns, and bitterness followed! How much the devil shook the Works of the Cross down to their very foundations! Rome, after having granted approval to the Missionaries of the Holy Spirit, withdrew it. Deaths, sorrows, calumnies, suffering, fighting and struggling with the powerful followed!

Unexpectedly, the day of the promised grace arrived on March 25, 1906, for which I prepared myself in the retreat, and during which Jesus suddenly freed me from a serious illness.

"I need you cleansed," Jesus told me.

So I made a general confession. At the second Mass in the upper Chapel on Mirto Street, I was sitting at the back, on the left, when Jesus suddenly presented Himself to me, clothed in white, radiating light and joy, carrying a scroll of paper in His hand. Standing near me, He told me:

"I accomplish what I promise: I want to incarnate mystically in your heart. *Receive Me.*"

"I have already received You in communion," I answered.

"It is not like that," He answered, "because in communion My real presence passes, but in this grace, it does not. My union with the soul is eternal. I give you a new life, receive it. It is a life of purity; it is holy; it is the life of Jesus. It is He Himself who is Life." And so on.[132]

He continued telling me beautiful things which I wrote in my Account of Conscience. I was trembling with emotion, and ineffable, indescribable happiness, because I was feeling Jesus intimately united with me, without knowing what to do but love and give thanks, and His possession was burning my soul.

At breakfast time, I went to tell it to Fr. Maximino Ruiz y Flores, then chaplain of the Oasis.[133]

What an incredible recourse to God! I did not want to separate myself from the Tabernacle. His divine presence in my heart was so clear, so evident that I sought only silence, solitude, peace, and being far away from everything which was not Him!

That same afternoon, at the foot of His altar, He asked for and explained the "Chain of Love"[134] to me. He wanted me to start it without losing a single day, which I did with the permission of my director.

Then Jesus made me relive interiorly all the stages of His life, from His birth until His crucifixion and death.

Afterward, I experienced the mystery of the sorrowful solitude of Mary for years and I suffered *very much*. Then He wanted me to be as intimately united with Him as His own blood. He asked that both congregations should live these two experiences and explained them beautifully.[135]

The new stage was opened before me by asking for a more perfect transformation in order to be really able to offer to the Father the Divine Word: "This is My Body; this is My Blood." He in me and I in Him.

Jesus explained to me that the goal of the Chain of Love should be the offering, this ongoing offering of the Divine Word to the Father in union with the Word, entirely lost in Him. He insisted on it very much, asking for this devotion from both Congregations.

At that time, Jesus asked for the Covenant of Love, giving all explanations. (I do not remember the year.)[136]

Thereupon, He asked for the founding of the Fraternity of Christ the Priest as a very interesting association which would be of great help to the Works of the Cross.[137] (This was in Puebla, Mexico, in the chapel of the Sisters of the Cross.) Then Jesus wanted me to be offered as a victim on behalf of the Church and priests by Bishop Ibarra during the Mass on Pentecost.[138]

In Nazareth,[139] Jesus desired another new oblation to the Holy Spirit through the hands of Mary for the same goal. This offering was made at the altar of the Church of the Incarnation.

In that place, the Blessed Virgin assured me that the mystical incarnation was a real grace, and gave me some pieces of advice on purity and on protecting my heart because Jesus dwelt in it.

At the same time, Jesus was also elaborating on the mystical priesthood.

The Works of the Cross were growing.

In Rome, the Works of the Cross were discredited and met with much prejudice. We knew that they had condemned what they had been told about me, namely, that I had "incarnated the *Cross* in my heart."[140]

In Rome, the Lord explained to me very clearly, concretely and extensively what the grace of the mystical incarnation meant. He had me write it down so that Bishop Ibarra could present it in Rome with the aim of *clarifying* that grace, and thanks to this explanation the attitude toward me changed.[141]

My God! How can I not weep? How is this heart of stone not moved before Your unspeakable tenderness and gentleness?

Jesus told me that the tenderness of His love for me was such that as a reward for my deep suffering He wanted me to visit Nazareth, the cradle of the Incarnation of the Divine Word. How could I not die of gratitude?

And then the Missionaries came.[142]

And Jesus dictated the *Confidences* to me, with their heart-rending secrets.[143]

Then came the grace of remaining united to Mary during Masses.

And being a channel of graces for the priests.

Then the third love.[144]

The offering on behalf of the priests.[145]

Offering Jesus, delivering Him up to be crucified, even though it breaks my heart.

The interior sorrows, so many and for such a long time! accompanying Jesus with my agonizing pain.

The sorrowful union of my will with that of the Father.[146]

The lights and mysteries of the Divinity into which He deigned to introduce me. *All* due to the great grace!

The renunciation of His consolations, caresses, sensible presence, for the salvation of His priests.[147]

The lights on the holy mysteries of the Incarnation and the Holy Trinity.

The recent explanation that the mystical incarnation has not passed but is *operating*, which frightened me and moved me profoundly.

My God, my God! Is it still possible to doubt, to stop, and not to want to look *directly* at that grace, to evade it? Should I not cry over all these years I had kept the grace in the closet because it seemed to me impossible?

Bishop Ruiz, Fr. Ipiña, and other priests assured me that the grace was new but certain. And I still had doubts?[148]

But then came my director,[149] and he drew back the veil, and overcame my fears. I promised to *fully* accept the grace with gratitude, and I hope my accepting will be total in this retreat, forgetting myself and *living* only from this central grace of my soul and the Works of the Cross.

What a meditation! My God! My spiritual director hit the nail on the head. The retreat on the mystical incarnation!

And Jesus is delighted with this subject!

I have wept with gratitude and love, unable to make any comments.

Everything that the meditation says *deeply* touches my soul!

Here I am, my Jesus. May it be done to me according to Your word. Let's turn the page of my life and forget my ingratitude.

The memories of this grace came crowding into my mind, and that is why I have written them down.

Could I doubt now?

Conchita's Reflections on a Retreat

OCTOBER 17, 1935
FOURTH DAY

Meditation of Archbishop Martínez

Mystical Incarnation

St. Thomas Aquinas explains that all things find their perfection on returning to their source and consequently, your spiritual life will achieve perfection on returning to its principle and source.

The source of your life is God, whose loving bosom you will fully enter in eternity, but insofar as it is possible on earth, you should enter into it from this moment. The primary source of your life is the outstanding grace of the mystical incarnation which you received thirty years ago, and which sprang forth, so to speak, from the inmost depth of your soul, as a fountain welling up to eternal life.[150]

Everything you have received from God after that grace, all the numerous and fruitful stages which your spirit has passed through during these thirty years, are but the triumphal development of that precious grace. Just as the vigorous stalk, the fresh leaves, the fragrant flowers, and the tasty fruit of a tree are the rich growth of the tiny seed hidden in the womb of the earth.

Thirty years ago, amidst intimate joys and heavenly splendors of that unforgettable day of the mystical incarnation, it was impossible for you even to suspect what would come about later, what the heavenly seed deposited in your soul by the divine Sower would work in your life.

Do you remember? The divine feast left in its wake love and peace in your soul; the gentleness with which your soul was burning after the unspeakable solemnity;[151] the mysteries of Jesus mystically renewed in your soul; the great solitude which is a reflection of the divine solitude of Mary;[152] the beginning of the mystical priesthood,[153] the spiritual fruitfulness which shook your soul with the sudden wind of the Spirit of an intimate Pentecost.

Jesus deposited His confidences of love and suffering in your soul. Just like germinating seeds, priestly souls are sprouting in your soul; a new love and a new source of martyrdom appeared in your life; the third love[154] expanded your soul, and the intimate sorrows of Jesus, in which you share mystically, immolated your heart; your soul was introduced into the mysteries of God, and the deep and incredible extension of sacrifice was revealed to you; as the practical consequence of these most high graces and deep revelations, your life became a terrible martyrdom, because you had to sacrifice the gentle Son to cruel crucifixion; you also had to sacrifice the consolation of His caresses and even His sensible presence on behalf of priestly souls, the children of your spiritual fruitfulness, for they are mystical images of Jesus.

I have just presented to you, in broad strokes, the rich development of that outstanding grace. It is rather easy to draw an outline, but who can count the abundance of heavenly graces which this development required, the conflagration of love that it produces, the suffering which it causes and the spiritual riches which it pours into souls?

In order to perfect and consummate this spiritual richness, it is necessary that it be merged into unity by returning to its origin. Just as the waters of the ocean, after having formed delicate clouds, refreshing rains, mighty rivers, rushing waterfalls and tranquil lakes, return to the place from which they welled up, losing themselves in the immensity of the ocean.

For this reason Jesus, so silent during this year, spoke only to explain to you this important grace, to tell you that it is not simply a memory, but the reality; that it is not the first link of the chain of graces and wonders, but that it is the entire Chain, the only reality that extends, develops, and enriches itself, becoming immense without losing its unity; that it is like a ray of the sun after splitting up into the seven colors of the spectrum and returning to the simplicity of the wonderful sun's light; that it is like a wonderful symphony which, after developing brilliant cadences of rich harmony, fuses, before merging into the triumphant unity of the awesome theme. Can you understand God's thought?

He desires that the richness of His wonders in your soul, which welled up from the source of the mystical incarnation, return to its source without losing its richness, but manifesting its divine unity.

Now you can begin to discern the magnitude of this wonderful grace, contemplating it from today's vantage point and seeing the development of this grace in the course of thirty years. Now you can grasp better the richness of this awesome development and gaze at the prodigious source in its simple and, at the same time, very rich unity.

Consequently, your retreat has as its theme the mystical incarnation, considered not in a fragmentary way as an unforgettable memory, or as a link of the mystical chain, or as a basic but passing stage on the divine journey. Rather, it is considered permanent, living, as something that does not pass nor will ever pass, but continues to be enriched and to reveal an abundant range of heavenly nuances.

Fundamentally, your spiritual life is the mystical incarnation, which encompasses all the graces and wonders of God, just as the sun's ray contains all the colors of the spectrum.

The mysteries of Jesus' life, the mystical priesthood, spiritual fruitfulness, the third love, sharing in the innermost, mystical suffering of Jesus, are all but one, very rich grace. The mystical incarnation does not pass, but remains and will be eternal. It will not stop producing wonders while you live, and will never stop manifesting the abundance of hidden treasures.

And not only while you live, but even after your death, this remarkable grace will continue to produce the fruits of life. Just as St. Thérèse of Lisieux is spending her heaven showering the earth with rose petals, so will you radiate upon the immortal Works of the Cross the inexhaustible fruitfulness of your motherly soul.

At the end of time, when the last soul of the Works of the Cross finds its path of purity, love and suffering, when Jesus receives the last act of consolation in His Oasis, in the desolate wilderness that is this world; it is then that the richness, fruitfulness and interior beauty of the mystical incarnation will be fully comprehended.[155]

Now, in the twilight of your life, after thirty years, the mystical incarnation is understood in a new and more profound manner, as a principle is understood better when its effects have been proven; as the value of a mine is realized when its riches have been extracted; as the fragrance of a flower is more intensely enjoyed when the exquisite essence of its crushed petals emanates from it.

In order to contemplate the mystical incarnation in the fullness of its beauty, it is necessary to establish that it is not merely a sweet memory, but a living reality.

All that is human passes, but what is divine is eternal. If in our human works there is something that survives, it is because we carry something that is divine within us.

When God sends something divine to earth, something which is the reflection of His Being, His perfections, something which is a mysterious emanation of His love, He envelops His gifts in the fragility of human vessels; His light in the opaque wrapping of our language; His grace in the passing and commonplace signs of our ordinary life; His wonders in our smallness; His life in the petals of our lives that wither; His providential victorious action in our passing history; His Kingdom in a society which is marked by human vicissitudes. And what else? He envelops the Body, Blood and Divinity of Jesus in the adorable but ephemeral Eucharistic species.

But earthly wrappings hide under their fragility what is divine and separated in an ineffable way from the changes of time and space. They hold immutable and eternal heavenly treasures in earthen vessels.

This is what happens with the mystical incarnation. God plants it in the inmost core of human life, which is inevitably subject to the changes of time, limitations of space, and to the commonplace conditions of everything that is earthly. Nonetheless, under the restless and passing waves of earthly life, the divine mystery remains immutable and immortal, without losing its unity, without being transformed in its essence, as a living reality.

The heavenly solemnity is over. The stages of the awesome development of the grace came one after another bringing consolation, martyrdom and fruitfulness, but what is divine does not pass or change. The Divine Persons, through their intimate and secret operations, ceaselessly accomplish the ineffable mystery in the blessed soul.

Personal Reflection of Conchita
FOURTH DAY

I reflected on the meditation on the mystical incarnation. It is *overwhelming* and touched the most delicate and deep fibers of my heart.

There is no doubt that Jesus desires to round out my life, to expand my soul to love this important grace ever more. In these days, I would like to ask forgiveness and to give thanks with millions of hearts, if I but had them.

Will this retreat be the last stone in the spiritual building of my soul? Whatever God wills, but I don't want to lose even one minute; rather, I want to make amends for my indifference, my lack of faith, and my little love.

My Mother! Make up for my deficiencies, fill the gaps of my material and earthly life, and ask Jesus to forgive me.

I copied a part of the Archbishop's meditation just to be moved more by this grace whose magnitude I have never been able to understand and *appreciate* sufficiently.

Once, suddenly, Jesus spoke to me on the mystical incarnation insisting that it had not *passed* but is *always present*. I was frightened and impressed and lately, He has wonderfully developed the same subject. It is in my writings.[156]

Now, in this retreat, they have hit a raw nerve. God has

willed it and my director has enlightened my soul with the very same light.

The Archbishop told me not to look back, but to look directly at the grace in all its splendor, peaceful and happy, although its light and magnitude may kill me. I offered it to God and to my director.

I continued reflecting on the meditation,[157] annihilated and happy, melting in gratitude, and *finally* anxious to correspond to Jesus' wishes insofar as I am able, that is, the plan He points out to me in the course of this retreat.

Lord, You know my weakness! You know what I am, but with You I will be capable of all, helped by my Mother who is also Yours.

Oh my Father![158] Help me to carry out what God wants from me; do not leave me; drive my soul even if I die of shame and love.

October 18, 1935

FIFTH DAY

Meditation of Archbishop Martínez

Mystical Incarnation (new lights)

The mystical incarnation is a special outpouring of the Holy Spirit, an intimate union with the Word and a fruitful gaze of the heavenly Father. These ineffable divine operations are continuous and not occasional, or rather, they are simple and eternal. They are like constant currents that bathe, enrich and divinize the soul.

For this reason, the mystical incarnation does not pass, but springs forth to eternal life. Surely the divine action neither produces these marvelous effects in one instant nor can these effects be discovered on one occasion, nor simultaneously.

Just as a stream of water, which irrigates a meadow and makes it flower slowly, first making the seeds germinate, and then de-

Conchita's Reflections on a Retreat

veloping stems and covering them with leaves and finally making the buds appear and blossom until they spread their fragrance and show off the petals, so also the stream of grace, which ceaselessly bathes the soul that has received the mystical incarnation, makes the marvels of God appear in it bit by bit. First, it delineates the image of Jesus, then reproduces His mysteries until the soul, like an immaterial flower, opens its petals, and diffuses the heavenly fragrance, perfuming the whole world with spiritual fruitfulness.

On the meadow as in the soul, even though the effects succeed each other and appear one after another, the stream is always crystalline, fruitful and constant.

Yet these practical comparisons are inadequate for understanding the divine operations. In the meadow the effects of fruitfulness succeed each other in due course, but in the soul, even though the mystical incarnation does not produce its effects in one instant, the outstanding grace is substantially the same.

This character of the mystical incarnation being an ever present and operative reality is of capital importance for you. Actually, on March 25, 1906, at the most solemn moment in which the heavenly prodigy was realized in your soul, could you think of anything else? Did you look for other nourishment for your interior life from any other source? Did not the divine presence and the mysterious operations which the Three Divine Persons were realizing in your soul totally absorb you?

Moreover, if these operations are constant, if the mystery is at work at every instant, if the grace is not a passing act but permanent, should not the mystical incarnation absorb your life, direct your spiritual energy, and be the only nourishment of your interior life?

No doubt, the sensory impression and awesome brilliance of the moment had to pass, because otherwise the soul would be unable to concentrate on other things and would give up its ordinary, everyday activities of life. Therefore, God Himself lessens the intimate impression, softens the spiritual light which dazzles, and hides the fervor as fire under the ashes, in silent serenity.

But the substance of this grace of necessity absorbs the life of the soul that received it. The soul cannot and should not think of other things, look for or seek other things, except the divine reality that it carries within. This grace must be the only source of your spiritual life, your only program and ideal, considered, certainly, in all its splendid development.

For a long time now you have been conscious of the mystical incarnation, after having forgotten it because of exaggerated humility. But it is not enough just to be conscious of it; it is necessary to live it fully. This grace should be not only one of the preoccupations of your spirit, not even the principal treasure, but the *only treasure* of your soul, the whole reason of your existence, of your destiny; in it and through it you should see, love, seek and do everything.

This is what God wants, and that is why He is pleased that this retreat should be dedicated to the study of this grace. So you must consider it in its full splendor, study it in its fullness, love it openly, and dedicate yourself to it *totally*, *constantly* and *lovingly*.

What should be your only goal from now on? It should be to carry the mystical incarnation to its full development, to its perfect completion.

What should be your program? The one which logically springs forth from this divine grace. What should be the principle of your action? The inexhaustible and fruitful source which you have had in your soul from the *25 of March 1906*.

Personal Reflection of Conchita
FIFTH DAY

During my corporal penitence Jesus enlightened me, and He immersed my soul in deep understanding, which is at the same time enlightenment and experience. I am unable to explain it. It was *petition, lesson, confidence,* and then in the chapel He expanded on it, saying:

Conchita's Reflections on a Retreat

The Glory of the Father

"I suffered the Passion in My Body, rejoicing in the suffering for the sublime goal of *the glory of My Father*.

"In fact, expiation was a joy to Me, not only because it wipes away the sins of the world, but also because it glorifies My Father, which is the highest goal.

"The glory of My Father, accomplished by My sacrifice and by all who sacrifice themselves in union with Me, *is not understood in the world*; the exterior part, the surface, is understood but what I do not allow to be felt is not appreciated.

"Was not all My suffering sweetened, when it had *the glory of My Father* as its loving goal, the glory which My immolation gave Him?

"And what is the glory of My Father? The greatest and most perfect thing that I could offer Him on earth was My most perfect praise and My most pure love. Therefore, the flogging, thorns and sufferings were My delight, because I knew I was glorifying My Father through them. By them, I was atoning for and blotting out what sin had deprived Him of.

"I was and I am happy glorifying My Father!

"For this reason, I seek souls with these same characteristics, that they may suffer as I did on earth. I seek souls for this reason, that being transformed into Me, having become one with Me, as My image on earth, they may continue this path of suffering for this perfect ideal: *the glory of My Father!*

"Fundamentally, in the mystical incarnation it should be like this. And why? Because of the transformation into Me; the more the soul becomes Myself, the more it should resemble Me in love for My Father, and in glorifying Him in suffering.

"It is holy and perfect to suffer all pains lovingly as coming from God's will; but it is more perfect to suffer only in order to glorify My Father secretly, lovingly and in close union with Me, selflessly, with the purity with which I did everything while I was on earth, suffering for *the glory of My Father.*

"If My Body suffered, the smile of My soul was always raised from the earth, glorifying My Father.

"May the souls from the Oasis rise to this highest perfection and likeness to Me, and may they lift themselves up in the spiritual sense, which, *if lived*, will bring them new light and countless graces.

"Thus, following this path, they will become like Me and will take on My most salient spiritual features, soaring to perfection. That is what I was on earth, a continuous thurible, joyfully offering Myself to glorify the Father, and that is what I am in heaven, the perennial hosanna to His glory."

As I was telling you, my Father,[159] when I was suffering on the "roses"[160] today, Jesus made me feel a new joy, the most pure delight raising my soul from the earth. He made me experience that His greatest joy is this manner of suffering, without the least interest, only *in union with Him*, as He inspired me, *for the glory of the Father*.

I told Him in the Chapel, "So how can I deprive priests of what I do and suffer on their behalf, as you have asked me, if I offer all *for the glory of the Father*?"

"What I ask of you is the most perfect and the highest and nothing is taken away from your basic suffering on behalf of priests; rather, it enriches the channel of graces on their behalf."

I reflect on and enter ever more deeply into the great grace of the mystical incarnation with these new lights.

What a meditation! I ought to die, and only because I am a *dimwit* I manage to resist these meditations, which would cause a delicate soul to die. Oh my Jesus, be merciful to me!

Conchita's Reflections on a Retreat

October 19, 1935
SIXTH DAY

Meditation of Archbishop Martínez

The mystical incarnation is the intimate and perfect transformation of the soul, that united to the Holy Spirit through the purest and most profound love, receives from Him the fruitfulness of the Father, and becomes Jesus in order to share in an ineffable way in His intimate priesthood, exercising this priesthood fruitfully on behalf of souls, especially on behalf of priests.

From another general description, which we will consider in detail, we conclude that the mystical incarnation has as its basis a special and ineffable action of the Divine Persons. It is essentially a transformation into Jesus, Priest and Victim. It is the renewal of the life of the purity, love and suffering of the divine Heart of Jesus, for the sake of souls, especially for priests. Finally, it is to console Jesus, to provide repose for the Holy Spirit, and to give glory to the Father.

Let us carefully examine the heavenly elements of this special grace.

The Holy Trinity is the source, model and goal of all spiritual life. It begins when the Holy Spirit is given and pours out His grace and charity in the soul. When the soul, as a consequence of this divine outpouring, is united to Jesus, and shares in His life, it becomes the adoptive child of the Father who gazes on it with divine pleasure.

Twice in the Gospel the mystery of Jesus' life appears with splendid solemnity and magnificent symbolism: at the Jordan and on Tabor.[161] It begins in the Jordan and is consummated on Tabor. The Church teaches us that in the splendor of the Holy Mountain, the perfect adoption as children of God is marvelously manifested, that is, the life of grace is consummated. Thus, the adoption which appears at the Jordan is the same life which begins with the baptism.

UNDER THE GAZE OF THE FATHER

At the Jordan and on Tabor the Three Divine Persons are present: Jesus who immerses Himself in the river or shines out transfigured; the Holy Spirit, who descends like a dove upon Him or a bright cloud which overshadows Him; the heavenly Father, who testifies that Jesus is His beloved Son at the baptism and at the transfiguration.

In its beginning, its development and its consummation the spiritual life has its source in the bosom of the Most Holy Trinity.

Even though the divine action in our souls is common to the Three Divine Persons, scripture and theology authorize us to attribute to each one of them a distinct phase in the ineffable and rich action, and even to distinguish a certain logical order which, by appropriation, corresponds to each Person.

The Holy Spirit, Love that sanctifies, is poured out in our souls and communicates to us the love of Jesus, who is Life. According to the Apostle John, "*God gave us eternal life, and this life is in His Son.*"[162] If our souls become Jesus by sharing in His life, the Father looks on us with His gaze of light, love and satisfaction, just as He gazes on His Son.

Basically the spiritual life is essentially the same from the Jordan to Tabor, that is, from baptism till the consummation of holiness, and essentially the outpouring of the Holy Spirit, the union with the Word and the gaze of the Father are the same.

Yet without losing the divine unity, who can tell how the spiritual life becomes enriched, and what heights it attains in its consummation?

The mystical incarnation is a perfect gift in the spiritual life, even though the beginning of it is just the door to the royal dwelling, an excellent and beautiful path which opens to the soul the first link of the royal Chain of Gold[163] which continues eternally in heaven.

In heaven, you will not do anything else but live the mystical incarnation in its full splendor, in its perfect consummation, in the eternal flourishing of its fruitfulness.

There above, you will enter into the joy of your Lord, into the ineffable mysteries of the Divinity. The Holy Spirit will possess you without fear of breaking the vessel which contains the heavenly treasures. The Word will unite Himself to your soul in an ineffable way and the delightful, profound gaze of the Father, sharper than any two-edged sword, will penetrate the inmost recesses of your soul.

Your spiritual fruitfulness will continue from heaven to radiate torrents of purity, light and love on the souls of the Works of the Cross and on priests.

I repeat it to you, start from now to live out your grace. If your heaven will consist in living the mystical incarnation fully, living this grace on earth should be an anticipation of heaven.

The outpouring of the Holy Spirit in the soul that received the mystical incarnation is something singular; it has three characteristics: unitive love, perfect possession and holy fruitfulness.

The Holy Spirit is the eternal and personal Love of God who is poured out in souls through love; or rather, it is Love that is poured out in souls. That is why the Holy Spirit is called Gift, because love itself is the first gift of love. But when love is poured out in souls, it produces different effects analogous to that of fire when it envelops a metal: it purifies, illuminates and melts it, or rather, transforms it into the same fire.

The love of the mystical incarnation unites the soul with God and transforms it into Him. God is love and when He fills, envelops and penetrates the soul, He makes of it the reflection of God to the extent of saying that the soul, in a certain sense, becomes love.

"Qui autem adheret Domino unus spiritus est." *"Whoever is joined to the Lord becomes one spirit with Him,"* St. Paul says.[164] Who could ever express the profound reality of these words, the wonderful union that love establishes between God and souls?

Therefore, among other consequences which we will study later, souls that received the mystical incarnation are considered brides of the Holy Spirit, because love in them is essentially unitive as spousal love.

If we compare the love of God with different kinds of love we know on earth, heavenly love far excels our poor affections, as the mother country exceeds exile.

The union which produces spousal love on earth is imperfect. When can we say that the spouses have one heart, and that one loves with the heart of the other, except as a figure of speech? But this mystical betrothal with eternal love is the blessed reality that this bold, down to earth figure of speech expresses.

"You have stolen my heart, my sister, my bride," says the Song of Songs in some translations.[165] The soul that has the mystical incarnation has stolen God's Heart; it has stolen the Holy Spirit from Him and keeps Him as a treasure in its own heart. The soul loves with this divine Heart.

Do you remember all that the Lord told you and explained about the way of loving with the Holy Spirit?[166] I will not repeat what I have said so many times, but I would like you to note what is proper to the mystical incarnation, to loving in this way; and I would like you to note how this way of loving makes us experience what is real, profound and divine in this ineffable union.

We love with the Holy Spirit and He loves with our heart, because one thing supposes the other, He loves in us; that is why our love can attain to divine characteristics.

St. Thérèse of Lisieux expresses this idea with respect to this love of neighbor in this delightful passage of her autobiography: "You know perfectly well that I can never hope to love my sisters as You love them, unless You Yourself love them *in me*. It is only because You are willing to do this that You have given us a *new* commandment, and I love it because it is my assurance of Your desire to *love in me* all those whom You command me to love."[167]

Is there a spousal love, is there a union which could be compared with this union and love that realize the miracle that not only God may possess the heart of the beloved soul and the soul God's Heart, but also that one of those in love may love with the heart of the other?

Numerous and important consequences flow from these

principles. If Jesus and the soul have the same love that is the Holy Spirit, are they not to have the same priesthood, immolation, and noble undertaking?

The links of gold of the Chain of Love, even though those of Jesus differ from those of souls, nevertheless have a similar quality, for they have the same source, *the Holy Spirit.* If souls love with the Holy Spirit and He loves with their hearts, is it strange that these souls give consolation to Jesus, if the Holy Spirit is the Consoler *par excellence*?

How could one fail to do good to souls if one possesses the Sanctifier, and loves with Him and lives under His divine influence?

How could the soul fail to spread purity if it is joined to ineffable Purity? There would be no end to enumerating the consequences deriving from these fruitful and comforting bases.

Logically, a full and most perfect possession corresponds to this unitive love. The Holy Spirit possesses each soul in grace, but how limited and narrow is this possession in imperfect souls!

In the beginning, the Holy Spirit is confined, so to speak, to the center of the soul, and He can hardly exercise His influence in some regions of the soul and only in some happy instances; but slowly, He extends His action and penetrates, so to speak, to different parts of the soul as His influence becomes more effective and frequent, until He finally reigns as sovereign in this interior kingdom. He penetrates to the core of the soul, and directs all its faculties, and inspires all its actions so that it is not the soul that lives but God in it, and the words of the Apostle, *"For those who are led by the Spirit of God are children of God,"*[168] are accomplished.

If one could only understand the possession of the Holy Spirit in the transformed soul! Some consider the expression "transformation into Jesus" excessive because they do not understand spiritual realities. If the Spirit who moved Jesus and inspired His life is the same Spirit who moves and guides souls, why is it excessive to say that souls become the reflection of Jesus and their lives the image of His life?

Let's imagine a hypnotist who continuously makes suggestions to the hypnotized person; that person carries out the thought and suggestions of the hypnotist like an automaton. One would rightly say that the hypnotist operates on the person and directs the person's life during the hypnotic state.

Something like this happens in the transformed soul, but with two radical differences. The soul is not an automaton, but acts under the influence of the Holy Spirit with all its vital energy and with its full liberty. Moreover, the life which the Paraclete inspires is not something artificial and superimposed, as happens in the case of the hypnotized person, but it is a life which springs up from the depths of the soul, adapted to its nature, according to its own activity. In fact, it exclusively pertains to God to move souls in an effective way without harming their liberty, without contradicting their nature, without distorting their action. Rather, the Holy Spirit elevates and uplifts what the Creator has bestowed on them, grafting into souls the divine and supernatural impetus so that their actions may be totally and profoundly theirs while at the same time they are really and admirably God's.

Personal Reflection of Conchita
SIXTH DAY

What Jesus said to me yesterday on the glory of the Father was engraved in my soul. And this thought, even more than the intimate joy of doing His divine will, spurs me on to *doing* and *suffering* all for the glory of the Father in union with Jesus.

It struck me to the depths of my soul and Jesus makes me experience it.

This morning Jesus said to me:

"Look, upon incarnating mystically in a soul, I *expand* and enlarge it. When the mystery is accomplished in it, this soul does not give Me life, because I am Life, but I give life to the soul through grace.

"The soul receiving Me in the mystical incarnation receives a new life, especially that of purity and light.

"That soul gives life to Me in the sense that it shares, in a mystical manner, in the fruitfulness of the Father; but when Jesus grows in the soul by this grace, so to speak, He absorbs it, and the creature seemingly disappears, and can truly say: *"Yet I live, no longer I, but Christ lives in me."*[169] It can truly say, to the extent of its transformation, as it offers itself in union with Me to the eternal Father: "This is my body, this is my blood," while it immolates itself in His almighty presence for the salvation of souls.

"When the soul becomes more and more perfectly Jesus, My Father gazes on it with pleasure and the Holy Spirit possesses it, infusing His gifts and precious fruits into it.

"The Father is pleased with these infrequent mystical incarnations seeing in them the reflection – even if remote – of the mystery of the Incarnation of the Divine Word in Mary and He delights in seeing the continuation of His divine reflection in souls. Why? Because, in giving Jesus, He delights in giving Himself. As His Being is *self-giving*, communication and diffusion, He is happy, so to speak, to see His image and the reflection of the Trinity in souls.

"All the Divine Persons necessarily participate in the mystical incarnation, working in souls, and receiving glory through My human nature."

I am going to reflect on the Archbishop's meditation. My God! Give me strength to endure what it says.[170]

Later – The Works of the Cross

Suddenly Jesus told me:
"That gaze of the Father upon you was a sign of predilection, the heavenly grace which would develop in your soul, and would attain to consummation in due time.

"The abundance of incredible graces prepared your poor soul to be the dwelling of the Word mystically made flesh in your soul, and now I reveal it to you. Those graces came simultaneously with the Works of the Cross, and thus, were of a dual nature. They were born and grew, developing in the shade of that gaze of the Father, without your knowing it, and due to that grace whose principal features are purity, love and suffering, became accentuated in your soul.

"The divine plan of the Works of the Cross was embodied, without your knowing it, in the grace of the mystical incarnation from the moment of the Father's gaze on you in time, but it was in the bosom of God from all eternity. That gaze with divine gentleness prepared the foundation on thorns and infused in you a new spirit, that of the Works (which you had already begun from your childhood) and which would save many souls through the Holy Spirit and the Cross.

"The Father's gaze is so fruitful!" Jesus said with delight. "He began His work in you; the Holy Spirit inaugurated it first through His apparition and then through His symbol on the Cross;[171] the Divine Word consummated it in your heart, and then diffused it in the Works, in vocations and in thousands of souls that belong and will belong to the Works.

"Did you ever suspect this before? Have you pondered over this and reflected on it enough?

"But now, before the end of your life, you should reflect on this grace in depth, give thanks for it, and treasure it. The retreat, which Satan tried to block, is to bring to perfection My work in your soul, that grace of graces, with yet another sensible gaze of the Father which will remain in your soul throughout eternity, thus making fruitful what He sowed on earth through you."

"My God, my Father! Why do You gaze at me?"

"My Father looks on His Word and in His Word He sees you and all things. He is pleased with Me, communicating His essence to Me from all eternity. He rejoices in Me and He loves Me through the Holy Spirit, thus establishing infinite and eternal love, the heaven of the Three Divine Persons.

"Has My Father ever stopped gazing on you, Concha?

"He never has, because He is God, but He gazes with special affection because of the mystical incarnation from which He never averts His creative sight, because I, the Word, His Son, am His delight, and where I am there is the Holy Spirit.

"What would you do if His fatherly, loving gaze did not envelop you? Certainly, this special and wonderful grace of the mystical incarnation is not always sensible, but it *is real*.

"That is why you are pure and loving and you become like Me. Through that gaze of infinite love that produced in itself the Divine Word, equal to Him in all things, all graces come to you, and through that gaze which encompasses the Church and priests you will be saved."

"Oh God of my heart and of all my soul! Oh dearest Father! Oh my Jesus, my Jesus! Do You repay in this way my disloyalties and thousands of vile acts?"

"Do not think about them, but love Me. Give glory to the Father in union with Me and with Mary; seek My glory, losing yourself in the unity of the Divine Persons."

I truly feel that gaze which penetrates me and permeates my soul gently. I hope it might purify me, so that I will be less horrible while I am so close to Jesus.

October 20, 1935
SEVENTH DAY

Meditation of Archbishop Martínez

Holy Spirit

How blessed the soul that is guided in its actions by the Holy Spirit! The soul does not need to inquire painstakingly about what should be done, because it is moved and instructed inwardly by the Holy Spirit, by the Spirit of God.

It is enough for the soul guided in this way to have full docility to this holy impulse.

The assurance of doing God's will at every moment is not the only and the best advantage of the soul possessed by the Holy Spirit, but there is another advantage even more precious, which makes all its acts divine. It is not a pious exaggeration but a happy reality.

St. John of the Cross teaches this in a precise manner and St. Thomas explains it, because the acts of the soul come both from it and from the Holy Spirit; they come from the soul because it carries them out, and from the Holy Spirit because He moves the soul to do them; and they are more from the Holy Spirit than from the soul, and being from the Holy Spirit they are divine, because He puts His own seal on them.

You have not been aware of this marvelous effect of the mystical incarnation, have you?

As you cannot doubt the grace which you received, so you cannot doubt the prerogative which proceeds from it. If the Holy Spirit guides all your actions – unless you withdraw from His loving influence – you should feel assured that you please God at every moment! What peace your soul should feel, living in this divine world!

At the same time, you are surprised because of what God and I tell you, that with your sacrifices and acts of love you can purchase graces for souls, and glorify the heavenly Father. But if you realize that your sacrifices and actions have the divine seal, by the influence of the Holy Spirit, you should not be surprised. For it is not strange that what proceeds from the Spirit is effective and has value, even through the worst instrument.

Thus when you offer Jesus to the Father, you achieve a reflection of Jesus' life, who *"through the eternal Spirit offered Himself unblemished to God."*[172] Your offering has the same foundation: the Holy Spirit who moves you as He moved Jesus; the same oblation, that of Jesus who lives in you; therefore, your offering pleases God from whom you snatch torrents of graces.

That is why the Chain of Love which you practice continues that of Jesus, because the same Spirit who effected that of Jesus

Conchita's Reflections on a Retreat

forges yours, placing in its precious links the gold of priestly love, and the precious stone of the immolation of Jesus.

How many things can be explained if we understand this constant influence of the Holy Spirit in a soul that has received the mystical incarnation!

You should be aware that this influence is constant, and it is not exercised only in some acts of singular fervor but in all, be they interior or exterior, pious or ordinary.

When the soul knows, the Holy Spirit illuminates it; when it loves, He sets it on fire; when it praises God, He puts perfect praise on its lips; when the soul addresses another soul, the Holy Spirit makes it fruitful, and even seemingly ordinary actions are not so, because when the Holy Spirit touches them He divinizes them, converts them into love and makes them efficacious.

What we should understand from this is that you should live in a divine world, in an anticipated heaven, attentive to receive the impulses of the Holy Spirit, putting into practice what the Psalm says: *"Like the eyes of a servant on the hand of his master, like the eyes of a maid on the hand of her mistress, so our eyes are on the Lord our God, till we are shown favor."*[173]

This constant attention should be followed by perfect docility to the motions of the Holy Spirit, so that what He inspires you to do should be done, and He should be truly the Life of your life, the Soul of your soul. Thus Jesus lived, guided and moved by the Holy Spirit. The Gospel and the apostles' writings underscore His great mysteries.

"Then Jesus was led by the Spirit into the desert to be tempted by the devil."[174] Jesus rejoiced in the Holy Spirit, praising the Father for hiding His secrets from the learned and the clever and revealing them to the little ones.[175] St. Paul tells us that Jesus *"through the eternal Spirit offered Himself unblemished to God."*[176]

Both expressions perfectly correspond to each other: to be Jesus and to be moved by the Holy Spirit, as the Apostle points out, *"Those who are led by the Spirit of God are children of God,"*[177] that is, other Christs.

It is necessary that the soul let itself be guided and moved by the Holy Spirit in order to be transformed into Jesus, to reproduce His life, and above all, to renew His sacrifice and share in His priesthood.

This doctrine shows us the coordination and harmony between the various rich elements of the spirit of the Cross. It should be stressed that this spirit can be realized in all its fullness only by the mystical incarnation. From a soul that has received that grace came the revelation of the spirit of the Cross, and the ideal to which this spirit leads is that of the mystical incarnation.

The Spirituality of the Cross encompasses some essential elements: devotion to the Holy Spirit, the desire to be transformed into Jesus, the aspiration to participate mystically in the priesthood of Jesus, participating in His sacrifice and especially in His interior sacrifice. These elements are bound together by strict divine logic.

It is impossible to participate in the priesthood and sacrifice of Jesus, according to the spirit of the Cross, if the soul is not transformed into Him. Bishop Gay observed: "To accomplish the work of Jesus, it is necessary to be Jesus." How, without being Jesus, could the soul realize the intimate and fine work of the sacrifice and the intimate priesthood of Jesus?

It is impossible to be transformed into Jesus without the influence of the Holy Spirit, because this transformation demands having the same sentiments as Jesus had: thinking, loving, working, suffering as He did and thus being fruitful as He was. To attain to this, the same Spirit, who guided and shaped the life of Jesus, should guide and shape the life of the soul.

Personal Reflection of Conchita
SEVENTH DAY

Today my Jesus wanted to talk to me. And I thought He would be silent during this retreat! As soon as I entered the oratory, He said to me:

"Now, do you know what your consolation will be after giving all for priests?

"To *do* everything and to *suffer* everything for the glory of the Father, following My example, enveloped in His gaze and saturated by that divine gaze which encloses all: purity, fruitfulness, light and desolations, fortitude, and unblemished love in all of its phases, nuances, forms, an infinite and eternal love.

"That is enough for you, and it will make you happy here on earth and in heaven. You will see all *within* this divine gaze; you will suffer all from *within* that heavenly perspective. Enveloped and pervaded by God, you will be happy if you dwell within that infinite gaze, without leaving it and within that gaze you will dwell and die.

"This is heaven on earth; this is the gift that crowns the mystical incarnation; this is the perfect interior life. The soul, with all it has and all that surrounds it, occupies itself only in *giving Me glory*, in doing everything *for My glory*, in consuming all its energies, desires and loves in the one desire and love, in the Holy Spirit, for My glory, offering itself in union with the Word to the Father as a victim of eternal expiation, only because of who He is, *only to give Him glory.*

"Tell those souls[178] also to begin this new life which is the most perfect one, to grow in it, and to sanctify themselves in this way, with this nuance which encloses all nuances, which encompasses all the steps of the spirit in one which is the holiest, the most perfect, all *for the glory of God.*

"They should offer everything in union with Me, *without breaking* this union, living and dying within the gaze of the Father, that gaze with which He has looked upon His Word from all eternity, and with which He continues to gaze upon Him and to delight in Him, since He is the same God with regard to the divinity – while the Holy Spirit unites them in the bond of love.

"This is the course I have traced for you today: enter this way without hesitation and with great faith and love, this way which will raise you from the earth and will make you live in a divine way."

In another meditation I told Him: "Lord, it occurs to me that all these things are not true. Since Your Father does not have eyes – for He is spirit – or in whatever way one can express it, so what is this gaze like? How does He gaze upon us?"

He replied, "God is Light, and this answer should be enough for you to understand, if you reflect on it.

"This uncreated light encompasses all gazes in one gaze; all understandings in one understanding; all things in their essence, in their principle; all lights in the one Light; all mysteries in one sole Mystery; all loves in one sole Love.

"This Light includes all the attributes of God: His wisdom, power, eternity and all His perfections; His plurality in one sole essence; His infinity in one sole substance.

"God always sees, listens, feels, and always embraces what exists and what will exist. He is a Space which contains everything. He is a Science which knows everything. He is a Fruitfulness which produces everything. He is an Embrace which contains everything, from eternity to eternity. He is a Principle without cause. He is a Cause which encompasses all, the divine fruitfulness which, beginning to produce itself eternally in the Word, does not stop irradiating, filling worlds, souls, lives, creations, reflecting itself in all that is created and will be created...."

I felt as if God, being God, could not contain His inexhaustible fruitfulness, could not stop producing Himself in all things.

He made me see that He does not make a thing, a soul, a life, a world, an atom, without giving *Himself* in all His infinite immensity.

He told me that God is in an atom, in an insect, in a flower, as well as in a star, a sky, in all that He creates, without leaving Himself.

What lights, my Father! My soul trembled before this multiplication of God Himself, without multiplying Himself, without leaving this union with the Word and the Holy Spirit.

Oh how great God is! How incomprehensible God is! How infinite, powerful and holy God is!

How is it possible that we offend Him, being such atoms, such microbes?

And, Father of my soul,[179] God made me see and *feel* the limitless depth of His infinite love in all creatures, in the heavens and in space and in eternity. As a boundless torrent He came to my heart, dazzling me, blinding me with His light which, nonetheless, *made me see* more clearly, the closer it came to my soul.

This light darkens the earth and illumines heaven.

I was seeing... and feeling... His eternal fruitfulness in His Word by way of love, as produced by a substantial love in Himself... and the ebb and flow of His perfections enveloped, produced and sustained by love... and the substance of the love of the Three Divine Persons.

My soul saw – I don't know how – the Word being begotten within the Father, and "as if being born" while being generated within the same Father through the infinite power of an infinite Love, and it saw the Word being "made" of the substance of Love, which is the same Being, the same substance of the Father.[180]

Oh my Father! What can we call these heavenly lights, which in their shining warm the soul, and melt it as if with its fire, and raise it up with its sanctifying and purifying efficacy?

What will heaven be like?

Heaven is God, my Jesus, isn't it?

My husband[181] communicated to me, when I asked him, after his death as he was leaving purgatory (he spent no more than ninety-two hours there), what heaven was like. His answer still vibrates in me, *"Heaven is the infinite bosom of God."*

Later on – Unity

Jesus said: "I am going to tell you something which you do not even imagine. All that comes from God returns to God."

"But how?"

"In the sense of unity, because all things He creates and which come from Him, are in Him."

"But, Lord, with regard to souls, I somehow understand, because even those who condemn themselves, according to Your words, fulfill the attribute of Your justice, and in this they glorify You. You have already explained it to me. But for example, an animal which dies, a flower whose petals are pulled off, how do they return to You?"

"In the sense that the mission I gave to them on earth has been accomplished, that of serving, perfuming, that of giving Me glory in My attributes of power and wisdom, in My *essence*, in My loving designs.

"In God, everything is perfect and in order. He creates everything for His glory – and how much more the souls to whom He has communicated the reflection of the Trinity – so that He must necessarily receive glory from them, either eternally in heaven or in hell!

"It is clear that My Father is satisfied and delighted more by the glory which a soul gives Him spontaneously and not under duress, offered without pressure, without self-interest, only because of who He is, simply recognizing Him as worthy of all honor, reverence, gratitude, homage and worthy of being loved above all things.

"Where My Father sees love, that is, where He contemplates His Word communicated by the one who is Love, by the Holy Spirit, there His gaze rests, there He pours Himself out, empties Himself, I would say, and delights in Himself, in the Divine Persons who are joined to Him, that is, in His divine Son and the Holy Spirit.

"My Father sees only His Word with the eyes of Love, and in His Word He sees all things. That is why in the mystical incarnations He rests His gaze in a special way on the soul in which the Word dwells, and He is pleased pouring Himself out by the Holy Spirit in charisms of graces."

With all these things He did not let me reflect on the meditation, and I will do it later.

Blessed be the Lord!

I am embarrassed that my meditation runs in such directions, so that I pass over them as a cat over the embers. It seems I can hardly face the logical consequences to be drawn from the mystical incarnation.

The effects of this grace overwhelm me. They would kill me if I did not have a hide tougher than an elephant's.

October 21, 1935
EIGHTH DAY

Meditation of Archbishop Martínez

Fruitfulness

Fruitfulness is the third characteristic of the outpouring of the Holy Spirit. Even though all fruitfulness is attributed to the Father, as the source, it is proper to the Holy Spirit, who is love, to infuse divine fruitfulness in creatures.

Because of this, His symbol is the dove, even though there are other analogies expressed in this symbol.

In the beginning of time, the Holy Spirit was hovering over the chaos and beauty and life appeared in the universe. In the fullness of time, He descended on the Virgin Mary and Jesus was conceived in her womb. In the Upper Room – and the Church is the continuation of the Upper Room – He descended on souls and filled them with beauty and life and made them Jesus.

Whenever the Holy Spirit descends on a soul, He gives it life and He gives it Jesus, who is Life. But in the mystical incarnation, the Holy Spirit accomplishes His perfect work in the soul, transforming it into Jesus, and giving it spiritual fruitfulness, so that the soul may give Jesus to other souls.

The outpouring of the Holy Spirit in the soul who has received the grace of the mystical incarnation takes two forms of fruitfulness, which are essentially one: the one consists of making of the soul the reflection, the living image of Jesus; the other one enables the soul possessed by the Holy Spirit to give Jesus to other souls.

The mystical incarnation is the transformation of the soul into Jesus, and two delightful consequences, at first sight apparently incompatible, flow from it: the soul is mystically Jesus, and the soul is mystically mother of Jesus. The soul is mystically Jesus, because the Holy Spirit, as divine Artisan, has established Jesus' characteristics in it, but not in a static way, as an image painted on canvas or sculpted in marble, but in a living way, so that He ineffably conveys to the soul the life of Jesus with its intimate sentiments, lofty intentions, heavenly light, pure love, unspeakable suffering, divine actions, and in a word, with all that Jesus' lofty and holy life contains in itself.

The soul so transformed can say with St. Paul, "*Yet I live, no longer I, but Christ lives in me.*"[182] But this living picture of Jesus is produced not only by the Holy Spirit, but by the mysterious collaboration of the soul, as in the way that Jesus appeared in the womb of the Virgin by the work of the Holy Spirit, but also with the collaboration of the immaculate Virgin who conceived Him.

Just as the Blessed Virgin is the true Mother of God because of her unique collaboration, so also the soul is mystically the mother of Jesus as a result of its collaboration with the Holy Spirit in the mysterious work which He accomplished in it.

That is why, in this blessed soul, the love and sentiments of the Heart of Jesus are renewed and at the same time, the love and sentiments of the ever Virgin Mary are also reproduced.

Being Jesus, the soul loves the Father, reflecting Jesus' love and seeking His glory as Jesus sought it so that the love, suffering, actions and life of the soul aim with perfect unity and intense concentration at one point, just as all the activities of Jesus' soul converged to the glory of the Father, the center and crowning of Jesus' life.

At the same time, because of the mystical incarnation, the soul shares in Mary's love, which is at the same time a participation in the Father's love, pure, tender, motherly love; because truly the soul has conceived Jesus mystically in its bosom.

If we enter more deeply into the mystery, we will begin to discover the meaning of this strange duality of love and sentiments, considering that the soul that has received the mystical incarnation loves with the Holy Spirit, who is the love of the Father and of the Son. Since the Holy Spirit is the love of the Father and of the Son, it is through Him that the Father is loved as Jesus loves Him and it is through Him that Jesus is loved as the Father loves Him and consequently, as Mary, whose motherly love is a participation and reflection of the love of the Father, loves Him.

One can understand this love (which is apparently twofold, but in fact, wonderfully one) better, when one considers the intimate characteristics of this love.

The Father loves Jesus with the mysterious and ineffable refinement in which the incomprehensible strength and unfathomable tenderness that delivered Him to the Cross are commingled.

Thus, keeping due proportion, Mary and the soul that has received the mystical incarnation love Jesus. They love Him in order to sacrifice Him, and loving Him in this way this poor human love seems to touch the boundaries of the divine, sharing in the heroic strength and mysterious tenderness of divine love. The soul could not offer the divine Son to the Cross if it did not love with the same love with which the Father loves, that is, with the Holy Spirit.

In like manner, if the soul did not love with the divine Spirit, it could not love the Father as Jesus loves Him, that is, sacrificing itself for His glory. In this love, there are two divine characteristics: First, pure intention for the glory of God which, if we examine it well, presupposes a heavenly light in this love; the light which enables the soul to see that the glory of God is the supreme good of the creature, without taking itself into consideration and without any trace of earthly selfishness; second, a disinterest, a purity which can hardly be imagined in a creature, and which I will now explain in detail.

There are in the soul two elements: the most profound, which is at its base, is divine, the image of the Holy Trinity; and the frame which encloses this image, which is the setting of the jewel, so to speak, is what is properly human in the soul.

When the soul begins to know itself, it admires the setting without suspecting the jewel it contains; it contemplates what is human in it, unaware of what is divine; and from this way of understanding selfish love springs up, which thinks of nothing other than its own good, with no thought for the divine good.

To the extent that the soul receives God's light, the vision of self disappears, and the image of the Holy Trinity, which the soul carries within, appears, firstly indistinctly and vaguely, then more clearly and precisely. With this light from heaven, the soul is transfigured and the love of God grows in it, and each day seeks with ever greater determination the good of God. But this divine love is still commingled with the selfishness of our heart until the setting disappears and the divine jewel stands out in its splendor and fills the soul's field of vision with its grandeur.

So love also discards all its sediment of selfishness and, in its triumphal purity, it forgets the good of the creature, and encounters itself fully and totally in the divine good of God's glory.

This does not mean that the soul stops loving its own good, which would be against its own nature, but that it has received the wonderful revelation that its real good is the divine good, the glory of God. This is because its real good does not consist in health of body, nor in clarity and richness of intelligence, nor in the deep generosity of heart, nor, to say it in a word, in the exaltation of what is human in the soul, but that the intimate image of God may become splendid, living, supreme praise, royal homage, and the sublime canticle to the glory of God.

Conchita's Reflections on a Retreat

Personal Reflection of Conchita
EIGHTH DAY

Today Jesus is silent. I have only placed myself at His feet gazing at Him... giving thanks... and offering Him my past, my present and my future for His glory alone.

"Lord," I told Him, "even if there were no heaven, I would still love You."

I feel permeated with this thought: *His glory*! And on it I want to center my whole life.

The Cross!

His glory!

I would like both Congregations of the Cross to have this very clear coloring.

How Jesus' words are at work in us!

How His desires open up vast horizons in my soul!

Indeed, I feel God in a very special way, even though His love is ever old and ever new!

When will I disappear so that only the Three Divine Persons may reign in me *fully* and without *qualifications* on my part?

What a meditation I have made today! It radiates light; it explains with supernatural precision, the outstanding grace of the mystical incarnation, *inspired*, *deepened* and *developed*.

Jesus fulfills His promise to give light to my spiritual director in order to explore the abyss of that grace of graces.

And, as never, I feel wiped out, completely annihilated, without understanding why I do not dissolve, melt in gratitude?

Why was it given to me? Because Jesus looks for the lowest of the lowest to make His glory shine out the more.

What coordination in the graces of God! How they develop and attain their goal without one's knowing or understanding it!

Just impossible to make comments!

UNDER THE GAZE OF THE FATHER

October 22, 1935
NINTH DAY

Meditation of Archbishop Martínez

Sacrifice

The other trait of Jesus' love for the Father is characterized by sacrifice, not only in the sense that Jesus loves Him to the point of sacrificing Himself for Him, but also as a love whose supreme expression is the Cross, the only adequate homage, the only praise which corresponds to the magnitude, the tenderness, and the immense force of that love.

How do we explain the divine mystery? I think that every love has its specific formula and proper expression. When I open my heart fully to my friend, the friendship finds its measure. When the bride gives her life to the chosen of her heart, spousal love makes its supreme gift. When a mother gives her child life, in all its fullness, that is, of the body and of the soul, her motherly love fulfills its immense longing. But the divine love has another specific formula, another ideal, and another infinite mold.

Since this is the most refined of friendships, it is not enough for this love to communicate the treasure of its secrets. Since this is ineffable spousal love, it is not enough to consecrate one's life to the Beloved. Since it is fatherly love, it is not enough to give the gift of one's full fecundity to the beloved, without communicating life in its integrity.

I say this because the human way of understanding these things is never sufficient, and because divine love is infinite, its expression is infinite, its gift is infinite, and its canticle is infinite.

In heaven, in the bosom of God, the expression of love is the ineffable communication of the Divinity in the inscrutable divine processions.[183]

When this love is transplanted on earth, as it was when Jesus appeared on it, what will its expression, gift and canticle be like? What will Jesus, who bears eternal love in His Heart, do in order to tell His Father that He loves Him, in order to intone the full and just canticle to God's glory?

On earth, there is no infinity! Here all expressions are narrow and all gifts limited, and all canticles are poor in harmony, faded and ephemeral, since they cannot fill the universe with sonority, nor contain in their poor notes the infinite fullness of harmony!

On earth, heavenly love found its expression and canticle in the Cross.

Can our spirit understand this? Does our heart have any premonition of this? The suffering and death which are symbolized by the Cross are the infinity of earth, the infinity of poverty and misery, but in the end, infinity. Death means stopping to be what we were and isn't this somersault infinite in a certain sense, given that between being and non-being there is infinite distance?

Suffering, according to the words of one holy Father, is *"quaedam prolixitas mortis,"* that is, a slow drawn-out death, we could say, death drop by drop.

If death and suffering are not something infinite for us, would they be for the Word made flesh? What distance is there between God and death, between the divine beatitude and suffering on earth?

In heaven, the infinite self-giving of the infinite being is the expression of love and the ineffable happiness of God is His canticle.

On earth, the expression of the divine love is the Cross, which is the self-giving of something finite made in an infinite manner and the canticle of this love is the *"Consumatum est"*[184] of Calvary. It is the voice of the Spirit which cries out, of the blood which is shed, of the water which flows out of the open side.

In heaven, three give testimony, the Father, the Son and the Holy Spirit, and these three are One; on earth, three testify, the Spirit, the water, and the blood, and these three are of one accord.[185]

Divine love has two specific formulas, two canticles, and two testimonies: in heaven, the Blessed Trinity and on earth, bleeding and sublime Calvary.

The soul that has received the mystical incarnation, by the divine outpouring of the Holy Spirit and loving with His love, copies these two traits of Jesus' love. The soul, in the triumphal purity of its love, thrusts itself swiftly and confidently toward the glory of God, the center of the soul's unity and the only mover of its ardor, tenderness, longings and activity.

And in order to show its love for the Father, in order to find its expression and canticle, the soul seeks the mysterious and unspeakable canticle of the Cross. On the Cross, the soul offers Jesus and nails itself to it with Him.

Notice the harmony, the heavenly logic which links last year's retreat with this year's; to each one corresponds one of the characteristics I have just mentioned.[186]

Last year, you received from God the supreme formula of love, that of offering Jesus to the Father to be crucified. Today, the glory of God, which is the only and delightful goal of this love, is revealed to you.

Both revelations complete each other. They are two notes of the same chord, two nuances of the same fragrance, two facets of the same splendid diamond. Both show us the mystery of perfect love, whose source is the Holy Spirit.

Love has only one end: *the glory of God*, of which *the Cross* is the highest expression.

When a soul has received the full revelation of God's glory, it seeks the Cross with divine eagerness. When it has nailed itself on it, *the glory of God* shines over its head like a splendid crown.

The Cross of the Apostolate[187] symbolizes this mystery: below, the Cross with its infinite richness of suffering; above, the light of the Divinity covers it with its glory; and the heavenly dove as a magnificent link between earth and heaven, the eternal love which makes divine glory well up out of the bloodstained Cross and which bathes suffering and death with heavenly splendor.

In the center of the Cross, the divine Heart appears surrounded with light; this Heart, which accomplished the prodigy of salvation through the Holy Spirit. In this same Heart, I dare say, the soul of the Cross is symbolized, that is, the transformed soul which, fused with the Heart of Jesus, sings with Him the canticle of suffering and death to the glory of God on earth.

Personal Reflection of Conchita
NINTH DAY

Today also Jesus remained silent. Anyway, I love Him very much, even when He is *silent*, too. I want what He wants.

If He is glorified by my self-abandonment to His will, I will be happy in any case.

I have received a light, radiations of a grace....

I have felt and seen the richness Jesus has deposited in my soul *because of His sheer goodness*, and I am so grateful. The graces are His and they are granted to my soul for His service and glory.

I contemplated what I am from outside, and it is like *bark* which covers pearls, like a plain case which contains these jewels. It seems to me that I have hit the nail on the head. With this is destroyed the overdone humility which did not allow me to see the mystical incarnation as it actually is and in its full splendor.

Now, what is beautiful is within, where only God and my spiritual director see it. And what is ugly, the external self, remains unchanged in its deformity and faults, which I will use to cover the heaven of my soul like a black cloud which covers the sun; but the sun which radiates on behalf of souls, priests, especially focusing, above all other things, on *the glory of God*, remains untouched underneath.

I am reflecting on the Archbishop's meditation on sacrifice...

What a beautiful meditation!

Each point of it elevates my soul, opening up infinite horizons before it, sweet consequences and a bottomless abyss of love.

Oh God of my heart and my entire soul! Be blessed!

October 23, 1935
TENTH DAY

Meditation of Archbishop Martínez

Fruitfulness on behalf of souls

Upon pouring Himself out in the soul by the mystical incarnation, the Holy Spirit not only makes it Jesus, but also communicates spiritual fruitfulness to it, so that the soul may give Jesus to other souls.

One's motherhood of Jesus has as its logical consequence one's motherhood of souls, for the *whole* Jesus, so to speak, also includes His Mystical Body.

For this reason, Mary is Mother of all humanity, because she is Mother of Jesus. Analogically, the soul that is mystically mother of Jesus because of the mystical incarnation is also mother of other souls, according to the measure of Christ's gift.

It is a characteristic of the soul that has received the mystical incarnation to have a special influence upon other souls, into whom the fruitfulness of the Holy Spirit, who formed Jesus in this soul, also overflows.

Certainly, every soul that possesses God communicates Him to a certain degree, just as a vessel filled with perfume scents what is around it, given that God by His nature is diffusive; but the soul that has received the mystical incarnation, by the nature of that grace and the mission which it bears, has a special gift to give Jesus, to be mystically mother of other souls.

The gift of giving Jesus to other souls belongs to souls that have received the mystical incarnation in a singular manner for two reasons.

First, these souls have a special relation with Jesus because they have as their source the reflection of the fruitfulness of the Father. Being mystically mothers of Jesus, they not only form Him in themselves but also in others.

Secondly, for these souls, sacrifice is the center of their lives and mission. As the Word was made flesh in the womb of Mary to offer Himself in sacrifice, so the mystical incarnation of the Word in souls is also ordered to sacrifice.

What an amazing thing! Wherever Jesus is born, He is born for sacrifice; in Bethlehem, on the altar and in souls, the words of the Nicene Creed are fulfilled: *"For us men and for our salvation He came down from heaven; by the power of the Holy Spirit, He was born of the Virgin Mary, and became man."*

The Word of God descends from heaven and becomes mystically incarnate in souls in order to continue and renew His sacrifice. It is not by chance that the grace of the mystical incarnation is at the very center of the Works of the Cross,[188] because that grace and the Cross are inseparably linked by the divine logic.

Could we penetrate this mysterious link? As stated, Jesus has in His Heart a supreme longing for the glory of His Father, and this glory is also achieved by the supreme means of the Cross. Is it not logical that where Jesus appears in His fullness, sacrifice appears, and that He communicates His longing for God's glory and the mission to continue His sacrifice to souls in whom the perfect transformation into Jesus is accomplished?

A soul that has received the mystical incarnation is a victim soul and participates in the priesthood of Jesus, that is, it is priest, victim and altar like Jesus.

For this reason, the Father gave you the reflection of His fruitfulness to communicate to you His divine love, that love which offers the Beloved to the Cross. Jesus became mystically incarnate in you in order to renew His sacrifice. The Holy Spirit possessed you fully and accomplished His perfect work in you, in order to guide you to immolation as He guided Jesus, who through the eternal Spirit offered Himself unblemished to God.[189]

The Cross is fruitful not only because suffering is the necessary condition, even more, it is the source of fruitfulness on earth, as Jesus taught us: *"Unless a grain of wheat falls to the ground and dies, it remains just a grain of wheat; but if it dies, it produces much fruit;"*[190] but also because the sacrifice of Jesus on Calvary, on the altar and in souls is destined to bring abundant life to souls, because sacrifice by its nature is offered on behalf of others, *"to offer gifts and sacrifices for sins,"*[191] according to the words of the sacred author. The victim is offered on behalf of others, and the altar is precisely the place on which, not only the sacrifice is made, but also on which the fruits of the sacrifice are placed, and from which they are poured forth to the world, so that souls may share in them.

Therefore, there is a very close relation between *incarnation*, *sacrifice* and *fruitfulness*. In the mortal life of Jesus, His sacrifice is the golden link which joins the mystery of His Incarnation with the mystery of His fruitfulness. And in His Eucharistic life the mysterious trilogy is reproduced: Jesus descends onto the altar to sacrifice Himself, He sacrifices Himself to give life; and in His mystical life in souls the threefold mystery is renewed: *mystical incarnation*, *intimate sacrifice* and *spiritual fruitfulness*.

Thus spiritual motherhood is the characteristic and mission of the soul that received the mystical incarnation.

The life and mission of that soul is the reflection of the life and mission of the Virgin Mary, and the three phases of the divine mystery appear linked in it. Mary is Mother of all because the Word was made flesh in her, because she shared in the sacrifice of Jesus and because she was the depositary of the divine graces.

Three titles constitute Mary's sweet maternity with regard to souls: Mother of God, Co-redemptrix of the human race, and Mediatrix of all graces, and these three titles are linked, complement each other and make Mary our gentle Mother.

The soul that has received the mystical incarnation is the reflection of Mary, and through the divine link, the three titles of Mary are reflected in it, certainly in a lesser degree and with the limits marked by God, but nevertheless in their mystical reality and harmony.

When we consider the doctrine which I have just explained, how much your life is illuminated and the graces which God bestowed on you are clarified, and the harmonious whole of the work of God in your soul is admired!

Conchita's Reflections on a Retreat

Don't you see how the numberless and marvelous graces which you have received hold their place in the awe-inspiring whole and link and complement each other, giving the impression of unity and beauty, like countless and rich notes of a magnificent symphony which harmonize and fuse in most beautiful unity?

Your life could be synthesized in this admirable trilogy and grouped around each one of the phases of your spiritual life, in each of the mysteries of your great grace, the torrents of divine gifts, the cascades of precious charisms which form the mighty river of your life which culminates in the bosom of God.

Many deep and useful affections should spring from your heart as the result of these considerations.

First, a great gratitude, which should turn into a great love. The better the gifts received are known and appreciated, the deeper and more extensive should be the gratitude, which necessarily kindles the fire of love.

Second, since all graces link and unify themselves in a beautiful whole, they cannot be separated to the extent that some of them are accepted, while others are not; that some of them are looked at directly while others are viewed sidelong; rather all should be believed; all should be accepted and looked at directly, with simple boldness and with holy naturalness.

Third, since the law established by Jesus in the Gospel is that one should work and thus multiply the talents received, so you should not forget even one of your graces, but strengthen and develop all of them, and gather the fruits of eternal life from all of them.

Since Jesus is at the heart of all divine graces, each of them *prepares* for Him, *contains* Him, and *diffuses* Him. Therefore, to strengthen and develop these graces means to make Jesus grow in the soul, and to diffuse Him, to cooperate in fulfilling the words of the Apostle, "*for you are all one in Christ Jesus,*"[192] so that through the soul the supreme and final word of the Apostle may be accomplished, "*that God may be all in all.*"[193]

UNDER THE GAZE OF THE FATHER

Personal Reflection of Conchita
TENTH DAY

The Glory of the Father

Today Jesus wanted to talk to me. Some days ago, He made me see a ray in the cloud of what He wanted to share, but still it remained cloudy.

Today He told me: "Look, I don't want you to glorify Me only in suffering, penance, interior sorrows, in all that is exterior and interior and carry the sign of the *cross*, but also in all your actions, joys, satisfactions and consolations, focusing everything on giving Me glory.

"You will discover in this new period of your spiritual life a new nuance of special love with which all works get perfumed, wafting to heaven the divine fragrance, that of your Jesus, who glorifies His Father in you.

"However, I want and require this new passage of perfection not only of you but also of the Works of the Cross.

"I want them to have this splendid orientation and deep substance, *the glory of My Father*!

"Especially in certain souls of these beloved congregations this most holy facet, the glory of God, should shine as a star of first magnitude."

"But, Lord, who are these *certain souls*?"

"All in general should saturate their acts with this divine gold, but especially those souls transformed in Me, and the few that receive the grace of the mystical incarnation. Those souls will be especially raised to these heights, permeated with this substance, oriented first and above all to this goal, *the glory of My Father*.

"There are many degrees in seeking this glory, until the soul, lost in Me, stripped of all human interest and selfishness, purified by many crucibles and by degrees of transformation and inward martyrdom, throws itself into seeking this goal alone, *the glory of God*, and making of it its whole being and life."

"Lord, according to what You have said, is this not the crowning of the mystical incarnation?"

"It is and its full development in heaven and on earth; with regard to God and creatures, because by doing *everything* for the glory of God, through that soul, God diffuses Himself in other souls. And for this reason, what ascends from earth to heaven, *in union with Me* returns, through Me, from heaven to earth, enriched in graces.

"This is the Chain of love in all its perfection. The Divine Word is its center, the channel that carries to the Father the glory which creatures give to Him in Me, and which returns to creatures converted into charisms of great value.

"For that, what you will offer from now on for the glory of the Father will return to priests to whom you belong, converted into graces for their souls.

"As you see, one thing does not impede the other. Forgetful of self and transformed into Me through the mystical incarnation, you offer and suffer everything, totally lost in Me, for the glory of My Father; and I convert into graces for priests and souls your golden, vivid, intense and zealous acts.

"Do you know what these graces entail? They encompass the divine fruitfulness, which will produce more graces and multiply the links of the Chain of Gold which ascend through Me to heaven and descend through Me to souls, after having offered to the adored Trinity the delicate, loving incense of the earth."

Later on, Jesus continued:

"This loving attention on your part to give Me glory *always* in all you see, hear, speak, suffer, enjoy, whether asleep or awake and in all your acts, will keep your soul ever in My divine presence and you will live enveloped and absorbed in a divine and heavenly atmosphere, without losing sight of Me, in suffering or joy, in prayer or at work. And your soul will be invaded not only by the thought of Me, of My human presence, but also by My divine presence, which is inseparable from My human one, which embraces the Holy Trinity.

UNDER THE GAZE OF THE FATHER

"Is it not true that you did not even suspect the richness I have disclosed to you, the light and grace I have given you in this perfect step of your life that I asked of you, that of *the glory of My Father*?

"Enter, lose yourself on this path, I repeat it to you. May the souls of both congregations open themselves to receive the dew from heaven, which will give them vigor, freshness and strength to follow the paths of God, thus fulfilling the lofty designs of their vocation."

More and more, my Father,[194] I perceive the enveloping of this new grace. It is as if Jesus turned my soul toward a divine Lighthouse, *the glory of the Father*, and by this light, I apprehend a great perfection, a rare path.

Shall I tell you how? As if walking not with shoes or just walking, but flying with wings, and always ascending toward heaven, God. Is this holy effect real?

I think it is, because it envelops me in light; it permeates me with peace because, in all this, I perceive God.

Oh how subtle and real spiritual things are!

I distinguish *two things* in me: enjoying the beautiful which God has put in my soul and trying to ignore the ugly, despicable bark.[195]

As is the case with a walnut, enjoy the fruit and throw away the shell.

Look, Father, how once again today, while I was "on the roses," Jesus made me experience with vivid, ardent and holy love the delight of offering *this little thing* to the glory of God? This thought spurs me on to a suffering permeated with purest love, a love without self-interest, without egoism, a love elevating the soul, delighting in *God's goodness* even at the cost of the poor creature.

Do you understand me? Can I clearly explain the inexplicable, if it is not experienced?

How good Jesus is!

If I only gained from this retreat this new step in my spiritual life, I would be satisfied.

At the moment, I cannot reflect on my meditation easily, because Jesus hasn't let me. I will do it later on. Blessed be He!

Oh Mother of my life, oh Virgin incomparable, help me to give thanks to my Jesus!

Today, during Mass and communion, I told my Jesus I would offer all in thanksgiving, if it pleased Him.

I am meditating on fruitfulness on behalf of souls...

How does my soul respond to all these graces? For how many things did I not pay attention and should I ask forgiveness?

Oh what teaching, what lights the mystical incarnation contains!

How much Jesus suffered because of my stupidity, indifference, and carelessness because I did not give this grace *its proper place* in my life?

Oh Virgin Mother of my soul! Ask Jesus to forgive me, to forget my past full of ingratitude, to turn the page and begin a new life of light, love, gratitude, finally becoming what He wants me to be!

Is it not true, my dearest Jesus, light of my existence, breath of my soul, heart of my life, is it not true that You will refashion me?

October 24, 1935
Eleventh Day

Meditation of Archbishop Martínez

The Holy Spirit – His mode of working

Like every work which has its term outside of God, the mystical incarnation is produced by the Three Divine Persons; but being the work of love and sanctification, it is attributed to the Holy Spirit.

Consequently, studying the outpouring of the Spirit in the soul that received that grace, many characteristics of that grace have appeared and even more could appear.

But this admirable grace has other most important traits which are proper to the Word and the Father, and which it is appropriate to study with loving concern.

In the mystical incarnation, as we have already indicated, there is a close union with the Word of God, a transformation into Jesus. Jesus appears in this grace as the term of the transformation of the soul, and thus, as I have already said, the soul is mystically Jesus, and at the same time, Jesus is also the Son of the soul, in the mystical order.

Transformed into Jesus, the soul has a reflection of Jesus in itself. The soul thinks, loves, speaks, works, suffers as He does and shares in His mission, according to the measure and form of the divine design.

Hence, the transformed soul should live in a divine world, seeing everything: the Father, souls, creatures, divine and human things, through the eyes of Jesus. Its judgment is that of Jesus, its doctrine, the Gospel, or rather, the soul should be the *living Gospel*.[196]

In a special manner, the soul received the secrets of Jesus, *"the truth that He heard from God"*[197] and with the divine light, now penetrates the intimate confidences of Jesus.

Even though any soul united to Jesus receives all this precious treasure of light, each one has its special secrets in which God's light focuses, so to speak, on some truths more while on others less; and He reveals to the soul a particular region of the divine world, so that, even though the whole Gospel is accessible and clear to it, some pages of this immortal book are especially limpid and luminous, according to the particular mission of the soul.

How many of Jesus' secrets you have received! But even though He has manifested to you the riches of His Divinity, the marvels of the Incarnation and the treasures of the Church, Jesus' confidences to you bear their own seal, since all of them form *one* marvelous whole which we could call the doctrine of the Cross.

This doctrine embraces heaven and earth, it envelops the entire Gospel in clarity, but it makes you see all from the unique perspective which tinges everything with colors of loving sacrifice, with the bloodstained reflection of Calvary, with the candid beam of the Eucharist, with the gentle hues of the intimate sacrifice. It might be said that your soul sees everything from the perspective of the divine Heart of Jesus and because of this, everything appears to your eyes tinted with the mysterious color of the flames which burn in the divine Heart.

When the *Confidences*[198] scattered in your *Account of Conscience* will be collected and organized in a perfectly coherent system, the magnitude of the treasures of light, which Jesus has deposited in your soul, will be understood, their transcendence will be perceived and their harmony admired.[199]

Drink always from this fount of life received from the Lord, and do not turn your eyes away from the heavenly treasures. The water which should refresh your soul and the souls of your spiritual children is the crystal-clear and life-giving doctrine of the Cross.

If the transformed soul thinks as Jesus does, it also loves as He does. We have already explained that this soul loves with the Holy Spirit, as Jesus did. Loving in this way has a divine source, the Holy Spirit, under whose motion the soul loves, and it has a divine goal because it loves what Jesus loves; and it has a divine mode of loving which is Jesus' mode of loving and is reflected in the soul through the influence of the Holy Spirit.

It was already stated that the love of the soul that received the mystical incarnation comes more from the Holy Spirit than from the soul itself and that this love is divine. Its goal is the same as that of the love of Jesus: the glory of the Father and the good of souls, which, at its base, are not two goals, but one, for the good of souls is the reflection of the glory of God.

In a transformed heart, there is no room for anything but love, or rather, there is room for all, for the universe; but loving all, nothing else is loved but God because, for souls transformed into Jesus, there is a kind of anticipation of heaven in which "*God is all in all.*"[200]

So, such a soul almost has the substance of the virtues because, according to St. Augustine, "virtue is the order in love."

It should not be thought that the simplification of the soul takes away the richness of its affection; rather, it makes it vast, deep and very rich.

St. Thérèse of the Child Jesus discovered in herself the wonder of this simplified love and expressed it admirably: "I no longer feel that I must deny my heart all consolation, for it is fixed on God… It has loved Him alone, and this has gradually so developed it that it is able to love those whom He loves with a tenderness incomparably deeper than any selfish, barren affection."[201]

But it is perhaps the divine mode which most specifically distinguishes love under the impulse of the Holy Spirit, and which corresponds, according to St. Thomas, to the principle which moves it and to the norm which directs it.

Personal Reflection of Conchita
ELEVENTH DAY

Today I was overwhelmed by a deep, very bitter sadness to the point of weeping, because of an inner kind of poison in my soul, which penetrates all the faculties of the soul. My God!

It has almost gone away, leaving my heart weak. Then I resisted a thousand doubts, that I am mistaken, that all this is farce and deceit, etc.

I did not pay attention to them, but I went to the feet of Jesus weeping, casting myself at His feet as a wounded dog, and asking Him to wring the last drops of gall out of my heart.

I seemed to hear: "What kind of retreat is this if not a constant self-praising, extolling, writing your own eulogy, and things like that, being you are what you are? They do not know you, and you want to abandon humility, ascending the heights from which you would easily fall down.

"What a strange doctrine is this of *ascending* instead of *descending*, of exposing yourself to ruin instead of following the sure

Conchita's Reflections on a Retreat

path of contempt of self and others!"

Certainly, I did not pay attention to it, but something like sediment was left in my soul. As best I could, I embraced obedience and faith, which never deceive.

In reality, how strange and unique is my life and my path. Not because I look at myself. I know that what impresses and is praised *is God and His graces* in me. He is the absolute Owner and can grant them to a pigpen like me. But I need firmness not to falter.

My God! I close my eyes, I cling to Mary, to obedience, and I know that with this I will *not be lost*, even though I die tomorrow.

Father,[202] help me to dispel these black clouds, but if Jesus wants me to suffer doubts and agonies, be it as He wishes, if my martyrdom gives glory to the Father.

I do not know why, Father, for some time I have in my heart a premonition of new crosses in different forms, kinds and ways.

Now, in this retreat, I desire to open my arms and heart to receive them and offer them – in advance, as I do today – *for the glory of the Father.*

Crosses from the congregations, which wound my heart....

Crosses in family.

Julia....[203]

Interior sorrows....

During this retreat, I accept all these forms of martyrdom in advance, offering these deep and bleeding wounds for the glory of the Father.

Today I offered Mass and communion for Julia's conduct and policies to dispel the kind of fear which her nearness causes me, in case there is something which I am unaware of, and I really do not know why; I offered to Jesus my will with regard to agreeing to her [Julia] founding a community in Mexico City, her relations with the Missionaries, the suffering that it can cause to the Sisters of the Cross, that she may triumph in some degree and earn the Archbishop's respect more and more; all in all, I accept everything that makes me suffer and could hurt me in many ways; I accept all, if it is for *the glory of the Father*, to whom I will not refuse anything, aided by His divine grace.

I also foresee painful diseases and thousands and thousands of things which I also accept today in *all* their fullness, if this glorifies God and obtains graces for souls, especially for *priests*.

Oh my Jesus, who listen to me in this delightful Little Cave where the hatred of men put You! I want to love You for all of them and give You glory for thousands of worlds, *no matter at what cost*.

Among other thoughts, the Archbishop's meditation says:[204] "When the *Confidences* scattered in your *Account of Conscience* will be collected and organized in a perfectly coherent system, the magnitude of the treasures of light, which Jesus has deposited in your soul, will be understood, its transcendence will be perceived and its harmony will be admired."

When will it be? Perhaps when I die, since up to now, not even out of curiosity has it occurred to them,[205] since they are so busy, to take charge of the treasures of Jesus written there.

Oh my Jesus! When will the Trinity receive glory from all *Your* treasures?

Whatever You want! This is a thorn in my life, *not for me*, my Jesus who listen to me, as You know, but because of You, so that they may make use of all this special doctrine in both Congregations of the Cross as their *nourishment, orientation, formation* and *life*.

But what can I do but suffer, weep, be quiet, conceal, and sometimes (and many times because You asked it of me) speak without fruit?

What can I do or expect, vile as I am? I can only hope that they may give You glory, knowing Your treasure, the richness You have given them.

I must die, my Jesus, but... whatever You want, the way You want me to glorify You, either joyously or in suffering.

I let my pen run on. Why did You let me, my Jesus, if this thorn is one of the intimate secrets of my soul?

I continue reflecting on the Archbishop's meditation.

Conchita's Reflections on a Retreat

October 25, 1935

TWELFTH DAY

Meditation of Archbishop Martínez

Purity – its mode

How can we describe the divine mode of loving? We can describe its different characteristics: it is *ardent, deep, delicate, unchanging,* etc. Yet I prefer, if it is possible, to describe only one characteristic which embraces all of them, to say in one word what constitutes this divine *mode* and I think that this comprehensive word is *purity,* if it is understood in depth.

My attention has always been drawn to the canticle of the blessed which expresses, so to speak, the impression produced on them by the beatific vision, insofar as it can be expressed in human language, that trisagion[206] which Isaiah and St. John heard: "Holy, Holy, Holy."

It is a hymn of ineffable purity; three words, which correspond to the Three Divine Persons, who are substantially One, which express the unity of the divine essence. And this one word of praise and love does not explicitly express all the divine attributes, but something ineffable which includes all of them, that which is divine and characteristic in all of them: holiness, purity, given that the Greek word used in the canticle means, etymologically, *without earth.*[207]

Our spirit encounters in God, in a perfect and eminent way, all the perfections which we find in creatures, but with a divine seal, that is, without the earthly or created element, which necessarily accompanies the divine reflection in them.

In God, there is love, wisdom, goodness and beauty which shine out in creatures. In creatures, all of these lofty realities are mixed with the earth of our imperfections while, in God, they are very pure, without composition or mixture, with an infinite and ineffable simplicity.

In God, wisdom is light without shadows, according to the

words of St. John, "*Now this is the message that we have heard from Him and proclaim to you: God is light, and in Him there is no darkness at all.*"[208]

In God, love is charity without selfishness, according to the same St. John. In God, beauty is without stain and goodness, without anything lacking. Everything is pure and holy in Him.

The divine mode [of purity] is unalloyed, is simply what it is. "*Ego sum qui sum*,"[209] answered the Lord to Moses when he asked His name.

The divine mode is an ineffable simplicity and marvelous purity. His light is simply light. His love is simply love. His Being is simply Being that contains all perfections of Being, because He is the purest Being, and in His light there are all the riches of light, since He is "*the refulgence of eternal light*";[210] and His love encompasses all the fullness of love with its infinite nuances, with its marvelous blaze, with its eternal delights, because He is all love and the purest love.

We believe that we know love, because we have seen the marvels of love on earth, but when we speak about divine love it seems blasphemy, as Blessed Angela of Foligno said: "The most sublime secrets of love on earth are so far removed from the mysteries of eternal love!"

God loves all things and in them all He loves Himself and, loving Himself, He diffuses torrents of light, life, love and beauty in the universe. The treasure which He diffuses around Himself, the countless graces which He pours out where He passes in His triumphal march, merge into the ineffable unity of love, in the royal simplicity of His charity.

In the bosom of the Trinity the Holy Spirit, who is love, consummates the ineffable life of God in divine unity. In creation, love walks victorious and fruitful above the chaos and places the richest unity of the glory of God in the immensity of nothingness.

In the order of grace, love begins and consummates the marvels of God, unifying this rich world in the royal simplicity of that glory which the angels sang in Bethlehem and which will constitute the victorious song of the last day of time, the new canticle which will resound for all eternity.

In heaven, on earth and in the Church, eternal love shines out unmistakably, in its divine mode of very simple, rich and limpid purity.

The love of Jesus is very pure. His Heart contains all of us, yet He loves but His Father. He walked the earth doing good, pouring out graces, giving life with generous abundance, setting the earth on fire with fire from heaven, but in reality, He did not seek anything other than the glory of God, nor did He accomplish other work than that of simplifying all things in the unity of His Heart in order to plunge the universe into the most pure bosom of God.

His love was simply love, carrying nothing extraneous in His breast, no trace of selfishness, only the divine simplicity of purity.

This is the divine mode of loving: purity in its source, essence and end. This love is one, it is simply love and it has no other end but God.

How far away from that purity our heart normally is! There are many affections in it, which at times fight among themselves. Every one of them is not simply love, but a kind of bizarre mixture of love and selfishness. To the multiplicity of causes, the composition of essence, corresponds the almost always inconsistent diversity of desired objects.

The discipline of the spiritual life tries to accomplish precisely this purity in love, and to give to our affections the divine way of loving.

First, God's love arises victorious from the ruins of our earthly affections. Then, passing through the crucible of sacrifice, this love is cleansed of all extraneous traces, and when it has attained to the fullness of purity, it becomes marvelously simple, fixed on God as its only object.

St. Augustine said that virtue is order in love. We could draw the consequences from this happy expression by saying that holiness is simplicity in love, perfect purity in love.

When heart and life simplify into one love, which is simply love, and which arrives at God as its only object, holiness is attained.

It is incredible! The more love is *one* and pure, the richer, fuller and more fruitful it is. When love multiplies, it gets narrower. When it mixes, it becomes stingy. When many things are loved, nothing is loved in depth.

Purified love becomes similar to God's love; in its simplicity, it embraces all; loving only God, it loves all creatures; and in its unity, all nuances, all richness, all mysteries of love are contained.

Pure love embraces all virtues, envelops all gifts and excels all charisms: it is true life, perfect harmony and the glory of God.

That is why St. John of the Cross said that the least act of pure love is of more value than all other works in the Church.

The soul that has received the mystical incarnation should love in this divine mode. It is not enough simply to have charity in order to attain to this *mode* of loving, because this sovereign virtue in its imperfect state coexists with other affections and does not cast out of the soul all traces of selfishness. Even if God is loved above all things in charity, one has not yet attained to loving only God in all things.

In order that we may love in a divine way, we need to love with the Holy Spirit, because He alone can seal our acts with the divine *mode*, as St. Thomas Aquinas teaches.

The act of love which proceeds from Him is pure because its source is divine. This love is simply love because the Holy Spirit excludes all selfishness from His divine impulse.

As a magnet which approaches earth which is mixed with pieces of iron attracts only iron and eliminates earth, so the Holy Spirit in His intimate impulse does not attract anything that is earthly in the soul, but through a mysterious selection, moves only what is divine in charity. This act of purest charity goes directly and exclusively to God, and even though it can embrace the entire universe, it does not lose its mysterious simplicity, but embracing

Conchita's Reflections on a Retreat

all, it reaches God alone.

In order to seek the glory of God as Jesus did, and only the glory of God, it is necessary to love with the *Holy Spirit*.

Personal Reflection of Conchita
TWELFTH DAY

Absences

Today Jesus wanted to talk to me.

"Lord," I said to Him with my heart heavy, "why haven't You let me feel Your presence during this retreat, as in the others? Why does it seem to me that You are veiled and have hidden so as not to let me see You clearly, as on other occasions? You know what I mean...."

"Don't you remember," He answered, "what I *asked* of you, what you *gave* Me?

"If you only knew that when you accept sacrifices, instead of consolations, forgoing the graces of My sensible presence on behalf of others, My Father receives glory!

"Is this not – *I repeat* – what I have asked of you in this retreat, mainly, the *glory of My Father*?

"And if, through My absence, through not letting you experience My sensible presence, other souls and priests give Me glory, then, do you not want it?

"Is it not true that you willingly and out of pure love for the glory of My Father, do without consolations, caresses, My nearness to your soul, for the sake of priests and *especially* for the glory of My Father?

"If you only understood what this detachment offered out of pure love is worth in the presence of God!

"Continue, yes, continue, in your hidden martyrdom, with this heroic charity of a motherly soul, who loves Me with selfless and pure motherly love.

"What does it matter to you if you remain like this until your death, knowing that other souls glorify God, My beloved Father, with what is *rightfully yours*?

"And now I will let your soul in on a secret:

"If in the mystical incarnation My Father gave you His Son, with whom He is well pleased, He gave Him as He gave Him to Mary, in order that you *may give Him* to others; and not only that He be given for sacrifice and crucifixion, but that you may offer yourself in union with Him, painfully deprived of what you hold most dear: My consolations, apparent absence, veiled presence and the sensible caresses of My pure love.

"I alone understand the magnitude of this hidden martyrdom; it is the supreme sacrifice of a soul on earth, and what gives My Father the most glory, because it is a loving, motherly sacrifice.

"It is what I appreciate most because, in My soul, when I was on the Cross, on behalf of My Church and specially of her members, I felt the cruel abandonment of My Father.

"How few souls penetrate the secret which I reveal to you today! They see the external, but do not arrive at the very depth of My heroic sacrifice on the Cross. How could I do without the love of My Father, which wrenched a loving groan from My soul full of bitterness, a cry of infinite suffering, because the divinity had hidden itself, in a certain sense, from My sight?"

Tears came to my eyes and Jesus, so good, gentle and compassionate told me:

"Weep, weep over this more or less intense apparent separation from what you love most; but even these tears, this very sensitive and holy suffering, unite it to My suffering and offer it exclusively for the glory of My Father. Promise you will do it, won't you?

"For this I brought you here to make you taste this bitterness, to make you know its salvific consequences in all its extension on behalf of so many priests, so that you may sprinkle the Church in her members with your tears, so that your soul, lifted up for the love for My Father, may thus glorify Him in yourself and in the Works of the Cross.

"So do not be surprised by what refers to the glory of the Father in the sacrifice of your heart; embrace this cross with all your soul, and continue the path I traced out for you, smiling in the midst of the sorrow of My absence, giving Me thanks and glorifying God."

Later on, He continued.

"I have given you other *fundamental* graces, whose value you are unable to measure: peace, abandonment to My will and the foundation of more than sensible love, *simplified* love, which brings you closer to God, because it is the reflection of God Himself.

"God is love, but most simple love! He is Love-Unity, the essence of the unchangeable, unmoved and eternal love!

"Give Me thanks for My benefits and let the Holy Spirit lead you for your good, for the sake of souls and the Works of the Cross, established to give Me consolation and glory to My Father through the Holy Spirit and Mary."

Prayer of Offering

Oh Jesus of the Tabernacle, Jesus of the Little Cave, Jesus of my heart! What can I say to You? I am in tears, for You have told me that I can weep. I say *"yes"* to this heroic sacrifice, and with all my heart I embrace it for ever if it pleases You, if it is Your will, if it is for *the glory of the beloved Father*, as it certainly is!

What does it matter that I die of suffering, if priests give You glory; if what was for me, as You have told me, is *rightfully* for them, for Your Church, for their spiritual good, if it moves their hearts, makes them grow in virtues, if it is for the glory of Your beloved Father?

Here, at the foot of this beloved altar, I make a new total offering of my will, *consciously* doing without any consolation, sensible grace, Your luminous gaze... Your most gentle words... Your very pure closeness... Your ineffable smile... Oh my Jesus, doing without everything Your divine closeness made me familiar with.

But if this is so that Your priests may grow in virtue, zeal and love, that the Missionaries of the Holy Spirit may acquire their own genuine spirit, grow in number and sow in the world the love of purity and sacrifice, I am ready to live in this way until my death.

You will help me, although in a hidden way, my Jesus. You will sustain me in my sadness and bitterness. You will lift me up when I fall. You will forgive me. You will cover me with Your mercy at the hour of my death.

Right?

Oh Jesus of my soul! Receive this offering wrung from my heart through the most pure hands of Mary, the Immaculate and Sorrowful Mother and pronounced by her lips, in union with me. Bless me, smile on me and offer me, in union with You, as a *living holocaust* of love to the glory of the Father. Amen.

I will ask my spiritual director if tomorrow at Mass he could offer me in this way.

I could not reflect on the meditation and I will do it later on.

October 26, 1935
Thirteenth Day

Meditation of Archbishop Martínez

Love – the mode

It is appropriate to consider in depth the divine mode of loving which the Holy Spirit inspires in our hearts. This is a love that is simply love. At first sight, we could say that our love is always like this. But how rare is love like this on earth!

Ordinarily, our love, even supernatural love, is mixed with selfishness, because pure love is self-forgetfulness, and even in the most ardent raptures of our poor love, we think about ourselves. Pure love, however, makes us turn away from ourselves to throw ourselves with what we are on the Beloved and usually in the most fervent impetus of our love we manage to half turn away from ourselves; we simply do not offer ourselves totally to the Beloved of our heart. Pure love has no measure; it doesn't keep anything back; it tolerates no compromises, whereas the gift of ourselves is almost always limited, timid and inadequate. Pure love consists in loving with all our heart and with all the capacity of our soul so that in one act of love we place our love and life, whereas this doesn't happen with human acts of love because they lack fullness. They do not entirely exhaust our virtue of loving. Pure love is not forgetful, nor does it eclipse anything, except what is inevitable in human life and in the vicissitudes of time it participates with simplicity and constancy in the conditions of eternal love.

When the Holy Spirit impels us to love, He brings about the miracle of pure love, that is, of selfless love, which carries in itself fullness of heart and totality of life. He makes perfect the gift of the one who loves. He fulfills the capacity of loving which the soul possesses and He gives Himself without keeping anything back, without limitations, without imperfections, with a very simple, lasting and immortal action.

The divine mode of loving makes the one who loves offer all his love and being to the Beloved without thinking of oneself, without seeking oneself. I do not say without love of self, because the one who loves in a divine manner knows how to love oneself with mysterious perfection.

The most perfect manner of loving is to forget ourselves and let ourselves go, because our real good consists in turning away from ourselves and casting ourselves into the Heart of the Beloved.

The divine mode of loving is the way the Divine Persons love each other, that is, with the very simple, total and eternal act in which they mutually communicate their infinite substance to each other.

When one loves with the Holy Spirit, who is the personal love of God, one should imitate this manner of loving insofar as it is possible for the creature.

When God became man, another divine manner of loving appeared. The sign of this new manner is the Cross: the Cross in the one who loves and the Cross in the Beloved. It could be said that God made Himself man to love in this way.

Jesus loved His Father even to the Cross and the Father loved Jesus also even to the Cross. Neither in heaven nor on earth does one love in this way. This new love was necessary in order to merge heaven and earth in the Heart of Jesus.

The purity of love leads to sacrifice and death, because sacrifice and death are on earth the perfect forgetfulness of self and gift of self. The one who loves can offer himself totally in two ways: in the glorious gift of self in heaven or in the heroic gift of self on the Cross.

In His earthly life, Jesus was impatient to sacrifice Himself, because the Cross is the summit of pure love which forgets itself even to the point of death and offers itself in order to give life.

But what is most amazing, what disconcerts our spirit, is not the Cross in the one who loves, but the Cross in the Beloved. To love even unto death is beyond our strength, but not beyond our concepts because, even though we are incapable of giving our life for love, we faintly perceive the grandeur and the heroism needed to achieve this glorious summit.

But to love to the point of nailing the Beloved on the Cross, exceeds the concepts of our intelligence and the dreams of our heart.

How can we conceive that the one who loves may offer the Beloved to the Cross?

We are amazed, because we are unaware of the deep meaning of the Cross; then, in order to enter more deeply into this sublime sense, we must see and love it in the divine manner.

After heaven, which is pure love in its essence, full in its offering, great in its delights and eternal in its offering, there is no other love like that of the Cross, which is so pure that it forgets itself even unto death, which makes the supreme donation of life, which finds in the Cross perfect joy, which places in the nothingness of the creature something great and almost infinite.

After heaven, which is the intimate and eternal possession

of God, there is no higher good or more complete happiness than the Cross because, after heavenly love there is no more perfect love than that of the one who lives on it.

Consequently, divine love, which seeks the supreme good, gives the Divinity in heaven and the Cross on the earth.

The Father loves His Son infinitely and in the most simple and rich instant of eternity gives Him His own substance with the richness of His attributes, the eternal fullness of light and the ocean of perfect happiness; but when the Word became flesh, He could offer Him another gift, which is the greatest on earth, *the Cross*; in the Gospel, we read astonished: *"Proprio Filio suo non pepercit Deus, sed pro nobis omnibus tradidit illum."* *"He did not spare His own Son, but handed Him over for us all."*[211]

In heaven, the Father gives His Son His Divinity and on the earth He gives Jesus the glory of God. Nothing can be compared with God's glory and the Cross is the supreme glory of God.

To love the Cross as God loves it, as Jesus loves it, it is necessary that we love in a divine way, that is, that we love with the Holy Spirit.

Thus, you must love in this divine manner, because this love springs out of the depths of the mystical incarnation. Your love should simply be that love. For this reason, you should forget yourself as perfectly as possible; you should give yourself unreservedly; for this you should put your whole heart in your love.

You must love as Jesus loves. He loves with all His Heart. You should love with all your heart. What I want to say is that Jesus loves as much as He can and you should love as much as you can.

There is an immense distance between the Heart of Jesus and yours, but the love which springs from the divine Heart and creaturely love, which springs from yours, correspond, respectively, to the capacity of the heart of each one. Both love insofar as they can.

Precisely because of the wholeness of love, it is pure, since there is no place for selfishness if one loves with one's whole heart. I will give an example: if the molten gold is poured into the mold, all is gold and in that mold, there is no alloy. When the heart pours out all its love in an action, there is no trace of selfishness in it.

One who loves in this divine mode loves the Beloved in the most unique and pure manner; that is, he loves only Him and seeks His good, His good exclusively, His entire and supreme good. To love in this way is to seek purely and exclusively the glory of God.

Personal Reflection of Conchita
THIRTEENTH DAY

Today Jesus was silent. The Archbishop's meditation made me continue to ponder upon the precious and lofty love one could reflect on for a lifetime. It considers the divine mode of loving, of loving with the Holy Spirit. The divine love, the love of the Cross.

I meditate on the divine mode of loving...

OCTOBER 27, 1935
FOURTEENTH DAY [212]

Meditation of Archbishop Martínez

To act

As the soul that has received the mystical incarnation should think and love as Jesus did, so also it should act as He did, or rather, let Him work in this soul.

Considering the works of Jesus, Scripture says: *"He has done all things well."*[213]

What harmony, what perfection in His actions!

Just as the love of Jesus, so also His acts have one source, the Holy Spirit; one goal, the glory of God; one mode, the divine mode with which the Holy Spirit unmistakably marks His works.

In souls that are not transformed, there are many sources of action; sometimes *passion* inspires them; sometimes it is human reason that guides them and sometimes it is the Spirit of God.

In souls that are transformed passion does not reign and reason is subject to God. The Holy Spirit almost always directs their actions.

Thus Jesus always acted, moved by the Holy Spirit, as has been stated. Scripture teaches us that Jesus, moved by the Holy Spirit, went into the desert. Moved by the Holy Spirit, He rejoiced, praising His Father, and offered Himself unblemished to God.

The Spirit of the Lord influenced the actions of Jesus not only in these cases which Scripture shows us, but further, He alone was always the fount of His action, the constant mover of the ineffable works of Jesus.

The life of souls that have received the mystical incarnation is the reflection of the life of Jesus, because they have the same Spirit of Jesus who moves and guides them and makes all their actions divine.

In these souls passion does not inspire their works. In them, passion is only moved by a higher principle in order to give their works human integrity. We see this in the life of Jesus: His anger when He drove the merchants out of the temple; His tears at the raising of Lazarus; His agony in Gethsemane; His lament over Jerusalem.

Pure human reason, moreover, could not move the actions of transformed souls, but this reason, along with its lights and demands, should be subordinated to the Holy Spirit, just as it was perfectly subordinated in Jesus.

The Holy Spirit should fully move the transformed soul, just as He perfectly moved Jesus and for this reason, the life of Jesus is reproduced in the soul and even in its mortal body, according to St. Paul.[214]

In the soul that has received the mystical incarnation, this divine principle of action corresponds to this unique and lofty aim: *the glory of the Father.*

When passion governs a soul, the outcome of its actions is

base. When reason guides its actions, its aim is somewhat human. When the soul operates under the impulse of the Holy Spirit, it cannot have any other aim than that which God has in His works, that is, the divine glory.

The more the impulse of the Holy Spirit in a soul is complete and unmixed, the more purely the soul seeks the glory of God.

That is why Jesus told you that the consummation of the mystical incarnation consists in seeking only the glory of God. When this grace is consummated, the soul does not love or strive for anything but the glory of God, because the Holy Spirit moves it without obstacles and guides it totally.

With this principle and lofty goal, the action of the transformed soul is perfect and is accomplished in the divine mode.

If we could fully understand just one action of Jesus, we would be enraptured with admiration and love! One action which is perfect, harmonious, without excess or deficiency, divine in its source, very pure in its intention, perfect in its execution, amazing in its manner.

Many virtues work together in order to accomplish such an action in splendid harmony and the gifts of the Holy Spirit work together with heavenly power. Yet neither does the simplicity hinder the majesty, nor the divine seal diminish its deeply human character.

Who could understand this expression of Scripture, *"He has done all things well"*?

The actions of the transformed soul should be the pale, but exact reflection of the ineffable actions of Jesus. Only the Holy Spirit can accomplish them in this way. Only He can give them the very pure intention of the glory of God, the marvelous balance so difficult, given our limitations, the exact measure which excludes deficiency and impedes excess. Only the Holy Spirit can accomplish this most beautiful harmony, in which virtues work together without obstructing one another and in which the gifts, without losing their brightness, join the human element with the divine mode, which elevates it and makes it heavenly.

Conchita's Reflections on a Retreat

It is of no importance whether the action itself is high or common, heroic or ordinary, for the Holy Spirit to accomplish this marvel. Those actions which seem insignificant are, in reality, prodigies of harmony and something heavenly and divine. Just as the Creator puts His omnipotent seal equally on a star of giant proportions which floats in space, or on a tiny flower lost in the grass, so the divine Artisan of holiness equally puts His seal on a heroic act which others admire, or on a simple action which goes unnoticed even to the one who brings it about.

If the chain of actions of a soul forms its life, the life of a transformed soul is the exact image of the life of Jesus, since the same Spirit inspires it, the same aim directs it, the same divine seal signs it with its character, perfection and beauty.

Actually, the soul that acts in this way lives no longer, but Christ lives in it. And because Christ lives in it, the actions of this soul have singular merit and remarkable efficacy.

Thus our attention is called to the fact that the saints' one word, one seemingly insignificant action, may be anointed, fruitful and work marvels. There is nothing strange about this if Jesus lives in them, if the Holy Spirit guides them, if their actions are divine and what is divine is fruitful.

The disciples of Emmaus observed: *"Were not our hearts burning within us while He spoke to us on the way."*[215] The word of Jesus makes our hearts burn.

In fact, with those words, He was opening to them the profound meaning of the Scriptures; but the simple action of breaking the bread opened their eyes and revealed Jesus to them. How would the mysterious traveler break the bread?

How would simplicity and majesty meet in that ordinary action? What sweet reminder of the Upper Room would the disciples perceive in the little corner of Emmaus? What heavenly brightness would spring forth from the venerable hands of Jesus which enlightened the dim eyes of the disciples?

Keeping the right proportion, there is the mysterious brightness which opens eyes in souls transformed into Jesus, the heavenly anointing which transforms souls, the secret virtue which inflames hearts, because Jesus lives in these souls; Jesus is always the same and wherever He dwells He accomplishes amazing deeds.

Whoever understands this doctrine never asks the meaningless question: How is it possible that my word has unction, that my actions are fruitful, that I have virtue which touches souls deep down if I am so little, fragile, unworthy and imperfect? It is not the soul that works marvels, but Jesus who dwells in it, just as the Eucharist is the source of life and love, although hidden in a poor, plain vessel.

Meditate on this teaching and many doubts, anxieties and perplexities will be dispelled.

Do not forget that Jesus dwells in you, and you will learn to look at yourself with respect, as we look with respect at the rough vessel which contains the Eucharist.

Let Jesus who lives in you divinize your actions, and show Himself through your poverty when it pleases Him, and radiate around you His love and life.

You must allow Him to act; you must not hinder the work of the Holy Spirit; you must, with simplicity, see what Jesus accomplishes in and through the soul transformed in Him.

If sometimes your weakness withdraws from the divine impulse, the raw and imperfect fruit of the creature will appear, the human dissonant and miserable mode. And these poor actions, full of commonness and inefficiency, will emphasize by contrast that what Jesus accomplishes through His fragile instrument is pure, excellent and divine.

Personal Reflection of Conchita
FOURTEENTH DAY

There is no choice. I have to jump through the hoop and bury the overdone humility, if in this way I glorify the heavenly Father.

What meditations!

Conchita's Reflections on a Retreat

What examples of Jesus!
What a perfect model of all virtues!
Oh Jesus of my heart! Fashion me as You want me to be.

Forgoing

Today, very sadly, I said to Jesus: "Lord, at least in these days of the retreat, talk to me. Why are You so scornful? I love You so much! My life is not life without You."

"Listen," He answered, "if I need to use what is yours on behalf of the Church during this retreat, do you not want it?"

"Yes, I want it, my Jesus. But tell me, why am I not to tell You my desires, if You are Life of my life?"

"Look, when Mary purchased the most precious graces for the newly-formed Church, she lacked My visible presence and My consolations after My Resurrection and thus, purchased graces for the spreading of My glory.

"Think about it and tell Me. Don't you want to be like her, in her great sacrifice? She who was accustomed to My sensible and real presence, to My sweet company, to My words and filial caresses, did without all of it for the glory of the Father, in the very moment in which the Father asked for the sacrifice.

"Will you refuse Me this? If you know that with this intimate martyrdom you obtain graces for Missionaries and priests, for the glory of the Father, do you want to diminish the sacrifice, preferring your contentment and spiritual satisfaction to what I have asked of you for the glory of the Father?"

"No, my Jesus, forgive me. With these reflections, help me more and more to suffer this intimate martyrdom, which makes me cry even if I do not want to, not only with resignation, but joyously.

"My Jesus, pay no attention to me, even if I die of sorrow.

"If I will no longer *see* You, *hear* You or *experience* You on earth, I accept this out of pure love, and to prove to You that I do not love You for *reward*, I will adore You in the *darkness*, I will gaze on the tabernacle *loving You always, only with faith*; even if I will feel icy *without Your warmth* and I will die of cold *without Your closeness.*

"Do You hear me, darling Dove of my heart?

"With Your help, I desire to suffer this martyrdom with a loving, smiling countenance, *being silent, giving thanks*, and patiently waiting the day in which the splendid Sun of eternity will shine on me. *With You*, my Jesus.

"Then, nothing and nobody will separate me from You, isn't that true? Then I will give glory to the Father, contemplating You, caressing You, loving the Holy Trinity, in union with Mary, ardently and perfectly."

I felt that my words moved Jesus, who is so good, so fatherly, *so Son-like*, so noble, compassionate, loving, holy and so all for me!

"I accept your sacrifice," Jesus answered, "but leave Me free, so I will always give you what is best for you and for souls."

October 28, 1935
Fifteenth Day

Meditation of Archbishop Martínez

Suffering

In order to think and act as Jesus did, it is a characteristic of the soul that has received the mystical incarnation to *suffer as Jesus* did, since the mission of such a soul is, above all, to share in His intimate sacrifice.

When one considers the subject on a merely superficial level, one does not even suspect the countless, very fine nuances and grades which the mysterious science of suffering encompasses.

Hardly is there a soul, one could say, imitating St. John of the Cross, that is similar to another in the way of suffering. It would be enough to know in depth one's attitude before suffering in order to evaluate precisely the degree of its progress and point out its specific features. "Tell me how you suffer and I will tell you who you are."

There is a wide range between the tragic and desperate way of suffering of a condemned person and the divine suffering of Jesus.

We shall not take into consideration the souls that haughtily rebel against suffering, those that sink into desperation under the weight of suffering, or those that suffer to the fullest extent without acceptance and without merit. Among souls that suffer best there is an incredible diversity, because souls have such varied features that one could say each has one feature that distinguishes it.

The suffering of each soul is characterized not only by its intensity, but also by its quality and origin, by the cause which guides souls to embrace the cross and above all, by their *mode* of suffering.

Precisely the *mode*, because it is of singular importance in spiritual matters, as St. Thomas explains in one of his works.[216] The difference between virtues and gifts of the Holy Spirit is due to their different mode. This amounts to saying that the ascetic and mystical life differ in regard to mode, which is human in the former case and divine in the latter.

Let us consider how Jesus suffered, carefully analyzing, as far as our limitations allow, the source of His suffering, its quality, the cause for which Jesus embraced it and the divine way of suffering. Hence, the suffering of Jesus is the model of suffering for transformed souls and especially for those who have received the mystical incarnation, the center of which is *the Cross*, as has been already stated.

The priest who immolated Jesus in His earthly passage and mystically continues to immolate Him as the Church sings in her liturgy,[217] is *love, priest-love*.

Jesus suffered *because He loved*. Love not only thrust Him toward suffering – nor was it the remote principle of His immolations – but it was the immediate cause of His sufferings. Love's immaculate hands broke His divine Heart, its victorious sword pierced it and its fire consumed it.

It is true that hatred and malice were also His executioners, but the immolation would not have been what it was, unless mixed with the immolation of love; nor could they have touched Jesus, if love had not thrown Him into His enemies' cruel grasp. "He offered Himself because He willed to, because He was moved to sacrifice by *priest-love.*"

As this love is very pure and divine, as has been said, it filled the immolation of Jesus with purity, heavenly fragrance and sublime beauty.

The *quality* of suffering depends on the cause which produces it. On the material level, the suffering which fire causes differs from that caused by the sword. On the spiritual level, suffering differs according to its source: ingratitude, hatred, sin or virtue.

How excellent and sublime will be the suffering occasioned by a heavenly and divine love!

One should not think that the exalted origin of Jesus' suffering made it any the less intense and cruel. Since nothing surpasses the divine, either when it beatifies or when it immolates, so the same love made heaven and dug hell.

The sorrows of Jesus have a heavenly essence and an infernal bitterness, because they are forged by the purest and all-powerful love.

The bride in the Song of Songs says about her Beloved: *"He is all delight."*[218] That is true. All in Jesus is most beautiful, even His suffering; I should almost say, above all *His sufferings.*

If we could penetrate them in depth, their splendid beauty would seize us with admiration and perhaps we would understand why the Father handed Jesus over to immolation, so that this ineffable beauty might shine forth in the holy soul of Jesus.

"There is nothing like Jesus Christ in the universe and there is nothing in Jesus Christ like His sacrifice."[219]

This is true not only because all good for souls comes from Christ's sacrifice, but also because that sacrifice is perfect and of sovereign beauty.

Conchita's Reflections on a Retreat

On earth, nothing is as beautiful as suffering, but what happens to it is what happens to ocean storms. They are sublime, but we rarely have the serenity necessary to enjoy their beauty.

Souls that suffer can hardly appreciate the treasure they possess in suffering and the supreme grace God gives them by sending it. Those who come near to the sanctuary of those souls, even if they somehow appreciate the beauty of suffering, they do not manage to grasp all its beauty. This is because when we see others suffering, we suffer either from compassion or because we appropriate it in order to understand it, or because a very special light from God is necessary in order to penetrate deeply into the mystery of suffering and discover what is divine in it.

No beauty can be compared to that of the divine suffering of Jesus, nor is there a greater grace than sharing in it.

The soul that received the mystical incarnation is destined to share them. The suffering of that soul is a precious reflection of what Jesus suffered, with the same source and quality, although far removed from Jesus'.

The suffering of this soul is brought about directly by love, since priest-love immolates this soul.

The characteristic of this soul is sharing in the intimate sufferings of Jesus, and the Holy Spirit accomplishes this sharing through His gifts. The Spirit is *priest-love*.

The soul sees what Jesus saw and what caused His suffering by the light of the Spirit. In some of the saints with the stigmata, the mysterious phenomena were produced by rays of light which sprang from Jesus' wounds. In my opinion, this is symbolic. There is light which wounds, immolates and causes a strange pain. Such is the manner in which the sharing of the soul in the intimate suffering of Jesus is brought about: an immaterial light envelops the soul, wounding and immolating it.

But light is not the only cause of these divine sufferings. Love, which comes also from the Holy Spirit, is added to the light and the new love is sharper than any two-edged sword which, together with the light, penetrates to the very core of the soul, as far as the division of the soul and the spirit.[220]

Because the soul sees with the eyes of Jesus and loves with His Heart, it shares in His intimate sufferings; and if they have the same source, they consequently have the same value and beauty; these sufferings are formed by the same heavenly emanation and the same infernal bitterness.

If only souls that suffer knew the gift of God! If souls only knew how precious this suffering is! What value the suffering which breaks their hearts has!

Certainly, there are other forms of suffering in transformed souls, which seem of lesser value, because their source is not so elevated: suffering caused by men, suffering which springs from within the soul, suffering whose source is in the body, the companion of the soul.

As it has been said, just as in the summit of the spiritual life the heart becomes simplified, merging all affections into triumphant divine love, so also at that summit the suffering becomes simplified. This is because the highest and divine suffering, as we have just described it, coordinates and absorbs all the sufferings of the soul and elevates and dignifies them, making them a precious sachet of myrrh, in which the heavenly fragrance of purest myrrh, which the soul has received as the fruit of sharing in the intimate sufferings of Jesus, predominates.

Just as in the chalice of wine of the sacrifice, that is Jesus, some drops of water, which we are, are commingled, so, in the chalice of the suffering of the transformed soul, the water of our poor sufferings is commingled with the exquisite wine of the suffering shared by Jesus and the one chalice and the one sacrifice result from this fusion.

Consider the great grace that Jesus gave you by sharing with you the bitterness of His Heart. To our nature, this is a terrible grace, it is true, but it has no equal in the supernatural order.

Appreciate it.

Love it.

Live this so that you may truly say with the bride of the

Conchita's Reflections on a Retreat

Song of Songs: *"My lover is for me a sachet of myrrh to rest in my bosom."*[221]

Personal Reflection of Conchita

FIFTEENTH DAY

Today the meditation is on suffering as Jesus suffered.

My God! May I know how to take advantage of these holy teachings, learning more and more about what Jesus is like in His thoughts, in His actions, in His way of loving and in all, in His suffering and in His incomparable Heart!

Would that I could accomplish His designs in imitating Him!

October 29, 1935

SIXTEENTH DAY

Meditation of Archbishop Martínez

Loves

It is appropriate to consider more thoroughly the two forms of the one love for which Jesus suffered in the course of His mortal life and for which He wanted to perpetuate mystically His sacrifice: *His love for His Father and for souls.*

Two longings arose in the Heart of Jesus out of these two loves which impelled Him to drink ceaselessly the most bitter chalice of His intimate Passion and to await with divine impatience the chalice of His exterior Passion: the glory of God and the sanctification of souls, the purest longings which explain His eagerness to suffer and for which He generously embraced the Cross.

St. Paul says: *"For the sake of the joy that lay before Him, He endured the Cross."*[222] The joy which was set before Him, as the ideal of His praiseworthy life, was to unite souls to Himself in order to purify them, to communicate His holy life to them, to sanctify and glorify them, so that He might present to His Father the new, regenerated, holy humanity which constitutes the supreme glory of God.

To accomplish this divine ideal, He endured the exterior and interior Cross and wanted to perpetuate mystically His sacrifice on the altar and in souls, in order to continue forming His Mystical Body in the course of centuries and thus filling time and eternity with the new canticle to the glory of God.

The souls that received the mystical incarnation were chosen by Jesus to continue His sufferings and thus, to realize His longings and fully attain the perfect and complete joy of Jesus, for which He endured the Cross.

Consequently, these souls should suffer so that Jesus may completely accomplish His joy and consummate His divine longings.

Could you conceive of a purer and higher and if we might say, more divine reason to suffer?

On the eve of His passion, Jesus spoke thus to His Father about His disciples: "*But now I am coming to You. I speak this in the world, so that they may share My joy completely.*"[223]

Jesus' joy is the glory of the Father for the sanctification of souls, and this joy is accomplished in His disciples if they continue, motivated by the same ideal and longings, to fulfill in themselves the interior and exterior Passion of Jesus.

How sweet it is to suffer, so that the joy of Jesus may be accomplished in us!

This is the suffering of the souls who have received the mystical incarnation; they suffer so that Jesus may rejoice, and His joy is the glory of the Father.

When we consider in depth this mystery, we perceive how appropriate was the happy phrase of St. Francis of Assisi regarding "perfect joy," as well as that of St. Thérèse of Lisieux: "Is there any greater joy than to suffer for Your love?" "I found happiness and joy on earth only in suffering."

At times, one thinks that this joy in suffering is a subtle and generous idea of saints, and not a tangible and exquisite reality. You know it is not like this, that it is a real happiness to suffer, and in a certain sense it is the supreme, if not the only, happiness in this world.

Shouldn't it be a source of happiness to complete the joy of Jesus? But in order to enjoy this happiness, it is necessary to have received from God an abundant light and a very true and pure love.

In these days Jesus has asked you to suffer for the glory of the Father, which is to say, to suffer for the complete joy of Jesus.

Will you not exchange your joy for that of Jesus?

(Certainly I will and with all my heart.)

Yet this joy does not come only from the realization of the deep longing of the divine Heart for the glory of God, but also from the other longing, which is the accomplishment of the sanctification of souls.

In effect, both longings merge into one, but it is better to examine them separately in order to better appreciate the mystery which we are studying.

The joy offered to Jesus and for which He endured the Cross is also meant to attract all souls and unite them to Himself, communicating His life to them and making them holy and happy in God.

What a joy for Jesus that all the elect owe Him their eternal happiness!

What an exquisite delight to purchase this happiness with suffering and death! Oh, there is no joy or delight which could be compared with this heroic joy, with Jesus' unselfish delight!

Even though Jesus' suffering was so great, I think His joy was greater, but both mysteries escape our poor understanding. Only in heaven will we receive the full revelation of two supreme secrets which Jesus was hiding in the depth of His Heart: the secret of His suffering and the secret of His joy.

As souls who have received the mystical incarnation share in the intimate suffering of Jesus, so they also share in His intimate joy. They thus complete the joy of Jesus by effectively collaborating, through their suffering, in the sanctification of souls. They also share in the divine joy because other souls owe them their eternal happiness.

Truly, they only owe it in part to these souls, as to the instruments of Jesus, of course. But this happiness is so divine that collaborating in bringing it about, even in the least part, makes us similar to God, and brings us the joy which is above all earthly joys.

To share in this joy, Jesus called you to give up all the legitimate and divine consolations of His sensible presence and His intimate caresses as a most loving Son.

It is the supreme sacrifice for your motherly heart. After giving up everything that is earthly for Jesus, after focusing your soul on Him as the only object of your love, the source of your life, the fount of your joy and happiness, your further sacrifice of His heavenly consolations constitutes the most bitter dregs of your chalice of suffering, the very pure and exquisite myrrh which your hands exude.

But if you enter fully into the inmost feelings of Jesus, as you ought to, in order to consummate your great grace, at the bottom of this bitter chalice you will find the drop of the ineffable and divine honey of perfect joy, of the complete joy of Jesus in your soul.

Your consolations will bring consolation and life to other souls. Forgoing His consolation will bring sanctification to souls and you will be able to repeat the wonderful expression of Jesus: *"For their sakes I sanctify Myself (or consecrate Myself), that they themselves also may be sanctified in truth."*[224]

These souls will be your joy and crown, as they were for St. Paul. In a certain sense, these souls will owe you their eternal happiness. The majority of these souls are those of priests, centers of radiation for many others whom they will attract by the fragrance of their lives and they will form a crown of glory for Jesus, and a crown of joy for you.

Conchita's Reflections on a Retreat

Jesus asks a great sacrifice of you, but also rewards it with unspeakable joy. You lose Jesus in His consolations, but you regain Him in the priestly souls which you raise up and sanctify with such a heroic sacrifice.

St. Thérèse admirably understood this doctrine; she understood inscrutable happiness in suffering, so that Jesus' joy might be complete.

"So in spite of the fact that this trial takes away all sense of joy, I can still say: 'Thou hast given me, O Lord, a delight in Thy doings' (Ps 91:5), for what can give such keen delight as suffering for love of You! The more personal the suffering and the more hidden from the eyes of the world, the more pleasing it is to You, my God. If, to suppose the impossible, You did not know about it, I would be no less happy to suffer, hoping that I might, by my tears, prevent a single sin against the Faith, or at least atone for it."[225]

To make Jesus smile, to make His joy complete, to render priestly souls holy – these are the lofty reasons for your intimate suffering, similar to Jesus' own. They will make you experience the exquisite consolation of *no consolation* and make you share in the supreme secrets of Jesus: the secret of His unspeakable sufferings and the secret of His divine joy.

Personal Reflection of Conchita
SIXTEENTH DAY

What a beautiful meditation! Each paragraph is a world of light and incentive, which prods the soul on with strength and irresistible delight to sacrifice itself for the love of the Father, on behalf of souls and to give a perfect joy to Jesus.

Not only in suffering

Today Jesus spoke to me, referring to a previous time:
"Yet, do not think that if I ask you now to do and suffer ev-

erything for the glory of God, you should put aside what you were doing before. Rather, all is brought to completion, all is crowned by this noble end, and all acts are gilded with perfect charity and end in the glory of God.

"You should continue to offer to the Father His Word, whom I am, and through whom all graces descend. You must also offer yourself in union with Me in order to be the vessel of My graces, of the graces of the Holy Spirit, especially for My priests. You must attend all the Masses celebrated all over the world in spirit and in union with Mary. You must *offer Me, hand Me over to be crucified*, joining your will to that of My Father. You must generously and heroically do without My consolations, My sensible presence, My words and caresses, on behalf of My priests in need.

"Now with all that and without subtracting from these graces, you must direct all *to the glory* of My beloved Father. May everything in you, in your body and in your soul, have this holy end, this perfect intention in *all* its parts; not including all in one single act, but abiding in each one, directing them to and *consummating* them in that goal which is *the glory of the Father*.

"While accomplishing them, simplify these acts in one unique love, with only one coloring, so that without giving them up, they all may converge in the unity in its substance: *the glory of My Father*!

"That is what I want from you in this retreat."

"Thank you, my Jesus, because You let me know Your adorable will, what You want of me. What return can I make to Your incomparable Heart for Your great sensitivity to me?

"Is it not true that from my childhood You were my teacher, guide, light, way, goal and my all? Who taught me the way of the spirit? Who explained to me and taught me even the names of the desolations and tunnels which my soul crossed?

"Who gave me the image of things, the *objective* teaching, so to speak, in many paths of the soul? Ignorant as I was, my Jesus, who opened the horizons of perfection before me?

"Soul of my soul, who showed me the sublime secrets of the

Conchita's Reflections on a Retreat

Cross, the delights enclosed in suffering?

"From my childhood, from as far back as I can remember, who gave me the priceless grace of the *instinct* for suffering, like that of cats towards mice, and gave me a taste and relish for the delights enclosed in the Cross?

"As soon as the light of reason enlightened my mind, my soul looked for suffering, as for sweets, as for refreshment, as for the secret necessity of my soul, finding my delight in suffering, seeking it in a thousand hidden ways, with the only goal of pleasing God.

"I do not know why some of my strong bodily penances did not kill me, as for example, jabbing myself with sharp knives, etc. I could not keep still before the Blessed Sacrament, I felt ashamed because I thought I should be looking for suffering. I felt it should be like that.[226]

"I did not know that bodily penances should be performed with the permission of one's confessor, and I enjoyed my freedom, but as soon as I knew it, I asked for permission and I was not allowed to do many of them.

"Oh how good is my Jesus! As I felt that physical suffering was my life, and I found myself deprived of it so, when asleep, without looking for it, I was suffering and in that way I was offering it to Him joyfully and being obedient at the same time.

"Now, I understand that it was a grace of God, because generally children and adults flee from suffering."

My Father, why would Jesus have given me this desire for suffering?

Certainly, it was stronger in some periods than at others, but it was the basis of my piety, of my love for Him and of my aspirations.

UNDER THE GAZE OF THE FATHER

October 30, 1935
SEVENTEENTH DAY

Meditation of Archbishop Martínez

Suffering – the mode

The divine mode with which the Holy Spirit marks the acts He inspires is as important in the mystical life as it is difficult to explain. In any case, we can understand something of the divine mode of suffering in contrast to the human one.

One's concept of suffering molds, so to speak, the attitude of the soul towards it. For human reason, suffering is inevitable in human life, which one has to endure with philosophical dignity; at most, it is a ladder to attain a higher good, which one accepts with magnanimity. For this reason, the highest degree to which one's heart can attain in suffering is to suffer with dignity and fortitude, the way the pagan heroes did.

Yet, in the light of the Holy Spirit, suffering is elevated and is embellished. It is no longer the fateful course of destiny, but a messenger of the love of God. It is not simply a rough path taken to reach the summit, but the summit of Calvary itself, on which the Cross rises, divinized by the contact with Jesus and in a certain sense, an indissoluble part of Him.

In the divine world which welled up from the Heart of Jesus, suffering appears penetrated with love, fruitfulness, beauty and life. It is not something to be tolerated, but something to be loved, as it is capable of inspiring fervent love and attracting hearts irresistibly.

Perhaps there is nothing else in this world which may be so ardently loved as suffering. Even more, the divine light makes the rough exterior of suffering limpid and through it we perceive joy and happiness hidden within.

All the heavenly prerogatives of suffering derive from the fact that Jesus espoused it indissolubly on the summit of Golgotha. He conveyed to suffering His beauty and sweetness and He made it something sacred, transforming it into sacrifice; and He made it

Conchita's Reflections on a Retreat

something fruitful, converting it into the perennial fount of true life.

When suffering appears in this way before the enlightened eyes of the heart, souls that received the revelation of this mystery upon embracing the Cross experience the anointing of holy things, the emotion of beautiful things, the fulfillment of fruitful things, the gentleness of deep love and the unspeakable delight of perfect joy.

For this reason, in the school of Jesus one suffers gently, with peace, gratitude and joy. This is the divine mode of suffering.

Thus Jesus suffered. He awaited His baptism of blood on the Cross, which was the joy of His soul, with divine impatience, as He Himself revealed; with intimate peace and heavenly joy, He ascended Calvary and offered Himself in sacrifice; and in order to perpetuate the mystery of His perfect and complete joy, He immortalized His suffering in the Eucharist and in souls.

As a precious inheritance, Jesus left His divine way of suffering for His Church and for chosen souls. This legacy filled so many souls, like exquisite fragrance, in the course of the centuries and was exhaled as an emanation from paradise through the lips of the Apostle St. Andrew, who embraced the cross intoning his sublime canticle: "Oh good Cross, you received your beauty from the members of the Lord, for so long desired, fervently loved, ceaselessly sought and finally prepared for my most ardent desire! Receive me from among men and return me to my Master so that, through you, He may receive me, He who through you saved me."

Could the human heart ever love suffering in this way by its own strength?

According to this model, the soul that received the mystical incarnation should suffer with ardent longing, holy impatience, and ineffable joy; as the one who embraces happiness, the soul should embrace the Cross.

Do we need another model?

St. Polycarp, already tied to the stake as a victim of holocaust, receiving the host of the Eucharistic sacrifice, looking up toward heaven, prayed as follows: "Oh Almighty Lord God, Father of Your beloved and blessed Son Jesus Christ, by whom we have received the knowledge of You, God of angels, powers, and every creature, and of all the race of the just that live in Your presence! I bless You for having been pleased in Your goodness to bring me to this hour, that I may receive a portion in the number of Your martyrs and partake of the chalice of Your Christ for the resurrection to eternal life in the incorruptibleness of the Holy Spirit – among whom grant me to be received this day as a pleasing sacrifice, such a one as You Yourself have prepared, so that You may accomplish what You, Oh true and faithful God! have foreshown. Wherefore, for all things I praise, bless, and glorify You, through the eternal High Priest Jesus Christ, Your beloved Son, with whom, to You and the Holy Spirit be glory now and forever. Amen."[227]

The canticle of St. Andrew is a hymn of love. The prayer of St. Polycarp is an anaphora, that is, a Eucharistic prayer of consecration in the divine liturgy. The soul of the Apostle is full of joy; the soul of the bishop martyr, filled with anointing and gratitude.

The first canticle is an epithalamium;[228] the latter, a Eucharistic hymn.

Both reveal to us the divine *mode* of suffering of the souls of the Cross, which is distinguished by divine joy and sacred anointing. So should it be, because suffering was transformed by Jesus into something heavenly that fills us with joy, and into something sacred that produces anointing.

You should suffer like this: smiling with joy, peace and the anointing of an intimate and solemn liturgy.

Suffering is a betrothal and a Mass for transformed souls.

Personal Reflection of Conchita
SEVENTEENTH DAY

How far removed I am from what I should be!
My God! You who can do everything, have mercy upon me!

Conchita's Reflections on a Retreat

My Jesus, increase and intensify in my soul the desire for suffering, so that in bitterness I may water it with the joyful thought and delightful happiness of giving glory to Your heavenly Father.

October 31, 1935
Eighteenth Day

Meditation of Archbishop Martínez

Love

We have studied what the transformation into Jesus means for the soul that has received the mystical incarnation. Yet, as was already explained, this soul is not only Jesus but, due to its cooperation in forming Jesus in itself, the soul is also mystically His mother.

It is appropriate, therefore, to study this latter characteristic, which is full of charms and fruitful in practical conclusions. In fact, as was mentioned, God's love, properly speaking, is not any of the affections we know on earth, but it encompasses and excels all of them. In each soul or spiritual family that unique love has special features, which make it similar to one particular nuance among the many which love takes on earth.

In souls that have received the mystical incarnation, love takes on the character of motherly love, as we have already explained.

If we would like to express that love in a word, it would suffice to say that it is an image, or reflection, of the love of the heavenly Father.

St. Paul teaches us that all fatherhood in heaven and on earth proceeds from the Father. Since the soul has real and fruitful influence on the mystical Jesus who is being formed in it, this influence is undoubtedly the reflection of the fruitfulness of the Father and with all the more reason this is so, because the goal of this fruitfulness is the same as that of the eternal, divine fruitfulness.

It is obvious that if, because of the mystical incarnation, the soul shares, in a certain way, in the fruitfulness of the Father, it also shares in His love. It is also obvious that that love which is poured into the soul by the Holy Spirit has the ineffable nuance and holy characteristic of the love of the Father.

This love is a deep mystery, but we can faintly see the traits of it from what Scripture allows us to perceive and by the analogy which other reflections closer to our intelligence have with this sublime love.

Of course, this is a love which is the first and total *offering*. All love is a giving, but there are loves which do not give life and being, and this love gives precisely these basic gifts. There are loves which give back after having received, but this one takes the first step.

The heavenly Father is the Principle, the first source of being and life, not only with respect to creatures – which is common to all the Divine Persons – but also within the Holy Trinity. Perhaps because of this, the reflections of the Father's love are characterized by exquisite purity and perfect unselfishness.

In spousal love, those who love give and receive. In motherly love, the mother gives without expecting anything in return, but the good and happiness of her child. Motherly love is the most unselfish love on earth.

Given that love tends toward union, the center of love is where union is. In spousal love, love is between the spouses, in their midst, so to speak, joining them and making them one. While, in motherly love, union abides in the child to whom this love tends and in whom the mother's heart projects itself.

Hence, the child is the center of that love and the mother goes out of herself perfectly to find that center, without seeking herself, without expecting anything in return. The only thing that she is concerned about is the child. All she seeks is its good and happiness. Motherly love is pure and selfless by its nature.

Souls that have received the mystical incarnation should love Jesus in this way. It is obvious that they do not give life to Jesus, but rather, they receive it from Him, because He is Life, the only

Conchita's Reflections on a Retreat

life of souls. However, having a mystical relationship of motherhood with Jesus – because they worked jointly, so that Jesus may be formed in them – their love is tinged with motherly coloring and consequently, takes on the exquisite traits of that love.

A soul that possesses that love totally forgets itself in order to think of Jesus, as any mother totally forgets herself thinking of her child. As we have indicated before, that love does not force the fundamental law of each heart in seeking its own good; rather, *Jesus is* the good of the soul. Making Him happy and glorifying Him, the soul feels happy and has found its good.

Such love has attained to great purity, reflecting the ineffable purity and holiness of the Father, who begets His Son in the splendor of holiness.

As motherly love is very pure, it is also self-denying.

Let us notice the first link of that love with *the Cross*.

All love on earth is linked with suffering, because in all sincere love, there is self-forgetfulness, desirous to give oneself and longing for the good of the beloved, even at the price of martyrdom. But when, by the very nature of love, the Beloved is the only center of union, the one who loves desires to annihilate oneself and disappear, in order to obtain the good of the Beloved. One's own sufferings, far from being an obstacle or delaying the gift of self, or one's own projection into the Beloved, so to speak, render this love deeper and more intense, becoming a blessed ecstasy when this good is obtained through one's own martyrdom; then the one who loves arrives at self-annihilation, so that the Beloved may be happy.

Therefore, motherly love does not seek consolations, but desires to console. It doesn't spare suffering, but seeks it. It does not ask, but gives. Rather, its consolation is forgoing consolations, so that the Beloved may have them. Its delight is to suffer, so that the Beloved may not suffer. Its happiness is to give, to offer itself beyond measure, to give itself in suffering and death, so that the Beloved may be perfectly happy.

You've always experienced this characteristic of the motherly love deeply. Has not your life been suffering in all forms, bearing trials and tribulations, in order to give mysterious consolations to Jesus?

Jesus Himself was asking you for ever more subtle forms of martyrdom and more refined sufferings every day. Your motherly heart has experienced all forms of human suffering and many divine ones and your motherly love has been tinged with a range of all the nuances of suffering.

In the last period of your life, you have endured two of them which were even more subtle, deeper and more divine, so to speak, both typical of the purest love, both common to motherly love: sharing in the intimate sufferings of Jesus and the renunciation of all consolation, which the sensible presence of Jesus brings along with it, so that He might accomplish in souls, especially priestly ones, His work of love.

If you had any doubt about the quality of your love, this twofold martyrdom which Jesus asked of you would be enough to prove your *motherly* love. These intimate and deep secrets of suffering can only be confided to a mother; only she can be asked to heroically forgo the consolation of the caresses of the Beloved.

Rejoice, because Jesus treats you as a mother, because He has raised your love to this degree of selflessness and purity.

No greater grace could Jesus give you in this retreat than that of increasing and perfecting this dual martyrdom of motherly love, that means perfecting and exalting this intimate tenderness to the ineffable summit.

Can you receive a greater grace than that of fanning the loving flames you carry in your soul?

Up to now, the retreat time has been an oasis for you amidst the monotony of ordinary life. During these times, Jesus used to speak to you, caress you lovingly and fill you with exquisite gifts.

In this retreat, Jesus' attitude has changed so that, instead of the bliss and consolation of former times, He has given you very solid graces, the lofty gifts of a very fine, heroic double martyrdom, which make your motherly love truer and more perfect.

Conchita's Reflections on a Retreat

Personal Reflection of Conchita

EIGHTEENTH DAY

Jesus asked for *the Crusade of Victim Souls on behalf of Families* for His glory.

Yesterday morning, I was profoundly sad, weeping at the foot of the Tabernacle, while at the same time, I was happy gazing at Him, and even happier because He looked deeply into my soul, curing it, cleansing and purifying it of its unworthiness.

All for His glory!

How happy I am in this charming Little Cave! Even though I do not come up closer to Him, even though Jesus does not speak to me, it is enough that I can be close and look at Him and empty my soul before Him; that I can bring Him flowers and send Him kisses and caresses.

Today's meditation made me weep!

It is beautiful and full of a thousand sentiments and knowledge of spiritual motherhood. Oh my Jesus, You enlighten my spiritual director so much!

Thanks be to God!

November 1, 1935

NINETEENTH DAY

Meditation of Archbishop Martínez

Sacrifice

Motherly love is not only self-sacrificing, but also strong, very strong; so strong that the soul that possesses it does not hesitate before any sacrifice, but in fact accepts any martyrdom of the beloved, and even encourages him on and hands him over.

Even human, motherly love possesses traces of that unusual fortitude. A good mother – and I am thinking of my own – doesn't hesitate before a sacrifice required of her son, but she even insists on it when she knows it is necessary for his good.

Other affections are timid. They have neither the intuition of motherly love, which sees in depth the genuine good of the beloved, nor the courage to accept sacrifice despite the breaking of both hearts; perhaps it is because other kinds of love are not so pure and selfless.

A good mother scolds, punishes her child, and imposes hard sacrifices on him when her heart senses that such suffering will contribute to the perfection, glory and happiness of her child. It does not mean she does not love him; she loves him very much; she really loves him; she loves him deeply.

Even if human motherly love were not like this, divine motherly love should be like this, because both of these forms of love are a reflection of the highest model: the love of the Father, who delivered Jesus up to suffering and death.

On a superficial level, or to a fainthearted person, this ineffably strong love seems cruel.

How could one allow one's son to suffer, to die? Above all, how could one deliver him up to the Cross? Yet, if we look at the mystery in depth, if our heart is filled with truth and purity, we perceive that this is allowed not out of cruelty, but out of the sublime love of the one who thus acts. If for the son suffering and death mean glory and life, how could one prevent his happiness by cowardly compassion? The mother of the Maccabees encouraged her sons to accept martyrdom and handed them over to death.

"*Son, have pity on me, who carried you in my womb for nine months, nursed you for three years, brought you up, educated and supported you to your present age. I beg you, child, to look at the heavens and the earth and see all that is in them; then you will know that God did not make them out of existing things; and in the same way the human race came into existence. Do not be afraid of this executioner, but be worthy of your brothers and accept death, so that in the time of mercy, I may receive you again with them.*"[229]

She understood what was really good for her sons and prodded them on to martyrdom, because it meant happiness and glory for them.

With His infinite gaze, the heavenly Father saw in the Cross the incomparable glory and complete happiness of Jesus, so that He handed Him over to suffering and death, because He loved Him with infinite love.

Your love is the reflection of the love of the Father and it should be very strong like the fire from which your love comes. Similarly, you should offer Jesus to be crucified in the way you can and as it was explained to you in a previous retreat.[230]

You should offer Jesus to be crucified not only out of love for souls, or for priests, or simply because God wants it, but because the crucifixion of Jesus in all its forms is *the glory of God*, because it is the joy, honor and happiness of Jesus, because it is the real and great good of His beloved Son.

It is the second link of motherly love with the Cross.

Personal Reflection of Conchita

NINETEENTH DAY

Oh my Jesus, may You be blessed!

Have You brought me to this retreat for *this reason*?

And why did You not reveal Yourself up to now?

What prevented Your love from doing it before?

Yesterday Jesus asked of me a beautiful thing, which will give much glory to His heavenly Father. He started in the morning, but I played the fool, because I was afraid to be wrong. Yet, in the afternoon, He caught me and overwhelmed me by explaining His will.

I'd better consult my spiritual director first, before I write it down.

Mystical Incarnation

Today He gave me some light on the mystical incarnation.

"Look, one of the goals of the development or explanation of the mystical incarnation that I desired in this retreat was to protect this important grace in the future by enlightening your spiritual director, because this grace will no doubt have its enemies."

Thank you, Jesus of my soul; may You be blessed and glorified in all.

November 2, 1935
Twentieth Day

Meditation of Archbishop Martínez

Fruitfulness

Motherly love has still another link with the Cross. As already said, the soul that received the mystical incarnation extends its spiritual fruitfulness to other souls and loves them with the same love with which it loves Jesus.

This love for souls demands new forms of suffering and crucifixion, because suffering is the indispensable condition of fruitfulness and we cannot do good to souls except by suffering.

St. Paul, who possessed this spiritual fruitfulness abundantly, tells us about his own sufferings: *"Who is weak, and I am not weak? Who is led to sin, and I am not indignant?"*[231] As an earthly mother feels all the sorrows of her children in her heart, so the soul that has received the gift of spiritual motherhood suffers all that her spiritual children suffer.

In fact, these torments are part of the intimate suffering of the Heart of Jesus, in which souls that have received the mystical incarnation share. And when this spiritual fruitfulness concerns priests in particular, undoubtedly sufferings increase, because the priest overflows with suffering, is the victim of cruel persecutions and is exposed to numerous and special dangers.

Yet, the suffering mentioned above is not the only one experienced by spiritual motherhood, because it is not enough for the

Conchita's Reflections on a Retreat

one who has received this privilege to feel the suffering of souls, but one must also seek to remedy their misfortunes, obtain graces for them and communicate life to them – and all these things require intimate and cruel suffering.

The same Apostle also said: "*I will most gladly spend and be utterly spent for your sakes.*"[232] This applies not only to the one who can influence souls in active life, but also and perhaps principally, to the one who, in a hidden but effective way, fruitfully exercises his influence upon them.

St. Thérèse of the Child Jesus wrote: "Indeed, all my strength lies in prayer and sacrifice. They are my invincible arms, and I know from experience that I can conquer hearts with these more surely than I can with words."[233]

In order to give life, one has to suffer. Just as a mother gives birth to her children in suffering, so the one who has spiritual motherhood gives birth to souls in even more terrible suffering.

Jesus gave us life with unspeakable suffering. Mary, in order to be our Mother, was the Queen of Martyrs.

This is how we give life to souls: *on the Cross.*

In spiritual motherhood, there is a singular martyrdom, which joins the two great forms of suffering we have indicated as proper to motherly love. To explain it I will use the thought of Bishop Charles Gay: "When Cain killed Abel, Eve had a twofold martyrdom, because she suffered for the innocent and for the guilty one."

In this way, the Blessed Virgin Mary suffered at the foot of the Cross for her innocent Son and for her guilty children. The torment that we are trying to explain appears clearly in Mary. She suffered the sorrows of all men to purchase graces for them and to be their Co-redemptrix. She suffered not only her own sorrows, but also for those of Jesus. She offered Jesus to the Father and handed Him over to suffering and death not only for the good of Jesus, but also for the good of souls. This brought the singular and immense martyrdom of Mary's heart: she carried within her the martyrdom of Jesus and of souls. She suffered for her Son who was Victim and for the miserable and lost children to whom she was giving life through her suffering united to Jesus' own, joining one martyrdom with the other and exalting the heroic martyrdom of His Heart, handing over her divine Son to the Cross so that, through His sacrifice, her other children might be redeemed and have life.

That sublime martyrdom was a summit of Mary's sufferings and marks the supreme fortitude of her motherly love.

In no other soul as in Mary's, apart from that of Jesus, the phrase of the Song of Songs is realized: *"For stern as death is love."*[234] Love's marvelous fortitude, which joins human and divine suffering in one heart, that of Jesus and that of souls, and it doesn't falter, as the Father didn't falter in handing Jesus over to save souls, according to the beautiful Easter Proclamation: "Father, how wonderful Your care for us! How boundless Your merciful love! To ransom a slave, You gave away Your Son."

The motherly love of souls that received the mystical incarnation shares in this admirable fortitude of Mary's love. Your soul should share in that loving fortitude.

Look at all the suffering your spiritual motherhood imposes upon you, which is the source of graces, or rather, the channel of grace for souls. You must suffer what souls suffer, especially what priests suffer. You must suffer whatever is necessary to obtain graces for them, to give life, to develop it fully and to hand Jesus over to crucifixion, to every form of crucifixion, even though it makes your motherly heart break, so that souls *"might have life and have it more abundantly."*[235]

Can you see how the Cross is the center of motherly love?

Do you not see that Calvary is where spiritual children are born, in the same way that Mary gave birth? And how, at the foot of the Cross, motherly love finds its consummation and glory in suffering the supreme martyrdom?

The inestimable privilege which God bestowed on you in granting you the grace of mystically assisting at all Masses is joined to this mystery of fruitfulness in suffering; or rather, this privilege is really the immense extension – according to divine logic – of the mystery I have just explained.

The Mass is the sacrifice of Calvary, which renews and perpetuates itself and Mary, who was on Calvary, exercising her sublime role, must renew and perpetuate her role in all Masses until the consummation of time.

Consequently, since you share mystically in Mary's sublime mission, due to the outstanding grace you have received, it seems logical that God has also bestowed upon you the admirable prerogative of mystically renewing and perpetuating the mystery of love, suffering and fruitfulness.

At the altar, you are to be neither a simple witness, nor only a comfort for Jesus, nor do you assist merely out of motherly compassion. You are there to offer Jesus, to give Him up to be crucified, and to gather from the blessed Cross, from the pierced Heart, treasures of graces in order to pour them into souls, especially priestly ones.

Personal Reflection of Conchita
TWENTIETH DAY

I am reflecting on my meditation on fruitfulness.

The Crusade

Today Jesus wanted to talk. He poured His Heart out to me, clarifying His wishes, requests, His sorrow and pain, because so many thorns are hurting Him.

He wanted the Crusade of Victim Souls.

It makes me suffer seeing Him in sorrow! Oh my Jesus, I will repeat it a thousand times!

My sorrows are not sorrows, your sorrows are my sorrows!

UNDER THE GAZE OF THE FATHER

November 3, 1935
TWENTY-FIRST DAY

Meditation of Archbishop Martínez

Tenderness

Tenderness is another characteristic of motherly love.

By blessed experience we know it, because we were born and grew up enveloped in this tenderness, which filled our life with its exquisite and pure fragrance.

If the reflection of the Father's love achieves such perfection in creatures, even on a natural level, what will the splendor that causes such reflection be like? What will the Father's infinite tenderness be like?

In the inaccessible light which surrounds the divine, our heart perceives the treasures of that tenderness in the words which the Father let resound over Jesus on solemn occasions, and in which we perceive the ineffable divine mystery through this expression.

At the Jordan and on Tabor, the Father gave testimony of His infinite tenderness, saying of Jesus: *"This is My beloved Son, with whom I am well pleased."*[236]

Each word is a condensed and sublime expression of very tender love. Did God ever say such a thing to any of the angels?

The accent of tenderness with which the mysterious expression was pronounced can be imagined. One can perceive the abyss hidden in each word *"beloved Son, with whom I am well pleased."* A breath of His heavenly love, of His unspeakable tenderness, envelops the soul when it inwardly pronounces the divine testimony, when the loving revelation resounds in it like an echo from heaven.

Any time that our hearts, not only our lips, say the word "son," we feel the radiation of tenderness; this word seems to be a canticle from heaven, even to the created heart which pronounces it.

In the Upper Room, when Jesus pronounced the words "little children," adding "little" to permeate the word "children" with tenderness, it is as though He opened His noble Heart to show us the Heart of God.

How the word "Son," pronounced by the Father, would have resounded over the waters of the Jordan! How it would have shone in the brightness of Tabor, "like a shining rainbow in the clouds of glory!" How it would have enveloped Jesus like an immense caress, like an infinite gaze!

The adjective "little" was not necessary, because God's words, infinite in their simplicity, do not need it. Even the expression from the Psalms does not need it, since it is an echo of the eternal word: "*You are My Son.*"[237] Yet, in order to reveal to our spirit the richness of the divine word, the profound qualifier "beloved" was added to the essential word at the Jordan and on Tabor.

Sometimes our lips defile this word; sometimes we diminish its majesty or render it sterile when we pronounce it, because our heart does not put its treasure in it; but on the lips of the Father, it is filled with eternal love; one could say that the Holy Spirit is contained in it.

"Beloved Son!" Yes, He is loved as no one else in the universe, neither angels nor Mary; He is tenderly and infinitely loved, loved with unique and incomparable love.

In order that the narrowness of our spirit might not limit the great richness of tenderness – as we know how to do it – which is poured out in the divine testimony, the Father was pleased to add the rich expression "*with whom I am well pleased.*"

What is the delight of God like? To be pleased is to put one's delight and heart in what one is pleased with.

The Father pours out His infinite Heart and puts His eternal delight in Jesus, the unique object of His delight. Yes, unique. If He is pleased with souls, with the universe, it is for Him, with Him and in Him.

On another occasion, too, the voice of the Father was heard in order to express His tenderness to Jesus. I think this was the only reason why His voice was heard on earth. It was the day of the transitory, but prophetical triumph of Jesus, as He entered

Jerusalem amidst the hosannas of the crowd: *"Father, glorify Your name; then a voice came from heaven, 'I have glorified it and will glorify it again.'"*[238]

It is the echo from the Jordan and Tabor, or rather the complement of those testimonies; Jesus and the glory of the Father seem to be equivalent in the prayer of Jesus and the testimony of the Father.

Jesus has just said: *"The hour has come for the Son of Man to be glorified."*[239] Dom Delatte[240] wonderfully expresses the meaning of the prayer of Jesus: "Glorify the One who is Your substantial name, the interior manifestation and the exterior revelation of Your being and splendor." In this mysterious voice, the tenderness of the Father bursts out in an explosion of glory.

Perhaps I have exceeded myself in such a long digression about the tenderness of the Father, but it sprang from my heart, although I have not yet managed to point out the mystery.

If the love of the Father is so tender, its reflection in souls that have received the mystical incarnation should be characterized by tenderness. This love of delight must repeat, like a muffled but faithful echo, the Father's unfathomable expression at the Jordan and on Tabor, and be consummated in a burst of glory, since it is His last testimony.

Undoubtedly, even the divinized tenderness of our heart lacks the breadth, the depth and the sublime strength of the tenderness of the Father. In the heart of the creature this tenderness becomes motherly, that is, gentle, sensitive, with the delicacy that we all enjoy in the heart of our mother.

This tenderness does not hover victoriously over life-giving waters, but is shed in precious tears of heavenly strength combined with human weakness, just as Jesus manifested His tenderness at Bethany and on the Mount of Olives.

This tenderness does not shine amid the clouds of glory, but, passing through the prism of the human heart, it splits into a spectrum of all the gentle affections, into all the soft caresses whose secret only mothers know.

Conchita's Reflections on a Retreat

With this exquisite tenderness, these precious tears, these caresses which have the softness and fragrance of rose petals, you should love, console, envelop and lull Jesus, the gentle Son of your heart.

Truly, you need no lessons for this, nor do you lack motivation. God gave you a tender and great motherly heart, and wondrous grace expanded it even more, enriched it more abundantly with tenderness, and filled it with the ineffable reflection of eternal love.

Thus you have loved Jesus.

Thus you will keep on loving Him for all eternity.

Jesus is the beloved Son with whom you are pleased and in your inmost heart, you can quietly, but gently, repeat the divine phrase as an echo from the Jordan and Tabor.

Now Jesus desires that the grace of the mystical incarnation and the motherly love which springs from it may be consummated in a burst of glory, so that the name of God may be glorified; that substantial name which was clothed with our flesh, and which is the same yesterday, today, and forever.

Personal Reflection of Conchita
TWENTY-FIRST DAY

I am reflecting on tenderness.

Yesterday Jesus spoke about the Crusade and today, He is continuing to develop His plan and will for it. All for His glory.

May He be blessed!

November 4, 1935
TWENTY-SECOND DAY

Meditation of Archbishop Martínez

Souls

This motherly tenderness is not for Jesus alone, but must be extended to other souls, because they are Jesus and you are their mother.

In God's divine design, He wanted us to love Him and our neighbor with the same love and charity. When this love takes on a special coloring, which is applicable to Jesus and to souls, your love for souls must be the same as that for Jesus. The profound reason for this unity is that the whole Jesus, so to speak, encloses and encompasses the souls that are one with Him in a mystical, but deeply real way.

Souls are members of the Mystical Body of Jesus and in this sense they are His hands, feet and eyes. Can they be loved in any other way than the way Jesus is loved? Even more, being His members, they are Jesus Himself, because He dwells wholly in each one of His members.

If souls that have received the mystical incarnation should love Jesus with motherly love, they should also love souls with the same love, extending their spiritual motherhood to them.

For this reason, I have said before that you should sacrifice yourself maternally for the sake of souls, especially for the sake of priests, obtaining graces through your sacrifices, because self-denial and genuine motherly love require it. Then you should love souls with this tender love, which reflects the divine tenderness of the Father.

St. Paul gives us an example of that supernatural tenderness. Does he not use motherly expressions for it?

He calls them "*my children*,"[241] saying they are his "*joy and crown*,"[242] "*beloved*," whom he "*holds in his heart*" and that he "*longs for all of them with the affection of Christ Jesus.*"[243]

Conchita's Reflections on a Retreat

St. Paul reveals to the Philippians that his heart is torn between contrary forces, struggling between the desire to depart this life to be with Christ and the longing to remain on earth for their sake.

He wrote to the Thessalonians: *"Rather, we were gentle among you, as a nursing mother cares for her children. With such affection for you, we were determined to share with you not only the gospel of God, but our very selves as well, so dearly beloved had you become to us."*[244]

Quotations which reveal the really motherly tenderness of the heart of the Apostle could be cited indefinitely.

And whoever has received the reflection of the love of the Father in one or another form should love souls in this manner. No earthly affection can be compared with the tenderness towards souls that has such a divine source and heavenly savor.

St. Thérèse of the Child Jesus wrote: "My heart has loved Him alone, and this has gradually so developed that it is able to love those whom He loves with a tenderness incomparably deeper than any selfish, barren affection."[245]

This is the reflection of that tenderness of Jesus, which allowed the beloved disciple to listen closely to the heartbeats of Jesus. Such tenderness, rich in consolations and gentleness, excels the tenderness of earthly mothers, because it is heavenly.

These holy affections, which God Himself forms in souls, have the purity and depth of divine love or rather they are the magnificent expansion of divine love. I think that they are part of that hundredfold which Jesus promised to those who leave all things for Him. Besides, these empty hearts, which have abandoned all earthly affections for Jesus' sake, these pure hearts which never opened themselves to a love other than the divine love, are the only ones that know the secret of this heavenly tenderness, which superabundantly compensates them for the earthly affections which they renounced.

In heaven, the blessed should love one another with this tenderness and, loving one another intensely as one can love on this earth, they love God alone, because in that delightful dwelling

"*God is all in all*,"²⁴⁶ according to St. Paul.

The mystical incarnation has its privileges and consolations; not everything in it is sorrow and martyrdom. Certainly, one can apply to this outstanding grace the words of the psalm: "*You changed my mourning into dancing; You took off my sackcloth and clothed me with gladness.*"²⁴⁷

One could write much on the divine consolations, which embrace all forms of perfect joy, for example, the consolations of:

Suffering for Jesus.
Sharing in His bitterness.
Consoling His sorrows.
Helping Him in His divine work.
Receiving His filial caresses.
Hearing your name… pronounced by His lips.²⁴⁸

It is worth suffering all the forms of martyrdom which the mystical incarnation implies in order to enjoy these divine privileges, for the love which accompanies this grace is very pure and selfless.

Divine paradox!

The more unselfish the love is, the greater and finer are the recompenses it obtains.

The one who leaves all things for Jesus becomes rich, because he "*has treasure in heaven.*"²⁴⁹ The one who appears to become a fool for Him, attains to the highest wisdom.

The one who renounces all other affections for Jesus' sake attains to the fullness of His love, and, as a divine addition, one is given back all lost affections, but purified, perfected and divine.

This tenderness towards souls is one of the prerogatives and consolations of the mystical incarnation, which in a divine way makes up for all the tears and sorrows suffered on behalf of souls, making every form of martyrdom that spiritual motherhood carries with it sweet. Nothing makes the suffering which motherhood requires more bearable than the tenderness which God places in the heart of mothers on the natural level. This tenderness is the powerful incentive to offer sacrifices ceaselessly for the children's sake.

Conchita's Reflections on a Retreat

What amazes us most is that when this tenderness is poured out into souls, they disappear and Jesus appears; that is, the holy and pure affection offered to souls does not stop in them, does not even find them, but in place of them finds Jesus. Souls seem to be only a pretext to get to Him, the way to seek Him, a kind of sacrament which puts us in intimate and delightful communion with Him.

Bishop Charles Gay[250] states that these divine affections expand the soul, enable it to communicate with others to receive their confidences and to transmit spiritual lights to them.

I think that one of the reasons that God, who Himself is sufficient to do good to all, wanted to make use of some souls to do good to others was precisely in order to establish intimate relations between them. These relations join the world of souls, making them not only isolated beings joined only to God, but also members of one well organized body, agents of perfect order, living exemplars of the incomparable beauty of the whole Jesus, which embraces, in its rich unity, the Church in heaven, in purgatory and on earth.

I consider that when the soul feels this motherly tenderness for other souls, it is aware of this union which exists between souls, owing to the wonderful and divine communion among them.

I have gone on at length about this very important but so little studied spiritual point, because it serves for a better understanding of the mystical incarnation and obliges you *to look at it more directly.*

In my opinion, two things have made you look at this grace with a sidelong glance. First and foremost, you must feel yourself a mother of souls in all of its consequences, so that you can exercise motherly tenderness more earnestly. But a misunderstood idea of humility prevents you from doing this.

Secondly, just as we must love Jesus with the third love, so we must love souls with the same love. But this requires a new and very interesting chapter.

Personal Reflection of Conchita
TWENTY-SECOND DAY

Today Jesus again talked about the Crusade. He asks for so much purity!

The sins of the world and of those who belong to Him offend Him so much!

He bemoaned the wounds of His Heart, the thorns which pierce it. He grieved that there is so much mud in the world, and He asks for purity, purity. And I would like to have thousands of seas of purity to console Him!

November 5, 1935
TWENTY-THIRD DAY

Meditation of Archbishop Martínez

The Third Love – Souls

What you called the third love is the most *pure, simple, self-confident* and *bold* love for Jesus, which simply receives the most marvelous graces and asks for the most intimate caresses from the Beloved without shyness.

(What a beautiful definition of the third love!)

In the course of your unforgettable retreat,[251] you came to understand very well that the roots of this love are total self-forgetfulness and a profound knowledge of God.

St. John says that *"perfect love drives out fear, because fear has to do with punishment, and so one who fears is not yet perfect in love."*[252] Fear and wonder spring from the lack of knowledge of the infinite mercy and goodness of God, who pours out His love, caresses and gifts on whom He pleases, no matter how miserable he or she may be. On looking at itself and impressed by its wretchedness, the soul considers its misery incompatible with God's graces and gifts.

Conchita's Reflections on a Retreat

These same roots hinder the third love for souls, which consists in such a pure, simple, bold love for them, that it places us in the truth; that is, it reveals to us the intimate relations which God has established between souls and our soul.

The soul that received the gift of spiritual motherhood from God has close relations with souls which it influences supernaturally. As a result, motherly love, with its own traits and holy efficacy, wells up from these relations.

In order for the soul that has received such a gift to live in the truth and offer itself to this holy affection without wonder and fear, it needs to be aware of its motherhood, of the rights and obligations which this privilege carries with it; among others, the right and obligation to love the spiritual children given by God with motherly care, self-denial and tenderness.

Now, if the soul looks at itself, if it penetrates into its misery and nothingness, but without full light from God, neither does it dare to feel itself mother, nor does it have the courage to love souls in this way; even less does it attain to the boldness of entrusting itself without reserve to this motherly tenderness.

The soul says to itself: Isn't it boastful to feel myself a mother, being as wretched as I am? How can I give the sweet name of son to one who is superior to me in so many ways? How can I approach certain souls with confidence and treat them with tenderness if I am incapable of confessing that I have given life to them, that they are my daughters, precisely because I am poor and my soul is empty of the gifts of true life?

Undoubtedly, by ourselves we can neither give life to souls, nor even do good to them. This is what Jesus meant when He said: *"Call no one on earth your father; you have but one Father in heaven."*[253]

Yet, through the reflection of this fatherhood which God can project into any soul from His ineffable condescension in order to associate us with His works, to make us instruments of His action and sharers in His marvelous deeds, we can do good to souls, give them life and even call ourselves fathers, as St. Paul did when he wrote to the Corinthians: *"Even if you should have countless guides to Christ, yet you do not have many fathers, for I became your father in Christ Jesus through the gospel.*"[254]

The spiritual fatherhood or motherhood of creatures does not originate from the depth of their misery, but comes from the Father: "*from whom all fatherhood, in heaven or on earth, takes its name.*"[255] It comes from something divine which the Father places in us, which has no other link with our misery than that of the ocean with the deep hole which receives it.

Why should one be amazed at being mother, if this motherhood is God's gift, the fruit of His grace and goodness? If this privilege sprang from our being, we should be amazed, because never did holm oak give figs. It is impossible not only for the wretched creature, but even for the most perfect, lofty and highly endowed one to give so much as a spark of supernatural life to a single soul.

God is the only one who can give this life. Who can prevent Him from taking a poor soul as an instrument, if He delights in using what is weak, most contemptible, what is naught, as St. Paul assures us?

If the loftiest of the seraphim could not obtain spiritual motherhood by itself, because it is God's free gift, why should one be amazed at possessing it, if this gift is not fashioned by the one who receives it? It would be as if the rod of Moses were to be surprised by the miracles which the leader of Israel accomplished through it, or as if the tassel of Jesus' cloak dared to confess that when it was touched a sick woman was cured.

The soul that does not think of itself and knows that God can raise up children to Abraham from the stones, admits God's gift without shyness or boasting. If God has made her mother, she feels herself to be mother most naturally and simply out of profound humility, which is the clearest light and full truth.

Being in truth, the soul that has received the mystical incarnation lets motherly love invade it and totally fill it. It allows its innermost being to be permeated with the gentle and divine fire which the Father pours into it with His marvelous fruitfulness so that, like a flower filled with exquisite scent, it may open its chalice to perfume souls with the heavenly fragrance of its tenderness.

This heavenly fragrance is divine and, as such, it is effusive. Why should its expansion be hindered? Why should one seek to look at it in a selfish way, or to smother it by unfounded fears or shyness?

Moreover, the fear that this love might be imperfect or dangerous could hinder the third love for souls. Indeed, it would, if a soul that had not received this precious prerogative of spiritual motherhood, presumed to undertake these very pure paths of love without discretion.

In fact, in the spiritual life nothing is so dangerous as affection for created things. God's love is so pure, so exclusive and so jealous!

Yet, the Lord gives these holy affections, which are simply the mysterious radiations of His love, to souls that give up everything for Him and attain to the fullness of His love through the heart's perfect self-emptying.

This motherly love is the superabundance of the divine love which, after filling one's heart, overflows into souls. This overflowing of intimate contemplation belongs to the apostolic life, according to St. Thomas Aquinas.

Of course, the state to which the soul that has received the mystical incarnation was raised eliminates all danger. St. Thérèse wrote: "I no longer feel that I must deny my heart all consolation, for it is fixed on God..."[256]

But above all, how can charity be dangerous? How can God's own love, which is poured out ardently and triumphantly into souls through divine motherly love, be dangerous?

In reality, it is Jesus who loves in us and is loved in souls with this love. If we consider it on the natural level, neither souls nor we have anything to do with this prodigious love. Neither do we love on our own, nor are souls loved for their own merits.

Through our motherly heart, the Father loves His Jesus, who dwells in souls given to us as spiritual children. This is the eternal mystery of love hidden within God for centuries. The same mystery was accomplished in the Blessed Virgin Mary and is renewed in souls in a mystical, but real way.

The Father, in making use of the very humble cooperation of a soul in order to give life to others, that is, to give them Jesus, who is Life, also makes use of the heart of this soul that loves with the Holy Spirit, so that He continues to love Jesus, whom He fashioned in this heart and in other hearts in which Jesus dwells.

Let us imagine a circuit through which a powerful electric current passes to produce light, heat and power. If we entered this circuit, the current would pass through us and we would have a part in the marvels which it produces.

By the mystical incarnation the soul "enters into the joy of the Lord," into the splendid divine life; the current of the divine love that flows in the bosom of the adorable Trinity passes, in a certain sense, through our heart and into the souls we love with motherly love.

But there is great and delightful difference: in the electric circuit, the thing which enters it has neither awareness nor merit. On the contrary, in this circuit of love souls are not only aware of and have merit in the mystery which is accomplished in them, but also, due to the marvelous supernatural economy established by God, the Father loves Jesus in such a way through our heart that we really love, and Jesus is loved in such a manner in souls that they are also really loved.

It is clear that this wonder cannot be realized unless we love with the Holy Spirit, the love with which the Father and the Son love each other in blessed and incomprehensible eternity.

Personal Reflection of Conchita
TWENTY-THIRD DAY

This meditation enkindled my motherly love, and expanded my heart, which I always tend to repress.

I have written letters to many Sisters, as never before; this will surely surprise them.

I feel that this retreat is permeating me.

Oh my Jesus, be blessed!

Jesus is bringing to perfection something He is planning for His glory.

Today Jesus remained silent. Fr. Jacinto came to say goodbye. I wrote some very motherly letters to the Sisters of the Cross as a response to the today's meditation.

I must be mother! I have to broaden my heart, looking *directly* at this great grace, living it, pondering it, tasting it, thanking God for it and spreading it.

I must only gaze at the diamond, Jesus, and forget that *I am* the bark. I need self-forgetfulness, specifically eliminating overdone humility, appreciating this heavenly gift with all my soul, strength and heart.

Oh Jesus, Jesus of all my life! Make me what You want me to be right away, please, for the sake of Your mercy, for the sake of Your love; make me what You need me to be in order to fulfill Your designs on earth.

November 6, 1935

Twenty-Fourth Day

Meditation of Archbishop Martínez

The Gaze

St. Paul says that *"every fatherhood takes its name from the Father in heaven and on earth."*[257] Consequently, as I have said so many times, the mystical incarnation originates in the heavenly Father, whose reflection it is.

And according to St. Thomas, things are all the more perfect insofar as they return to their principle. Therefore, the mystical incarnation is consummated in the bosom of the Father.

UNDER THE GAZE OF THE FATHER

Especially in these days you have felt the mysterious gaze of the Father, who continues to accomplish His great grace in you. How justly the mystery of this fruitfulness is ascribed to the gaze of the Father!

The Virgin Mary attributed the great wonders accomplished in her to this gaze: *"Quia respexit humilitatem ancillae suae."* *"For He has looked upon His handmaid's lowliness."*[258] This is the deepest source of all graces: the infinite gaze which rests on the abyss of our nothingness.

The all-powerful gaze of God!

God looks on the earth and it trembles.[259] He looks upon His handmaid's lowliness, and she becomes the Mother of God, a wonder of grace and beauty.

The first page of Genesis says: *"God looked at everything He had made, and He found it very good."*[260] I would explain it in this way: because God looked at everything He had made, He filled it with abundant goodness. God's gaze is always the fruitful fount of grace and beauty.

> *"And having looked at them,*
> *with his image alone,*
> *clothed them in beauty."*[261]

He always delights in gazing upon the abyss, as Scripture says: *"Humilia respicit."* *"The Lord looks on the humble."*[262]

If each grace has its origin in the divine gaze, then those which are mysteries of fruitfulness are born especially from that gaze of the Father, since He is the principle, the fount and the model of all fruitfulness.

The mystical incarnation is not just any fruitfulness or vestige of the Father's fruitfulness, but it is like an image of the Father's fruitfulness, because it has the same goal: Jesus.

The Father begets His Word in a soul and Jesus appears in it in a mystical way. In his Epistle to the Ephesians, St. Paul, on his knees, begs the Father that, *"Christ may dwell in our hearts through faith."*[263]

Conchita's Reflections on a Retreat

The Father is the origin of all transformation into Jesus, the only one who begets His Word wherever He wants Him to be.

One should not think that it is arbitrary to attribute this grace precisely to the gaze of the Father, as if it could be attributed in the same way to His right hand or to His Heart; this is so because the Father begets His Word through a gaze, or rather through the gaze, His unique, infinite and eternal gaze.

The Church teaches us that the Son proceeds from the Father by way of the intellect, that His Word is the personal end of knowledge of the Father. And the gaze is the metaphorical term to express this unique act of notional knowledge, according to theologians.

He sees us and all things in this gaze, and, looking at them, He puts a trace in them, a likeness of His Word and, in the order of grace, He puts His image in them, by which we are made His children by adoption.

Transformed souls receive the perfect image of His Word through the intimate gaze of the Father, who gives them perfect adoption as children and makes them Jesus in an ineffable manner.

The Father gave testimony of Jesus twice, at the Jordan and on Tabor, and in both mysteries He saw us in Him, and this signified the mystery of our adoption. Yet, the liturgy of the Transfiguration clarifies the mystery, teaching us that perfect adoption is signified on Tabor, while it helps us to understand that that at the Jordan was imperfect.

The first we receive in baptism, the latter in glory. The first one makes us Jesus, but the second one, that of Tabor, perfects and consummates Jesus in us.

This perfect and consummated Jesus in us is Heaven, but it is also the transformation which God accomplishes in us in this life.

The Father gazed upon us, or rather gazed upon Jesus in our souls the day of our baptism. This unique gaze of the Father, when it rests on the purified soul, produces in it the fullness of light, love and divine fruitfulness. It transforms the soul into Jesus and in some chosen souls becomes the *mystical incarnation*.

It is impossible for our poor human language to describe, even suspect, the treasure of light, love and fruitfulness which is poured out into the transformed soul when the Father fixes the gaze of Tabor on it, when Mary's words are accomplished in this soul: *"Respexit humilitatem ancillae suae."* "*For He has looked upon His handmaid's lowliness.*"

In this gaze, there are the splendors of holiness in which the Father begot His Word,[264] and made Him the refulgence of eternal light, the spotless mirror of the power of God, and the image of His goodness.[265] The infinite fire of love, with its perennial flame and fruitfulness of life, burns in this gaze. The end of this fruitfulness is the Word of God.

All the divine splendor, the immaterial fire and eternal life are in the soul that receives this ineffable gaze because the Word is in this soul, and the soul is mystically Jesus.

Undoubtedly, the person retains his or her personality and misery, even in receiving outstanding grace, because God, even in His most intimate communications with souls, maintains His divine transcendence; He does not commingle with earth and continues being He Who Is; but the soul is enveloped in divine splendor like a cloud which shines with the glory of the sun and burns without consuming itself in the heavenly fire, possessing in its inmost being true life, eternal life.

The Father's gaze enlightens and embellishes the fortunate soul in order to transform it into Jesus, because He forms His image in it, the image of heavenly light, which gives to the soul the very beauty of the Beloved.

As the bride of the *Spiritual Canticle* of St. John of the Cross, the soul may say:

> "When you looked at me
> your eyes imprinted your grace in me;"[266]

Conchita's Reflections on a Retreat

The soul does not only possess:

> *"the eyes I have desired,*
> *which I bear sketched deep within my heart."*[267]

But the whole image of Jesus, all the traits of His beauty, all the richness of His majesty, have been engraved in its inmost being.

The Father loves the soul because He gazed upon it and clothed it with His grace.

> *"When you looked at me*
> *your eyes imprinted your grace in me;*
> *for this you loved me ardently*
> *and thus my eyes deserved*
> *to adore what they beheld in you."*[268]

Its misery does not prevent the soul from being beautiful and loved, just as the bride of the Song of Songs is *"dark, but lovely"* [269] as the result of the divine gaze. Perhaps the King loved her all the more for being dark and beautiful.

> *"Do not despise me;*
> *for if, before, you found me dark,*
> *now truly you can look at me*
> *since you have looked*
> *and left in me grace and beauty."*[270]

The Father loves the soul, because He loves Jesus who dwells in it by means of the efficacious virtue of the ineffable gaze.

With the light of love, the gaze of the Father brought the soul to life, it brought Jesus who is true and eternal life, so that the blessed soul can say with St. Paul: *"I live, no longer I, but Christ lives in me."*[271]

UNDER THE GAZE OF THE FATHER

Personal Reflection of Conchita
TWENTY-FOURTH DAY

Oh my Jesus, my Jesus! And even before that moment when I had arrived, even from the time when You had spoken to me, when I had heard Your voice in the Church of Our Lady of Mount Carmel in San Luis Potosi[272] telling me: "The Father is gazing upon you," from that time *that gaze* had left in me the holy germ of the mystical incarnation; that same gaze penetrates my soul, body and my whole being. What should I do, if not be annihilated, give You thanks, and invite heaven and earth to give You thanks for me?

Oh God of my whole soul, be blessed!

And with this insight which my spiritual director puts in his meditations, I sink and would like to melt in gratitude.

Neither do I know how to thank God for this retreat which has touched my soul very deeply because I can already experience its fruit for me and for others.

I feel the holy fruit of my retreat deeply in my soul. I am as if permeated with the graces of God and grateful for His infinite goodness.

My God! "*Quid retribuam Domino?*" What return shall I give to the Lord?

I meditate on all the graces of my life, and I am crushed by their weight, being at the same time raised from the earth while being within God, in an entirely holy and divine atmosphere.

Lord! I beg You, by what You love most, by Your divine Father and Mary, that I may be penetrated with what You want of me, and that You may grant me the grace to correspond. Humiliated and repentant, I ask You to forgive me my past so that, raised up and relying on You, I will soar above the earth, living out this life in the heavenly regions and giving You glory.

Conchita's Reflections on a Retreat

November 7, 1935
TWENTY-FIFTH DAY

Meditation of Archbishop Martínez

The Gaze

If the Father had looked at you with His ineffable gaze just once, it would suffice for you to be eternally grateful. Yet this gaze is constant and everlasting. You may feel it or not. It may produce different effects, but it always shines in the heaven of your soul. It is not a ray of light which opens its way from time to time amidst the clouds of human vicissitudes, but rather it is perpetual and radiant midday light, which bathes your soul with divine splendors.

What a delight to live always under this infinite gaze! What a life of light, love, fruitfulness and peace!

Is it not an anticipated heaven? Heaven consists in receiving eternally the gaze of the Father and corresponding to it, merging the soul's gaze with this gaze, filled with light of glory, in order to contemplate the divine essence in the unspeakable wonder of the beatific vision.

This gaze, which gives us Jesus, is enough to make a soul happy. St. Paul wrote: *"Thanks be to God for His indescribable gift!"*[273] This gift is Jesus, and the gaze of the Father gives Him to us so that He may be our gift, our life and our happiness.

In order to exist and to shine somewhere, a beam of light needs an emitter which becomes a point from which it emanates, so that we do not receive light if the emitter does not send it to illuminate us. Hence Jesus does not appear or shine in any soul if the Father does not look at it, if He does not send out the refulgence of eternal light by His fruitful gaze.

To live under the gaze of the Father is to receive His gift constantly; it is to possess Jesus, the end and precious fruit of this gaze.

Thus your soul lives under the gaze of the Father, enveloped in His light, bathed in His fruitfulness, intimately and sweetly joined to Jesus. I will not get tired of repeating that the transformation into Jesus and the gaze of the Father are two aspects of the same incomparable grace. Thus there are two aspects of the same phenomenon: being bathed by the light of the sun and shining with the gold of its splendor.

To be gazed upon by the Father is to receive Jesus from His infinite intellect: Jesus, the splendor of the Father and the reflection of His substance. Since you are gazed upon constantly, you receive this infinite splendor constantly.

Would it not be enough to live in a rapture of gratitude for the grace of the mystical incarnation?

Certainly, you do not constantly experience the divine anointing, the heavenly delight of this gaze. Nor could you feel it constantly in this desert, because the happiness of experiencing it would impede the process of earthly life, and it would render impossible suffering, which is fruitful, holy and irreplaceable.

Yet, even though you do not feel this gaze, the mystery remains. Heaven has descended on earth and has settled itself in a hidden but real way in the blessed soul that truly possesses *"the substance of things hoped for."*[274]

Let us look closely at the divine mystery. On earth, when somebody looks at us, not only do we perceive our image in the eyes of the beholder, but we also experience the mysterious sensation that the light of that gaze brings us a kind of reflection of the soul that looks at us through its eyes, as though the splendor and fragrance of this soul reached us by the impalpable and subtle ray of its gaze.

More, much more than through the common gaze of our eyes, something divine comes through the divine gaze of the Father; or rather, God Himself communicates to us the treasure of His Divinity in His gaze since the divine, being very simple and perfect, gives itself totally when it seems to be reflected in us.

It is not a fragrance of God, a simple radiation of the divine; it is God Himself whom we receive in the ineffable gaze of the Father. To live under this gaze is to live enveloped in the light of

Conchita's Reflections on a Retreat

the Divinity; let us repeat it, it is an anticipated heaven.

But on earth, not all gazes are equal. There are gazes of indifference, admiration and love. There are gazes which move our whole being because the most wonderful mystery is accomplished in them, the fusion of two souls.

What is the Father's gaze into the transformed soul like?

It is a gaze of love, and not of just any love, but of the love of predilection. It is the gaze of infinite love which chooses the fortunate soul out of millions and which envelops it in an incomparable tenderness.

On earth, a gaze of love makes our soul tremble and reach its depth and brings it not simply a message from the other soul, but the soul itself, which becomes fused with it. The loving gaze of the Father is more, much more than this. It is not simply the revelation that the soul is loved, but the outpouring of divine love.

St. John used to describe himself as *"the disciple whom Jesus loved."*[275] The soul that receives this gaze is "the soul whom the Father loves."

It is not a simple gaze of love, but a gaze which transforms, divinizes, which fuses the soul with God in an unspeakable embrace.

I will repeat it: this gaze is not simply a harbinger of a love which comes to announce the triumphal entrance of the one who sends it; but it is the victorious love itself which arrives, which envelops the poor creature with its heavenly emanation, which possesses it, fills it, and submerges it in its unfathomable mystery.

Oh, how good, how delightful, how divine it is to live under the gaze of the Father! It is the everlasting Tabor, on which it is good to dwell and on which it is not necessary to make tents, since God dwells in the sanctuary of the soul and the soul dwells in the bosom of God.

On earth, there are gazes which give life. When Esther presented herself before King Ahasuerus in spite of the prescribed death penalty, the Scripture says that: *"when the king saw Queen Esther standing in the court, she found favor in his sight, and that gaze gave her life."*[276]

How many souls feel reborn to life when they receive a gaze, and something like the daily resurrection of nature is accomplished in them when the sun appears on the horizon!

But it is a figure of speech that these earthly gazes give life. The gaze which gives true life is the gaze of the Father because it gives Jesus, who is the Life.

The divine gaze which brings about the mystical incarnation in souls is especially fruitful and vital. It not only gives life, but also communicates to the soul the gift of giving life in a mystical, but real way. In this very secret way, the soul gives life to Jesus and to other souls, because the Father has gazed upon it with His inscrutable gaze.

The Song of Songs says that the bride is beautiful as the moon. A magnificent symbol! The moon, bathed by the light of the sun, spreads silver glow in space. Not only does the sun illuminate it, but also communicates to it the capacity of illuminating what is around it and that is why it is beautiful.

The soul that has received the gaze of the Father is as beautiful as the moon. The divine gaze not only bathes it with the light of life, but also grants to the soul the privilege of diffusing this fruitful light in other souls.

For this reason, the transformed soul does good wherever it passes; for this reason, it communicates Jesus; for this reason, it gives life, because being enveloped by the gaze of the Father and possessing Jesus, who is Life, it emanates the divine radiations.

To live under the gaze of the Father is to live a fruitful life in divine light and eternal love; it is to possess Jesus and to give Him to souls in the splendor of the divine gaze.

Personal Reflection of Conchita
TWENTY-FIFTH DAY

The Fruit

My Father,[277] for some days I have been experiencing the holy

Conchita's Reflections on a Retreat

fruit of this retreat deeply in my soul, in my inmost being. I perceive it not as a particular and self-centered experience, but as a kind of universal one with deep desires and a zest for spreading the good I carry in my soul, for embracing thousands of worlds, for quenching the thirst of millions of hearts, above all, of priestly ones.

And how? I don't know. But two loves have matured in my heart: love for God and impelling love for souls. I can clearly see that I lacked them, but they were out of my reach and I couldn't obtain them on my own.

Now with God's grace, I hope to be able to start a new life, more intensely interior, more firm and vigorous, and full of intense, holy zeal toward souls.

For the first time, I really feel like a MOTHER, ready to give to Jesus my full vitality, offering Him millions of souls. May I be allowed to do this for the glory of His beloved Father!

I feel like a real MOTHER and with all the motherly characteristics: *self-giving*, emptying myself on behalf of others, even though this means sacrifice, destruction and death itself.

Now, my Father, I really feel full of light for other souls, full of self-denial and generosity till martyrdom.

Now I am really enveloped, penetrated and *compenetrated by the gaze of the Father* which makes me tremble delightfully, delicately, and with an *absorbent* intensity and depth. The same gaze of so many years, now *understood* not as the result of the meditations you gave me, but rather, from my recent experience.

Inwardly and outwardly I feel His light, presence, splendor, fire, gentleness and a divine power which raises me from earth, prods me, impels me toward heaven, and fills me with an ardent thirst to glorify the beloved Father. I would give my life and thousands of lives so that other souls, millions and millions, at least those of the Works of the Cross, would ceaselessly glorify Him.

This is the state of my soul, my Father. Come close to it and have a look at it. Even though it is covered with the bark of my roughness, I feel it white; I feel it rich; I feel it to be in grace. I feel it *to be a real MOTHER!*

Can you see, my Father, how since that time long ago when I first heard: "The Father is gazing upon you," Jesus has shed light for me on my spiritual life, that life which I crossed *without understanding* it and *being grateful* for it?

I remember that I wrote in my *Account of Conscience* how often at that time I felt the image of Jesus being delineated in my soul, and step by step imprinting itself and taking form and *life*. And no doubt, it was Jesus. "What is it?" I used to ask myself. And now, in this retreat, I realize that the divine Father had already established Him in my soul, making me fall more and more in love with Him through those vivid and transforming images.

After this, I had an irresistible attraction toward everything that spoke of the "Divine Word" along with so many lights and insights into the mystery of the Holy Trinity. The divine promise was made and then fulfilled. All that followed is the effect of the grace. My God! I only can abase myself and weep out of gratitude.

My Jesus, why were You and are You so good to one who deserves nothing and has paid You back with so much ingratitude?

November 8, 1935
TWENTY-SIXTH DAY

Personal Reflection of Conchita

The happy day of the foundation of the Crusade of Victim Souls on behalf of Families.

Today the day was *full*, because the Work which Jesus asked of me on October 31, and then on November 1, 2, 4, was inaugurated.

My God, is it possible so quickly?

It was accepted and approved by the Church.

It was inaugurated in the Little Cave before the Blessed Sacrament and with exposition and benediction.

The first three people[278] to make their consecration as victim souls for the sake of the success of the Work did so without any personal interest – only for the glory of God.

The endeavor to counterbalance many and great sins has begun.

Soon other souls will join them to swell the Crusade of these chosen souls.

Early in the morning, I prayed the *Te Deum* "on roses," and two more later on. Could it be otherwise, seeing my Jesus *served*, fulfilling His wishes and giving glory to the heavenly Father?

My spiritual director says that he also felt his soul bathed with special joy upon inaugurating this Work for the glory of God.

This occupied my whole day, so I could not write.

Today I am continuing my retreat.

Lord, when You want something, You provide all the means to accomplish it. This Work weighed upon You; You have promised to bless it. Put it in Your Heart full of love. Offer it as pleasing and fragrant incense to Your beloved Father. May sins be taken away, the world be converted and all families be Yours, giving You consolation and much glory to the heavenly Father with the Holy Spirit and Mary.

Today is my 51st wedding anniversary. Does it have any connection with what we celebrated today? Nobody remembered it, but Jesus' delicacy is unlimited.

Thank you, my Jesus! Thank you, Archbishop Martínez, for responding so readily to the divine will.

November 9, 1935
TWENTY-SEVENTH DAY

Meditation of Archbishop Martínez

The Gaze

On earth, a gaze does not achieve its full perfection and charm unless it is reciprocated by the gaze of the other in full accord and then both merge into perfect harmony.

It is a delight for the one who loves to gaze on the beloved and it is a pleasure to know by secret intuition of the soul that one is being gazed upon. How often those who are in love glance at each other, engaging in those clever games common to love. But when the gazes meet and merge, mutual love attains its delight and fullness, because when the gazes meet, the souls merge.

This law of human love is also common to divine love, according to Fr. Lacordaire: "Love in heaven and on earth has the same name, essence and law."[279]

Oftentimes, God delights in looking at our souls, even though they do not respond to His divine gaze. This is similar to a mother who delights in looking with tenderness at her son who sleeps or is distracted and unaware that the tender gaze of the mother envelops him. This is very frequent, because God always gazes upon us and, being absent-minded and weak, we manage to look at Him only from time to time.

Sometimes, it seems that the gazes which our spirit directs toward God do not meet His divine gaze, not because His infinite eyes ever turn away from us, but because God veils the light of His gaze in order to take satisfaction in our looking for Him in the shadows, just as a mother who plays with her child, hiding herself from his eager gazes. Or again, the Lord refuses us the fire of His eyes in order to refine and purify our love and longing for Him, and in the martyrdom of not seeing Him.

But sometimes, both gazes, the one that comes from heaven and the other that ascends from earth, the one of the infinite love and the one of earthly love, meet, link, become fused, and in these gazes God possesses a soul, and it is submerged in the bosom of God.

So the mystery of love is consummated, and in the fusion of the gazes God finds His glory, and the soul finds the fullness of its delight and its complete joy.

Undoubtedly, the soul's gaze is the fruit of the heavenly gaze. We would never manage to raise our eyes to God unless He first looked at us and with the light of His eyes enflamed in our eyes the fire of our intimate gaze.

St. John of the Cross explains it in this way in his *Canticle*:

> *"When you looked at me*
> *your eyes imprinted your grace in me;*
> *for this you loved me ardently;*
> *and thus my eyes deserved*
> *to adore what they beheld in you."*[280]

God's gaze gives the soul the ability to gaze on Him, the secret of that intimate gaze which is immersed in the divine. The soul sees the eternal light in the light of the divine gaze.

The gaze by which the Father bestows this gift to the soul that received the mystical incarnation reveals to this soul the mysteries of the Divinity and communicates to it the capacity to contemplate them.

Do you remember that last year the Lord invited you, especially during your retreat, to enter into His intimate treasure?

It is a consequence of the Father's gaze. This invitation means: "Look at Me, because I have looked at you with the gaze of predilection and fruitfulness. Enter the abyss of My light, because My light penetrated the abyss of your misery."

Do you know why the Father's gaze begets an intimate gaze in the soul? Because the Father's gaze is pure and Scripture says: *"Blessed are the pure in heart: they shall see God."*[281] His is a loving gaze, and love produces insights of which the intellect is unaware. It opens *"the enlightened eyes of our hearts"* in our inmost being, according to the expression of St. Paul.[282]

Since the Father's gaze bestows the Word, and the Word is light and wisdom, so the following words of the Psalms are applied to Him: *"In Your light we see light."*[283]

When our eyes receive the light of a gaze, they also see the eyes which emit it and through them, they see the other soul. Something like this happens when the Father's gaze brings about this other gaze in the soul. The soul is elevated to contemplation of the divine and enters into the mystery of God.

Yet, there is something special in this fusion of the Father's gaze with the soul's gaze; they form only one gaze as they contemplate Jesus, looking upon Him in a singular way, as only the Father and souls that have received His fruitful reflection look on Him.

Let us imagine, or rather, reflect on what happened in Bethlehem when the Virgin Mother looked at Jesus for the first time.

Many looked at Jesus: those of His time with their mortal eyes. There were those who in the course of centuries loved Him with their intimate eyes, but the gaze of Mary is unique. She looked at Him as at someone who was her own; certainly, as at the God from whom she received everything, but also as at the God who received human life from her. She looked at Him as a part of her heart, as her reflection; she looked at Him in the same way that the Father gazes upon Him.

Both gazes ineffably merged and converged on their mutual Son and upon joining their gazes, their hearts merged in the affinity of love, in the unity of ineffable and unique affection.

All hearts that love Jesus enter into communion of love with the Father. Yet, for no other as for the motherly heart, this communion is so full and perfect, because the love of her heart is not only in harmony with the Father's love, which comes from the unity of purpose, but it also has a wonderful similitude of nuance, because the divine Heart and the human one love the Son with analogous tenderness: the divine Heart with infinite fatherly strength and the human heart with fire and motherly gentleness.

Who could describe the intimate relations which exist between the Father and the soul who has received the mystical incarnation?

Who could conceive of, or much less express, the mysterious affinity of love which fuses both hearts in divine unity?

The Father and this soul have the same Son, even though by titles that differ infinitely, but at the same time, they are closely united. They have the same object with which they are deeply pleased, the same longings, the same divine passion. They both can say: "*This is My beloved Son, with whom I am well pleased.*"

In fact, the passion of their gazes and the affinity of their intimate affections establish between the Father and this soul unique relations, which on the soul's part, are permeated with refined spiritual modesty and with holy and heavenly rapture.

Why do we continue trying to express what is unspeakable? You have experienced this divine sentiment of the mysterious affinity with the Father. You will never be able to express it, but you savored it in your inmost soul. Savor it, expand it and bring it to holy fullness; the more it grows, the more your heart expands, the more perfectly the mystical incarnation with all its happy consequences, will be consummated.

Personal Reflection of Conchita
TWENTY-SEVENTH DAY

You are...

"Listen!" the Lord told me, "even though, in view of My goals and due to the mystical incarnation, etc., you must be the source from which the Works receive life, even though you head them in a hidden way, as their spiritual mother, you belong especially to priests in all your acts and in union with the divine Incarnate Word.

"You belong to the Church and, even though the Works of the Cross have this fundamental end, they have different exterior missions. But inwardly and outwardly, you belong to and give life to all of them, the life you receive from the Father and the Holy Spirit in Me. Your special mission is to sacrifice yourself and to be a victim with Me, the Victim, on behalf of priests, at every moment on the altars and always in your exterior and interior life of suffering. Belonging to all the Works of the Cross, you especially offer yourself on behalf of priests."

"Lord, I would prefer to be more a part of the Oasis, like the Sisters."[284]

"But you are."

"But how, since I'm outside?"

"For Me, you are not outside, but in the very heart of the Congregation and in the other Works of the Cross. Who is the spiritual center of them?"

"You, my Jesus."

"From whom were they born by My will?"

"From You."

"Who gave them life, if not the Father's gaze on you, the Holy Spirit in you, the Divine Word mystically incarnate in you? You cannot escape from this spiritual foundation and, on the contrary, you should be *divinely grateful* for it and exploit it to the full, but more on behalf of My priests, because you were born for this. This is the mission of the Works of the Cross, whose center is the Church and whose goal is the priesthood, enriched by the sacrifices which come from these Works which obtain graces from heaven."

November 10, 1935
Twenty-Eighth Day

Meditation of Archbishop Martínez

The Gaze

The fruitful gaze of the Father introduces the blessed soul that receives it "into the joy of the Lord," into the bosom of the Holy Trinity. As was said, this gaze produces in the soul another intimate gaze which is like a reflection of the divine gaze, and makes the soul contemplate heavenly realities.

Through this intimate gaze, the soul sees Jesus as the Father sees Him – of course, taking into account the immense disproportion which exists between God and the creature – and sees the Father as Jesus sees Him.

The soul sees in Jesus the splendor of the Father, the wisdom of God, the incomparable beauty of heaven, the Teacher of men,

Conchita's Reflections on a Retreat

the King of hearts, who is all for us.

The soul sees Him as its own, as the beloved Son of its tenderness, the object of its care, the Lord of its self-denial and the sole reason for its life.

Each one of these titles deserves special meditation, but as we are unable to study them singly, we can divide them into three parts with common features:
1. Jesus contains all the treasures of God;
2. Jesus is wonderfully adapted to our smallness;
3. Jesus Himself deigns to become the Son of the soul that has received the mystical incarnation, encompassing all the delights and all the forms of martyrdom that this title implies.
4. Our soul is made for God. Its infinite longing finds perfect fullness only in God. It is an immense capacity of God, an unquenchable thirst for God.

Goodness, beauty and light attract us insofar as they are the reflection of God. And if the pale, divine reflections transport and enrapture us, what will the focus which emits them be like, the supreme source from which they flow?

Through the sacred humanity of Jesus, we enter into the divine treasures, and possessing them, our soul experiences the fullness of its total longing and the achievement of its happiness.

And what impresses one most is that the divine satisfies but never tires one, according to Scripture: *"For association with her involves no bitterness and living with her no grief."*[285]

The soul that enjoys the divine experiences full happiness, with the beauty of desire, the freshness of newness, with the exquisite aroma of old wine, which, like love, has deeply penetrated our being. What is divine is ever old and ever new, according to the unsurpassed phrase of St. Augustine.

In this world desire and possession have their own advantages and disadvantages. Desire, like an ardent dream, idealizes and embellishes its object, but it also feels emptiness and expectation which sadden and torture it. Possession brings joy and fullness, but it begets annoyance and fades quickly. Only the divine joins the ardor of desire with the joy of possession in ineffable delight, the fragrance of spring with the richness of autumn.

The soul that contemplates Jesus in the very depth of His divinity, that loves Him in His limitless beauty, that possesses Him in His ineffable, divine richness, enjoys a complete happiness without slaking its thirst, without exhausting its longing; and every day it finds its Beloved anew, with enrapturing newness. Every day it experiences the exquisite sensation of a fragrance from heaven which becomes finer and more concentrated with time, of a love which, as a result of long intimacy, becomes deeper and more delightful. The inaccessible light of God becomes accessible to our smallness because the limpid humanity of Jesus tempers it to our capacity.

We cannot taste the new wine of the Divinity unless it is served in the chiseled chalice of that sacred humanity that can be brought close to our lips because it is flesh of our flesh, bone of our bones; insofar as it is possible on earth, unveiling the Divinity to us instead of veiling it.

Jesus adapts this light to our fragility, so that it may enlighten us without dazzling, fill us without overwhelming us, be totally ours without ceasing to be what it is, and without breaking the fragile vessel of our life with its immensity.

Oh, let us thank God for His unspeakable gift!

Yet, to penetrate the deep mystery of Jesus, so that we may *"comprehend with all the holy ones what is the breadth and length and height and depth"*[286] of this incomparable mystery, it is necessary that the Father of Our Lord Jesus Christ, *"from whom every fatherhood, in heaven or on earth, takes its name"*[287] look upon us with the brightness of His infinite eyes, and bathe us with the ineffable clarity of His divine gaze.

That gaze reveals Jesus to us, and introduces us into His unfathomable mystery, revealing *"the love of Christ that surpasses knowledge."*[288]

But to the soul that has received the mystical incarnation, the divine panorama that surrounds Jesus is illumined by this singular and sweet light.

The Son is the God who is so wonderfully adapted to our soul because He desired to take on our human nature. Without ceasing to see in Him the infinite Majesty – rather seeing it with greater splendor than other souls do – the soul looks at Him in a more intimate, familiar way, just as the Virgin Mary must have seen Him, as an extension of herself, as a part of her heart.

Who could ever express this most beautiful contrast, this mysterious perception of that divine, motherly love, which joins the adoration of infinite Majesty with tenderness for the Son of her heart in such amazing unity?

This gaze has something from heaven and from earth; it is a fusion of strength and weakness; it is the love of the Father reflected in the delicate substance of the motherly heart.

You have felt it. You have enjoyed it. You have suffered it, because earthly love is suffering; and the more specific and cruel this suffering is, the more intense, deep and divine the love is.

This vision of Jesus, this unique love, this unspeakable impression, would be impossible for the soul if it had not received the gaze of the Father, or in other words, if the soul did not see through the eyes of the Father, if its gaze were not the mysterious extension of the divine gaze.

Let the Father gaze upon you, and let the intimate, motherly gaze, which merges in its light the majestic beauty of God and the delightful charm of the Son, spring from the depths of your spirit.

Personal Reflection of Conchita
TWENTY-EIGHTH DAY

Oh my Jesus, my Jesus, how much I owe to Your beloved Father! Enlarge my heart to love Him a million times more and unite my heart with millions of priestly hearts to love Him more.

May both Congregations and all the Works of the Cross love Him deliriously to the end of the ages on earth and eternally in heaven, giving thanks with me for that gaze which bathed me that day and which continues gazing upon me because the Father sees His Word incarnate in my poor soul.

Oh, my spiritual Father,[289] how can I repay God for His infinite goodness for me?

The Crusade

Jesus told me today:
"Tell your spiritual director how very grateful My Heart is for the establishment and the launching of the Crusade; tell Him that His soul will experience a special grace from My bounty.

"This Work will grow with My blessing. It is to honor My Father! How could I not bless it? It will expand to give Him glory."

"Lord, did You not tell me that few souls will enter this Work?"

"There will be few in each part, but there are many parts where there are also pure and self-denying souls that love Me, and the Crusade will be established, yielding fruit for heaven. May your spiritual director, other bishops and prudent priests, who understand the depth of My will, help you in this. Also some Missionaries of the Holy Spirit can establish it."

"Are you glad, my Jesus?"

"I brought you here primarily for this. Tell Archbishop Ruiz that I wanted this place to be the cradle of this great and much needed Work of atonement and of selfless and pure glorification of the Father.

"Yet, I brought you here not only for this, but also to give your spirit rest, solace from certain sorrows and an incentive for your soul, filling it with peace.

"I wanted to remind you of the gaze of the Father, revealing to you the source of the mystical incarnation, and directing your life to the glory of this beloved Father.

Conchita's Reflections on a Retreat

"In this retreat, I wanted to refine your motherly tenderness for Me and for souls and, with the help of My love and strength, to prepare you for future martyrdom, if this should be My will."

"Thank you, thank you, my adorable Jesus, my *incomparable* Jesus, so generous with me in Morelia. Close to You and in union with Mary, under the delightful gaze of Your Father, I am not afraid, because He is all tenderness, goodness and infinite charity."

Later on, thinking of the countless sins which offend God, I told Jesus that I was sorry for the persecution of the Church.

"Lord, why do You always create difficulties? Why don't You exercise Your infinite power so that all people may know You, surrender to You and love You?"

"Because I gave freedom to man and because one sacrifice, one spontaneous act of praise pleases God much more. Man makes a thousand uses of his free will, using his liberty against himself, *because he wants to*. He has My gentle and sweet laws, but he does not want to follow them, and in a certain sense I let him, but don't think that I abandon him. I try to gain entry into his soul in many ways; I struggle, I beg, but sometimes with no result, and then My loving Heart is torn.

"So, what do I do? I look for victim souls who, in union with Me, atone for this world of sins before My beloved Father. I look for souls not because I cannot atone for and save a thousand worlds, but so that they may deserve more heaven by cooperating with Me.

"It is a mark of My predilection to associate souls with My redemptive sacrifice. In order to make the offering of those souls perfect I must transform them into Myself, so that they might be one with Me for the glory of My Father, thus completing My perfect Mystical Body.[290]

"My Father sees everything in Me, forgives everything through Me, loves everything in His Incarnate Word. The more souls are transformed into Me, the more they glorify Him and gain more graces on behalf of other souls, and they are unified more in the Trinity."

November 11, 1935
TWENTY-NINTH DAY

Personal Reflection of Conchita

My spiritual director was out today and there was no meditation.

Jesus remained silent, and I spent my day looking at Him... remembering His benefits... and reflecting on the previous meditations.

One of the Missionaries of the Holy Spirit was taken prisoner because the authorities found him administering the Sacraments. How fortunate! I was glad that someone from the Congregation would suffer for God's sake in this way.[291]

November 12, 1935
THIRTIETH DAY

Meditation of Archbishop Martínez

The Gaze – Confidence

By virtue of this intimate gaze of the soul, produced by the gaze of the Father, the soul not only sees Jesus the way the Father looks upon Him, but also sees the Father the way Jesus looks upon Him.

How does Jesus gaze upon the Father? To begin to understand how Jesus looks upon Him, one has to think of how He loves Him. That is:

With immense confidence;
With deep tenderness;
With divine passion.

This shows us that He looks upon infinite Majesty, supreme Love, and the greatest Goodness; in a word, He sees Him *as Father*, considering that in this heavenly word merge Majesty, Love and Goodness.

Conchita's Reflections on a Retreat

At first sight, we would think that the greater the majesty, the less would be the confidence, because majesty demands respect and adoration, and our prejudice is that these things impede or diminish confidence.

But this is not so. The greater a person is, the greater confidence he inspires, provided we are not dealing with superficial and pompous human grandeur, but with the genuine and profound grandeur of God and its every reflection.

If we think deeply, we discover that a limitation always impedes confidence, be it in understanding, or in loving, or in forgiving.

We cannot be confident if we do not feel ourselves to be understood – and the lack of understanding is born out of ignorance.

A broad-minded and elevated spirit understands all souls with their deep miseries and intimate longings, but nobody understands them like God, who is infinite wisdom. Therefore Scripture says: *"Quoniam tu laborem et dolorem consideras,"* "You observe this misery and sorrow."[292]

His penetrating gaze can see the most secret sorrow which lips do not express, and heroic effort hides to human cleverness. How can we have confidence in someone who does not understand us? Can we not trust when we feel understood?

We feel uncomfortable with human beings limited in love, since we can't be sure of their love. There are simply two ways in which imperfect and wretched creatures can be loved: either a veil – even if the noblest – hides our deficiency or a fullness of love fills these creatures with its richness.

Human love corresponds to the first way. Earthly love always has a bandage over its eyes, as the ingenious Greeks personified love in painting it; the bandage represents ignorance, generosity or passion, but there is always a bandage.

The second way refers to God, who is the only one who can love us with open eyes, because His love is fullness and looks for void, because His love does not depend on what we are, but on what He is.

UNDER THE GAZE OF THE FATHER

When we approach a creature, our confidence hesitates, because we do not know if his eyes have a thick enough bandage so that his heart may love us.

If we only knew God, we would always approach Him with immense confidence, because His light always beautifies whatever our ugliness may be and His fullness always fills our emptiness and His Heart always loves us, whatever our goodness and misery may be.

What primarily hinders our confidence is the awareness of our offenses and ingratitude. With this weight on our soul, we dare not approach with trust him whom we have hurt with our malice, unless we are sure of his generosity – and even then we hesitate. Is the generosity of the creature perhaps unlimited?

God is the only one in whose arms we cast ourselves with absolute confidence, even if we are stained with all the crimes of the world, because we know that His forgiveness is infinite; because we know what we can expect from His love and mercy, according to St. Thérèse of Lisieux.

We have examined only the negative part of confidence. Its source is light, love and generosity. When this light is infinite and this love is divine and this mercy is eternal, a secure, very delightful and unlimited confidence arises in the soul.

With divine light, Jesus' soul knew the Father, who is rich in goodness, great in mercy, fount of all consolation and bottomless ocean of love. For this reason, Jesus felt divinely filial confidence for Him and cast Himself into the Father's bosom with even more trust than a child into his mother's lap.

The soul that has received the gift of penetrating divine things with the gaze of the Father sees in the Father the reflection of what Jesus sees: His majesty formed of bountiful light, by inexhaustible love, by infinite mercy. Since the soul feels understood, forgiven and loved in this heavenly perspective, it casts itself into the bosom of the Father with indestructible and victorious confidence.

Isn't it true that you have felt this ineffable confidence in the depths of your soul? Perhaps in moments of darkness and anxiety the heaven of your confidence gets temporarily clouded, but when the gaze of the Father becomes more manifest, the intimate gaze of your soul is perfected; in your sight the divine majesty appears as attractive as it is great and an intimate, irresistible impulse prods you to cast, to immerse, to lose yourself in these depths which are the fount of immense confidence – this is the wonder of infinite majesty.

Undoubtedly, not all souls discover the secret of this confidence because they have not received the secret of light, the gift of that gaze which reveals the treasure of God since it has its deep source in the eyes of the Father.

Do not turn your spirit away from these shining eyes; do not cover this intimate gaze in your soul; look through the eyes of your Son, immerse your interior pupils in the bosom of God and you will trust beyond measure, and you will dwell in confidence, and you will sleep in peace, wrapped in the immense pleats of the royal coat of divine confidence.

One could object against the doctrine just presented, that on earth there are souls that inspire unlimited confidence in spite of the inevitable limitations of the creature and without having the traits of human grandeur. These souls have something divine. There is a reflection of God's grandeur in them which is the source of the confidence mentioned before. Jesus dwells in them and He exercises an intimate attraction over souls through them and makes them confident.

This divine element which inspires confidence is found in priests according to God's Heart and in holy souls, especially in those who have a mission for others. It is the divine light which makes them understand souls intimately, which makes them transparent to those who received the gift.

It is the reflection of God's Heart that offers them the secret of loving imperfect creatures with eyes wide open. It is the reflection of infinite mercy which gives them the key to generous forgiveness, and broad and discreet sensitivity.

Blessed are the souls that find the fullness of confidence in a human heart in which Jesus dwells! Blessed are those who have received the royal gift of inspiring holy confidence!

This gift is intimately linked with what we have called the "third love" for souls. Both prerogatives are the sign that there is something divine in those who possess them: that it is Jesus who inspires in a soul a love similar to His for other souls and in souls a confidence similar to what He inspires.

Personal Reflection of Conchita
THIRTIETH DAY

Today has been a very painful day for my soul, with many temptations against the retreat, like a hailstorm from heaven, and with intimate, unexplainable and sad suffering.

Blessed be God and I offer all for His glory!

This afternoon, three other charming souls joined the Crusade. Gathered in the living room, Archbishop Martínez was really inspired and gave an explanation again about this Work. The ladies were very enthusiastic and happy. We all went to the "Little Cave," where they made their consecration with the door of the Tabernacle open and the Archbishop concluded by giving us benediction.

With all my heart I offered those souls to Jesus, asking for His blessings for this Work of the Cross, so that it might spread for the glory of God.

Now I think that perhaps the sorrows of this day were for the triumph of the glory of God.

I feel happy amidst my tears if Jesus smiles, if He is content because His adorable will is accomplished.

Conchita's Reflections on a Retreat

November 13, 1935
THIRTY-FIRST DAY

Personal Reflection of Conchita

Today I have not had a written meditation, because my spiritual director was busy.

Sins

Yesterday, at daybreak, Jesus wanted to talk, even though I did not ask Him anything and today He continued.

He told me, "I want you to bear, in union with Me, the sins of the souls for whom the Crusade atones."

"But, my Jesus, is it not the same to atone for sins, or to bear them?"

"No, it is more to bear this enormous weight and at the same time atone for it. That was My mission on earth: to bear the enormous cross of the sins of others and at the same time, to offer Myself as a pure and unstained Victim in order to obtain forgiveness. Bear them with Me."

"Lord, besides the sins of priests which I bear, as You have asked, do You want me to bear these others also?"

"Yes, because if you are Jesus, *in a certain sense*, due to your more or less perfect transformation into Me, you should bear what I bear, and atone for what I atone."

"So, my Jesus, do I have this additional part in the Crusade?"

"Yes, in a hidden way and in union with Me."

"But, my Jesus, do You still bear all sins?"

"I will never stop being the Redeemer for ever, and in the world, as long as there is a single soul to be saved. What are Masses for? Are the same mysteries of Calvary not at work there? Is it not the same sacrifice; am I not the same Victim that is immolated to obtain graces?"

"But, listen, my Jesus – adulteries, divorces, hidden sins which I do not even know – should I make these sins mine?"

"In a certain sense, yes, you should make them yours – not the acts, but the malice of them – and with the same atoning martyrdom, you glorify the Father."

"But, divine Jesus, won't these hidden sins I am unaware of stick to me? Even adulteries, divorces, etc.?"

"Do they stick to Me? I deplore them, I cry over them, so to speak, I atone for them, and I glorify My Father by renewing My Passion and thus obtaining His forgiveness and compassion for souls."

"Well, all right, my Jesus, let it be, even though this steamroller may crush my heart. If You want it, I want it."

"Look, my Jesus, at what happens to me. I just want to please You; I want You to see my soul as beautiful, white. How will Your Father gaze upon me if I have this very black burden on my soul, with all these sins for which the Crusade atones, and which make me feel ashamed and horrified?"

"My Father will see Me in you, and you must understand that it is not the same to carry coal and to be coal."

"I agree, heaven of my soul. But tell me, why do these things come to Your mind, my candor and eternal light?"

"Due to the mystical incarnation, which is working in you and transforming you, you are no longer alone, but with Me – with Me in you, and you in Me – as I have told you. You have not yet understood its extent."

Later

I asked the Lord: "How is the disinterestedness which characterizes the Crusade combined with indulgences which one day will be bestowed on the souls that form it?"

"In this case, indulgences can be offered on behalf of the souls in purgatory, stained by faults which the Crusade expiates and the great benefits of this heavenly Crusade – born out of the infinite mercy of My Heart, which does not desire the death of souls, but their eternal salvation for the glory of the Father – will reach them there.

"One of the means is the communion of saints, since they are the merits of victim souls that merit in union with Me (because of My infinite merits) and in this way glorify the Trinity, in union with Me."

"Lord, are You pleased with the souls that joined the Crusade yesterday?"

"Yes, I am and I will reward souls of the Crusade with special graces."

"My Jesus, please remember the special grace which that soul was to experience."[293]

"Do I not keep My promises? Why should you ask Me about it?"

November 14, 1935
Thirty-Second Day

Meditation of Archbishop Martínez

Tenderness

Since Jesus' soul knows the Father's majesty profoundly, it feels immense confidence in Him. Since this majesty is all love, it inspires a delightful tenderness.

You have already meditated on the Father's tenderness and examined the characteristics of this ineffable love, which you should imitate as much as possible, since you have received a reflection of His fruitfulness in the mystical incarnation. Still it is appropriate to reflect on it again, to find in it the divine basis of the tenderness of Jesus for the Father.

Divine love has delightful nuances:
It is fullness which seeks the void;
It is grandeur which descends to littleness;

It is majesty which lowers itself to wretchedness;
It is omnipotence which protects weakness.

One can perceive how deep, delicate and tender this love is. One can sense the delight, as we say in our language, the delight of God who loves His creatures.

From a distance, from a far distance, our heart sometimes feels the delight of loving in this way. Even though we are small and miserable, we meet weaker and smaller creatures than we are, and before them we experience an exquisite feeling which is a pale reflection of God's love.

We also feel the delight of approaching the miserable, of protecting the weak, of adapting to the little ones, and when this noble sentiment is transformed into love, it takes on the gentle and profound tones of *tenderness*.

A mother's heart feels this tenderness for her child when she bends to his smallness, and speaks his language, and shares in his likes and herself takes on a childlike heart to beat in unison with his. Generous hearts experience this when they leave everything to share in the woes of others. They renounce all their own joys to share the joy of weeping with those who weep, suffering with those who suffer, becoming perpetually childlike to love children and to live their innocent lives.

Such is God's love for His creatures. Let us say it once more, such is the Father's love by appropriation; let us say it once again, such is His love, which descends, protects, hides His innate majesty with loving self-annihilation so as to be childlike, in order to be in unison with the hearts of His children.

Are we not the Father's children? Laden with years, filled with wisdom, virtue or power, we are still children in the eyes of God due to our native weakness, our creaturely smallness and our ignorance before infinite wisdom.

Yet the Father stoops to us and makes Himself divinely childlike in order to adapt Himself to us, just as a mother makes herself delightfully girlish in order to be in harmony with her children.

In spite of our age and maturity, we are always children for our mothers; and serious, deep and self-sacrificing motherly love seems somewhat childish and leaves a pleasant and perennial savor of childhood in our soul.

For this reason, motherly love is very tender because it is majesty that is inclined; greatness that protects, because its noble richness always hides a kind of mysterious weakness, a kind of candor and childlike gentleness.

If we raise motherly love to the infinite, we will have an idea of the divine tenderness of the Father's love, because it is infinite fullness which is lovingly annihilated in order to adapt to our indestructible weakness, to our everlasting childhood.

Tenderness generates tenderness and when in mutual love there is weakness on the one hand and greatness on the other, love is tinged with the gentle tonality of tenderness.

For this reason, Jesus' love for the Father is a wonder of tenderness. Jesus gazes upon the Father as He is, the ocean of infinite love and His delicate and great Heart is permeated with heavenly and exquisite tenderness.

In order to perceive this tenderness, it is enough to read Jesus' prayer to His Father on the eve of His Passion with the enlightened eyes of the heart.

In the account of St. John, one can admire Jesus' touching accent, which twenty centuries could not extinguish. Beneath the profundity of the words throbs the emotion which upset the divine serenity of Jesus that night. In this incomparable prayer, tenderness differs slightly from our sensible, superficial, exuberant tenderness, because the divine tenderness is deep as the abyss without losing the delicate charm, typical of tenderness, making it rather intense and divine.

It differs slightly from our tenderness, because Jesus' divine tenderness is also human, as the Apostles could notice in the heavenly light, in the ineffable expression of Jesus' eyes raised toward heaven. And we can confirm it by penetrating into the mystery of the Gospel, observing the way in which Jesus pronounces His Father's name, and the epithets He attaches – holy Father, righteous

UNDER THE GAZE OF THE FATHER

Father – words so unusual in the clearly sober language of Jesus.

Oh, yes! Jesus loved His Father with a tenderness which we will only be able to appreciate in heaven, sounding the depths of its gentleness, delicacy and royal richness. In the splendid light of glory, one of the deepest feelings, one of the most beautiful visions, one of the most marvelous delights must be to immerse the radiant eye of our soul into the intimate relations of Jesus with the Father, when we approach the divine mystery.

While we are on the way to our homeland, it is an incomparable delight to perceive this mystery amidst the shadows of our faith, and even more, to enter the divine joy as deeply as it is possible in this exile. Through the divine gift and fruitful gaze of the Father, we may share in this mutual love, in this ocean of tenderness which breaks with the ebb and flow of its great waves on the Heart of the Father and of Jesus, in the divine unity of the Holy Spirit.

Especially you should look upon the Father as Jesus looks upon Him and feel in your heart the fascination of this incomparable tenderness.

Did the Lord not give you a mother's heart? Did He not expand it, attune it and perfect it through the mystical incarnation? Do you not feel the tenderness of heaven invade you when you call Jesus with the delightful name of "Son" in a rapture of love and when, in heavenly moments, you have heard from His mouth the mysterious name, the divinely wonderful name of mother, which in its short syllables encloses a poem, an idyll and a canticle of tenderness?

Look at the Father through the eyes of Jesus the way His eyes gazed upon Him that night in the Upper Room and through this heavenly light, raise the tenderness of your heart like a gentle fragrance to the Father. Receive from Him the heavenly dew, the divine bath of the holy, eternal, infinite tenderness of the Father.

Conchita's Reflections on a Retreat

Personal Reflection of Conchita
THIRTY-SECOND DAY

Today Jesus wanted to talk. He is so good! Now He is so close to me, so kind!

I asked, "Lord, do You want me to love You thus, with great refinement? You understand me, and I want to be very correct."

"I prefer you to talk with Me with the simplicity and confidence of a child."

"Listen, my Jesus, when will the *day of the graces* be which You grant to me every year?"

"Tomorrow, I will give you what you will ask Me."

"You know what I would like best: to love You more each moment, doing and suffering everything for the glory of the Father. But I want so many things for the Works, the Church, my children and souls!"

"My Heart is an ark from which you can draw what you wish. It is a treasure with which you can enrich millions of souls without using it up."

"But will You give me some words for those for whom I ask? They are so useful for them."

"I will do what you wish, letting you enter the dwelling place of My secrets."

"So I want to cleanse myself in order to enter that dwelling without staining it, my Jesus."

"This is a dwelling place of light where the Holy Spirit, who is Light, radiates."

"Lord, are You pleased with me?"

"And you, are you pleased with Me?"

"I am, even though You have laid the 'garbage' of the sins which the Crusade atones for on me."

"Then I am also pleased, because you are open to My will, and all for the glory of the Father."

"Lord, reward my spiritual director for the very many beautiful meditations which he wrote for me about You, Your Father and the Holy Spirit."

"I am not short on giving, and return a hundredfold what is done for Me – and shall I tell you? – what is done for you."

"Oh my Jesus, but why do You love me, if I am so horrible?"

"I do it for mother."

"I would rather not ask You; but my director does not want me to have overdone humility. Will You take it away?"

"A part of it, but not all."

"Then he will not write a sonnet for me on the death of overdone humility, which I would like. Don't you see that this bad humility hampers me?"

"A part of it – but you should work on it and be obedient to him; tell him that in part it pleases Me and he knows very well to what extent."

"Lord, I am so happy in this beloved Little Cave where the Crusade was born, that I would not like my retreat to end, but it is almost one month, and it seemed to me like a day. What will heaven be like?"

"I don't want you to go either, but whenever your spiritual director decides, I will go with you."

"Jesus of my soul! Does this mean I will never return?"

"Whatever I want."

"I suffer from having to drag myself out of here, even though I'm sorry that it was such a long time, but You know that You are so often silent elsewhere. And why, if You are my Life, if Your words are the happiness of my soul? If You are the center where my heart dwells, where it finds warmth, from where it receives the divine life, why would I want things which are not You? And if I leave You, and if You veil Yourself, and if You stay silent, and if You hide Yourself, it is hard to find You. What shall I do, my Morning Star, who enlightens my path on the way to Calvary?"

"At all times be convinced that you do My will, giving glory to My Father in every situation of your life."

Jesus did not say anything else. I made my confession in order to be cleansed and exposed all my remorse to my spiritual director and remained in peace so as to enter tomorrow "*into the dwelling of Jesus' secrets,*" as He told me today.

November 15, 1935
Thirty-Third Day

Meditation of Archbishop Martínez

Passion

As has been said, Jesus saw the infinite goodness of His Father and felt a great passion for Him. Indeed, this was the passion of His life. The usage of the word passion might seem incorrect, because normally it denotes a love which is too sensitive. Yet by using this word intentionally in reference to Jesus, I'm trying to underscore that His love for the Father is as ardent and overwhelming as a passion.

To the extent to which a human being is good, beautiful and attractive, he or she inspires love and exercises influence over hearts.

No creature on his own can captivate the human heart, because no one wholly fulfills the desires of our souls, which are infinite in a certain sense. In order to captivate, the heart must supply with its own free will what the beloved lacks in goodness and beauty.

Consequently, as has been said, we must be blindfolded in order to love a creature. In order to give our heart to someone, we must first consciously captivate it, because no created being has enough power to become the lord of a human heart.

Yet, the infinite goodness of God totally captivates and His extraordinary beauty takes possession of our souls. We cannot stop loving Him and in heaven we will love Him with beatific love. If the shadows of the desert did not veil His divine perfection, we could not love Him even on earth.

UNDER THE GAZE OF THE FATHER

When God reveals Himself to a soul, He becomes its Lord. He enraptures its heart, irresistibly attracts its faculties and exercises His victorious and gentle power over its being.

The divine goodness imposes its unique and total love. When the soul discovers this goodness, it must pay the supreme homage, loving *"with all its heart, with all its soul, and with all its mind."*[294]

What fire there is in such love! Every creature, when it finds its true center, the goal of its deepest aspirations, the source of its longed-for happiness, casts itself upon the beloved object with unspeakable ardor, with all its strength and its love becomes aflame with overwhelming passion.

Its entire being is moved by an irresistible strength. No obstacle can prevent its union with the Beloved; no abyss can impede this delightful union. It gives up everything, it undertakes anything and it suffers all in order to cast itself with irrepressible strength upon the supreme goal of its longings. Who can explain the treasure of strength hidden in the inmost heart?

Let us approach the intimate sanctuary of Jesus. His profound gaze, filled with light, penetrates the abyss of God and He knows the Father as no one else has ever known Him. His royal beauty enraptures Him. He walks in that divine heaven in which all perfections shine in marvelous harmony like splendid suns, in ineffable unity.

Here, in this intimate sanctuary of Jesus, there is the inexhaustible fount of being and life; there is the ocean in which all beings are immersed and in which they find their consummation and rest.

His Father, who loves Him with infinite tenderness, who is infinitely pleased with Him, is this boundless treasure of beauty, goodness, and happiness beyond understanding. How would Jesus' very noble, delicate, great Heart, made for divine love, cast itself into the bosom of the Father with uncontainable strength, with superhuman ardor? How would Jesus consecrate Himself to the Father with total, irrevocable, eternal consecration from the first instant of His life?

Conchita's Reflections on a Retreat

Neither the gigantic waterfalls which cascade thundering into the void, nor the great meteorite which rends space with vertiginous speed, leaving light in its wake, nor the worlds which roll in the firmament with fantastic speed, nor the most zealous souls that accomplish heroic deeds and run to martyrdom, driven by a strange passion, give a remote idea of divine love, of the incomprehensible force with which the soul of Jesus casts itself into the arms of the Father, with a love more powerful than death, overwhelmed by the splendid, ineffable vision of the infinite goodness.

If we could know what Jesus saw and loved, neither the Upper Room, nor Calvary, nor the Church would surprise us. All these marvels would seem perfectly logical to us, if we knew the ardent love of the Heart of Christ and the refulgent light of His soul.

Your love for the Father must be a pale but exact reflection of this great passion, because what your eyes see when you are bathed by the divine gaze is the reflection of what Jesus sees.

Compared to this light, compared to this passion, your martyrdoms should seem to you perfectly logical, the burden of your immense Cross, light; your Calvary is fragrant with flowers, because love is like this. It sweetens and beautifies all because, for love, all is heaven, even supreme ignominy and suffering.

Fervently love the Father as Jesus loves Him; offer yourself to Him with full and irrevocable consecration, as Jesus offered Himself. May the glory of the Father be the passion of your life, the unique longing of your soul, your joy, happiness and crown.

It is true that sometimes – and how many times! – the heaven of your soul becomes dark and the sun of the divine gaze hides from you, and in your inmost spirit the radiant gaze goes out; however, the darkest clouds do not extinguish the sun, but only hide it, and the eyes of the soul manage to see the divine, even despite the shadows.

Neither does the gaze of the Father ever stop bathing your soul, nor is the light of the Holy Spirit ever extinguished. For this reason, the volcano of divine love is never extinguished in your heart, even though the ashes of desolation hide the interior fire and immense flames.

Your love, stronger than desolation, more powerful than martyrdom, will bear and suffer everything: abandonment, darkness, unspeakable heart-rending as a result of the triumphal virtue of your passionate love, the effect of the irresistible fascination of this heavenly gaze and that which also wells up from the depth of your soul.

For the sake of God's glory, everything is suave and light, and the more one suffers for its sake, the more one loves it and seeks it and consecrates one's heart and life to it.

Look upon Jesus as the Father looks upon Him. Love the Father with the ardor with which Jesus loves Him, and your life will be the reflection of Jesus' life, which was the harmonious, triumphal and great canticle to the glory of the Father.

Personal Reflection of Conchita
THIRTY-THIRD DAY

Petitions

Yesterday I felt a kind of fire in my heart. I spent the night on the "roses," etc. During Mass and communion, I prayed for all needs "as the one who entreats God"; and with Him, it is possible. I entreated a King, a compassionate and tender Father, *all love* for His poor creatures.

All petitions from the communities of the Sisters of the Cross, those of my spiritual director which he left for me later, and then those from other souls were placed during the night and at Mass near the Tabernacle. They are there, so that He may read them as I tell Him, warm them, and take care of them favorably.

"Lord, the Pope[295] who carries so many sorrows in his heart; the Apostolic Delegate[296] who celebrates his saint's day today; my spiritual director and all bishops, especially those who had to leave their dioceses; my Jesus, Fr. Félix, Fr. Edmundo, Fr. Treviño, Fr.

Conchita's Reflections on a Retreat

Tomás, Fr. Pablo, Fr. Félix Maria, Fr. Vicente, Fr. Manuel, Fr. Ángel, and all, all of the Congregation;[297] the Sisters of the Cross, Mother Manuela and her council, all superiors and sisters.[298] Lord, You know what I want and the needs of Your Congregations.

"I pray for the Covenant of Love and the Apostolate of the Cross, with their difficulties. Only You, my Jesus, can take care of them, guide them and make Your beloved Works of the Cross flourish in virtues.

"Lord, I pray for the Fraternity of Christ the Priest, the Sunday Communion, the Crusade; my Jesus, today sprinkle their members with the blood of Your loving Heart, so that they may fulfill Your designs and ideal on earth.

"Lord, save Your Church in Mexico, give her freedom and stop the bloody persecution of her priests. Have mercy on so many souls disoriented and poisoned by communism.

"Listen to me today, Jesus of my life, for Your Mexico, its children and souls."

"I have already told You that despite all the enemy's efforts, Mexico will not be lost. The faith will not be lost in Mexico, and the reaction will be greater than all the evils which make it cry. It is purified."

"Lord, may Your fatherly Heart have compassion on so many abandoned souls, without priests, *without a Tabernacle*! They are deprived of the Sacraments and You of glory. Why, my Jesus, why are Your priests persecuted, calumniated, disdained, detested? Do You not see that they are also mine?"

"I draw good out of evil, and My punishment in this life is mercy, even though this is not understood. To so much evil there are counterweights which give Me glory. I have My moments. My punishment and trials will finish. Do not think that I do not take into consideration the martyrdom and sorrows of those who are Mine. Those sorrows purchase graces and I am glorified in them.

"Do not be afraid. This satanic wave will pass, and I will make My great mercy shine out. My Church in Mexico needed this bloodshed, the *purification* which is at work now, even though in a hidden way.

"Do not be afraid; trust and wait for God's hour."

"Lord, help Archbishop Pascual Díaz, and fill him with fortitude and light. Bishop Maximino Ruiz, Bishop Rafael Guízar, Bishop Guillermo Tritscher. Give health to Rev. Juan Buitrón. And with regard to all the petitions I left close to Your Tabernacle, what do You tell me?"

"Tell them that I will take them into consideration *very especially*."

"Lord, fill Primitivo with graces.[299] Lord, my children, my daughters-in-law, my grandchildren; give consolation to the soul of Manuel,[300] and light so that he may *see* and *trust*.

"I especially want graces for the one You know, and You know which graces. At least a breath!

"*Particularly* for Fr. Félix Rougier, You already know what I seek for his dear soul. My good Jesus, have I already tired You?"

"Do I by chance get tired of listening, of giving and even of giving Myself?"

"So *give Yourself* totally and for ever to me."

"You already have Me."

"The more I have You, the more I seek to have You. Lord, I ask Your big blessing for Morelia, no?"

"Yes, mother, today I cannot say 'no' to you."

"Bless the Bishop and all who dwell in this house, his aunt Angelita and the girls.

"Oh my Jesus, the day became bitter with the news from Pancho. *Heal* him, and grant to his father the grace to visit him.

"Lord, Lupe. The new list I left You. The petitions of Fr. Ibarrola. Vocations for the Works of the Cross.

"They…, my Jesus… They, Life of my life. Those in Rome. Remember them all and bless them. The intentions of Mr. Reyes, Mrs. Candelaria; those who are present and absent; Maria Cecilia, Jesus of my soul; bless them and save them all.

"Today a special grace for the Apostolic Delegate."

"I fulfill what I promise and all your prayers will be favorably answered in one degree or another according to their needs and My will."

He deigned Himself to answer the petitions for the Sisters of the Cross.

Last night I had that devastating and agonizing interior sorrow. All for priests, souls and God's glory.

The day of graces is over. I await everything from the divine goodness. His promises are facts and Jesus' love is infinite.

Heaven of my soul, *thank you*!

November 16, 1935
THIRTY-FOURTH DAY

Meditation of Archbishop Martínez

Consummation

As the mystical incarnation has its source in the bosom of the Father, so it finds its consummation in this loving bosom.

On earth this consummation has two meanings, while in heaven the souls that received the wonderful grace will possess special glory.

Jesus showed you one of these meanings in the last retreat as He introduced you in the abyss of Divinity. To enter this abyss means the divine rest, the ineffable goal of the journey which is the holy humanity of Jesus.

Jesus ascended to the Father after accomplishing all His mysteries on earth, so that the transformed souls can also ascend to the Father, and share in the mysteries of Jesus, according to God's designs.

To ascend to the Father is to enter the joy of the Lord in eternal glory; but the prelude to that glory it is to enter that joy, that means, the soul is introduced into the divine bosom and enjoys there light, love and rest.

Sometimes your soul has felt the divine radiations like gusts of glory while it was introduced into the mysteries of God. You were bathed with light there, permeated with love, and rested in the bosom of the Father.

This grace is the consummation of the mystical incarnation, and marks the divine height which one can reach by the path of the Cross.

Do you remember the stages of the spiritual journey symbolized on the Cross of the Apostolate?[301]

First, the large cross, rough and bloody; then the royal dwelling of the Heart of Jesus, surrounded by light, aflame and enveloped in bitter suffering.

Through the wound of His Heart, you penetrated the sublime sanctuary; you barely had wings to fly in those immense regions, but the divine love made the wings of your soul grow and, guided by Mary, you traversed the temple of love and suffering.

One day, love introduced you into the ocean of bitterness, and permeated by it you reached the mysterious cross which crowns the Heart of Jesus, sharing in mysterious suffering. Climbing this cross, you arrived at the inaccessible light which the Holy Spirit sheds over it. This mystical ascension was consummated in the splendors of the Divinity, in the bosom of the Father.

Yet, while you are in this world, you will be unable to establish a perpetual dwelling on the divine Tabor, but your life will oscillate between two immensities: the deep sea of bitterness of the Heart of Jesus and the splendid light of the infinite bosom, between Tabor and Calvary. And obviously, the greater part of your life you will pass on the hill of blood.

From time to time, the light of heaven will transfigure your soul, and your astonished eyes will perceive the divine mysteries. These gusts of glory are preludes of eternity and the consummation of the central grace of your life.

As preludes to heaven, these delightful moments share in the prerogatives of glory as far as it is possible on earth.

When you enter the divine bosom, *"God is all in all."* Isn't that

Conchita's Reflections on a Retreat

true? You experience God with all His infinite perfections, His sovereign beauty and His ineffably mysterious life.

Sometimes you have dared to translate into our poor language what your soul contemplates. After trying to explain the divine, you are convinced that you have not said anything, that it is ineffable, and that the silence of adoration and love is the best homage the soul can pay to it, until the blessed moment of singing the eternal trisagion[302] comes.

Is it not true that when your soul is introduced into the bosom of the Father, it looks upon everything in a new way? Then *"God is all in all,"* is He not? In effect, the universe is full of God; the heavens sing His glory and the earth is full of His majesty; creation is a canticle to the divine glory. But who listens to this canticle? Who understands the deep and divine meaning of creation? Who hears the unfathomable harmony of the universe resound in the soul?

Only in heaven is the mighty hymn fully heard. On the earth, only chosen souls hear the sound-waves of the divine harmony in fleeting moments when they enter into the bosom of God, like those who listen to the sounds of a distant orchestra which waft on the waves of the restless wind.

More than the material universe, the little universe we carry within our souls has divine meaning. Above all, souls declare the glory of God, because they carry within the image of the Most High.

In order to understand the value of a soul it is necessary to dwell in the divine atmosphere in which *"God is all in all,"* because to understand a soul, we need to look with penetrating, deep, enlightened eyes upon the image of God – the gem of heaven set in the royal jewel of this soul.

If God dwells in each soul and if the mysterious canticle springs from each soul, what will the amazing whole be like, this spiritual heaven in which souls shine like splendid constellations in harmonious concert?

What will the Church be like, this Church in which all souls in union with Jesus, forming one marvelous Mystical Body, live a divine life and are linked with the blessed by indestructible, divine bonds?

To understand this world of the blessed, to hear the delights of the supreme canticle to the glory of God, it is necessary that "*God be all in all*" for the soul – either because the soul has established its eternal dwelling in the bosom of God, or because the boldness of love has introduced it into the joy of the Lord in fleeting, but happy moments.

St. Francis of Assisi looked upon nature from above and understood its deep meaning. Because of this the universe was, for him, the canticle which filled his soul with optimism and joy.

St. Paul contemplated the world of souls thus and because of this, he understood the mystery of Christ. He loved souls with passionate tenderness and spent all for their sake and spent himself.

In this way, Thérèse of Lisieux saw the abyss of her littleness and that abyss was filled with God, and she loved her nothingness, as we love the vessel which contains the perfume of beatitude, spreading her suave perfume on earth, so that little souls may approach the ocean of merciful love through the abyss of self-annihilation.

It fell to your lot to contemplate a different world and listen to a different canticle. From the watchtower of the Divinity, you saw the world which rises from the summit of Calvary, and you listened to the hymn which issues harmoniously from the wood of the Cross to the divine glory. Or rather, your world is hidden in the Heart of Jesus; yours is the divine canticle that wells up from it.

You received the revelation of the Cross from the Heart of Jesus. You knew the richness of suffering, the very beauty of immolation, the perennial source of purity and love which springs from the bitterness of the divine Heart, from the mystery of the interior Cross of Jesus. And you have intoned the amazing canticle of suffering which sings the praises of the glory of God.

The ineffable canticle will never be extinguished. The souls of the Cross will repeat it until the consummation of ages. Some of them will pass on the divine theme to others. Each generation will intone its powerful verse, and all will form a mysterious and harmonious symphony which will repeat the sublime theme of Calvary, the divine theme of the Heart of Christ, throughout the centuries, so that the Father may be glorified for ever and ever.

Personal Reflection of Conchita
THIRTY-FOURTH DAY

The foregoing meditation left me deeply impressed, speechless, annihilated, grateful, overwhelmed, but at the same time full of confidence.

Thank you, my God! I cannot say more.

NOVEMBER 17, 1935
THIRTY-FIFTH DAY

Meditation of Archbishop Martínez

The Glory of God

The second meaning of what has just been said, that is, that the mystical incarnation is consummated in the Father, consists in the fact that this grace attains to its perfection when the soul *understands*, *loves* and *seeks* the glory of God[303] in a perfect way which, by appropriation, is attributed to the Father.

This glory is the supreme goal of all works of God, the divine ideal of Jesus, and the supreme aspiration of the Church.

The essential glory of God is God Himself. His accidental glory, the only one that creatures can offer Him, is the image of God in themselves which is the manifestation of His excellence, so that spirits may know Him, hearts may love Him, and lips may praise Him.

After God Himself, there is nothing so beautiful and excellent as His glory, which is like the diffusion of the divine, the divinization of creatures. In creatures which lack intelligence, God's vestige is manifested in their activity and perfection. Intelligent beings are filled with God through knowledge, love, adoration and praise and share in Him, and are even gods by participation, as Scripture says: *"Is it not written in your law, 'I said, you are gods.'*? "[304]

It is clear that after being God by essence, there is nothing better than being gods by participation.

The perfect glory of God will be accomplished when the Mystical Body of Jesus is brought to completion, all enemies defeated, even death itself, and everything subjected to Him; then, according to St. Paul, *"the Son Himself will also be subjected to the one who subjected everything to Him, so that God may be all in all."*[305]

These final words are the supreme formula of the glory of God, because they express the full divinization of the entire universe in Jesus, to whom the Father handed over everything.

Until the day God's glory comes, those of us who walk through this desert longing for that splendid day, for the full revelation of the glory of Jesus, must go on preparing the glorious triumph through our faith, firm hope, fruitful love, holy activity and loving sacrifice, as the diligent and solicitous workers who raise up one large stone after another of the huge monument to the glory of God.

The whole purpose of our life is this glory. We must open our eyes so that His light may fill them, our hearts may burn with His love, and consecrate all our activity so that it may achieve blessed fulfillment.

Each soul's worth is in glorifying God, in cooperating in the divine enterprise of Jesus and thus, one's whole life is consummated in this glorification.

With greater reason, the loving life and sacrifice of a soul that has received the mystical incarnation is to be consummated in this glory, which must be known with more clarity, loved with more purity, sought with more perfection.

All that you have meditated on during this retreat proves it. Jesus has joined you more closely to His mission through your

Conchita's Reflections on a Retreat

transformation into Him, through this very noble mission He bestowed on you. The Holy Spirit is abundantly poured out in your soul, and He has given you a twofold spiritual fruitfulness. The Father, with His ineffable gaze ceaselessly fixed on your soul, has placed in it His divine reflection.

Yet the mission of Jesus is the glory of God. The course to which the impulse of the Holy Spirit leads is this same glory to which the soul, that has received the fruitful gaze of the Father, should look. This gaze introduces your soul into the abyss of the Divinity, that is, into the sanctuary in which one can see with singular depth how *"God is all in all,"* which is to lead you into the dwelling of the glory of God.

The outpouring of the Holy Spirit has enflamed your heart with true and very pure love whose supreme desire is the glory of God, which is worth more than all the works in the Church, as St. John of the Cross teaches.

Your transformation into Jesus consecrates your being and life to this divine glory to which Jesus' rich and divine life was consecrated in all His mysteries.

Yet the mode of knowing, loving and seeking the glory of God is very special for the soul that has received the mystical incarnation. To specify this mode it would suffice to say that the soul should fulfill the phrase repeated so many times that *"God should be all in all"* as well as possible on earth.

For the eyes of your soul, God has to be *all in all*. All earthly forms of things, people, events, should disappear from your gaze so that the divine may shine in your eyes. For you, the present form of this world must pass away and in turn, God will fill the field of your soul's vision with His majesty, beauty, concerns, in a word, with His glory.

Even very holy and perfect things, such as the good of souls, should become coordinated, or rather, subordinated to the glory of God.

Finally, the real good of souls is the reflection of the glory of God in them.

In your life, your children and the Works of the Cross, you should only see the ineffable splendor of the glory of God. Hell itself should appear to your eyes as it appears to the blessed, as a monument raised by "the divine power, supreme wisdom, and the first love" to the glory of God. May *God be all in all* for your understanding.

May it also be so for your heart. In all that you love you should love the glory of God: in souls, in works, in your children. Creatures can be loved in different ways, according to what attracts us to them. Worldly people love ephemeral bodily beauty, while noble souls love spiritual richness of souls. Those who love in a divine way should love the glory of God in souls.

Oh, this glory shines with clear splendor in souls. They all have the image of God within. Grace renews this image, elevates it and makes it grow. In order to make this image more vivid and brilliant, Jesus cleanses souls with His blood, and you should love this image in them, which is the germ of glory, so that *God may be all in all*.

Just as a picture is loved because of the image of the beloved, so the monstrance which holds the Eucharist is loved, so also souls are loved because they have the divine image, because the glory of God is concealed in them.

In the very activity of your life, God is to be *all in all*. To what do your efforts and sacrifices tend? Where do you direct your steps? Which is the deep significance of your actions? What do you work, live and suffer for? What do your longings tend toward? What is the goal of your aspirations?

The glory of God. You should not lift a finger but for this. You have received such marvelous graces! You carry such heavenly treasures in your heart that any other aim which is not the glory of God – no matter how noble and great it may be – *is not worthy of what you have received*.

The goal corresponds to one's being. It suffices for a one-day plant to spread its fragrance in the atmosphere for a few hours and give fruitful seed to the earth. For the birds of the sky, it is enough to sing in springtime and build their passing nests. A man of science is satisfied to leave the light of his soul on the pages of a book and an artist to sculpt his ideal of beauty in marble. But to the one who looks upon the divine in one's heart it is not enough to conquer the world and be admired by people for his immortal deeds, but one must raise one's eyes and heart to divine heights: *the glory of God, which is clearly known, purely loved and heroically sought*; this is the only goal worthy of all the treasures one possesses.

That is why Jesus has told you that the grace of the mystical incarnation is consummated in the glory of God, and this consummation means that God must be *all in all* for *your eyes, heart, activity* and *sacrifices*, as a prelude to heaven, as an anticipation of eternal life.

Personal Reflection of Conchita
THIRTY-FIFTH DAY

My God, what a meditation! I began my retreat self-emptied and I will finish it "wiped out," plunged into the bottomless abyss of the sea.

Virgin Mary, beloved Mother! Help me to give thanks for so many blessings.

Seeking love

Today I was blessed in assisting at the ordination of a priest at the "Little Cave."

Unexpectedly, Jesus said to me: "Here you have another son to offer sacrifices for."

"Lord, why is it only in Morelia that I happen to assist at priestly ordinations?"

"Because of My special love for you."

"Lord, are You happy in this 'Little Cave'?"

"I am happy everywhere."

"I would like You to have only cathedrals."

"I seek only love, and I delight and repose where there is love. But I also like to be among those who crucify Me, in order to forgive them. My Heart is like that and I want yours to be like Mine – all love and suffering – but suffering that saves and glorifies My Father, in union with Me."

"Lord, I really want to become holy and concentrate my life on the Father's gaze, giving Him glory in all the moments of my life and into eternity."

In my soul I experience an immense impulse toward God, who prompts my heart to give Him glory in every grain of the sea's sand, in every atom of air, in the firmament and in souls, and if I could, in millions of worlds.

It is not a passing fancy, but the *mature fruit* of this retreat, which seems like an immovable weight in my inmost spirit.

From the very moment Jesus told me about the glory of the Father, I felt as if a sun illumined my path, as if I were on fire with zeal, but not with an exterior zeal, rather, a spiritual and intimate one which overwhelmed my whole soul.

My Father,[306] weeping, I ask you to pray to the Lord that I may really become holy only for Him. What does the world mean to me or even I to myself! He alone is my dominant passion, and I want to give all my blood and thousands of lives for this beloved Father.

I need gigantic souls to help me, to complete me. I feel *like nothing*, but with heaven itself in my soul, with divine vibrations; and with the sea pouring itself into a thimble which seems to break if someone doesn't help me, if someone doesn't receive it into his bosom from the same fount.

Lord, Lord, give me these souls to help me, complete me, go beyond me and die out of love to give You glory.

May these souls be those of the Missionaries of the Holy Spirit, Sisters of the Cross, all the Works of the Cross, to quench my thirst, to glorify Your Father here and there… in time and eternity. The souls of my children, family, the souls of the priests.

Oh my God, my God, have mercy on me!

Conchita's Reflections on a Retreat

November 18, 1935
THIRTY-SIXTH DAY

Meditation of Archbishop Martínez

Conclusion

Rather than making a full summary of all that has been written on the mystical incarnation, I will emphasize the points which have made the greatest impact on your soul, because they correspond to the intimate movements of God.

This important grace – with its development in your soul and the characteristics which God has placed in it – forms a well-defined spiritual life, which you must live.

Every spiritual life comprises: *light, love, activity* and *sacrifice*. And the mystical incarnation gives a special coloring to each of these elements.

Its Light

It is the intimate gaze of the heavenly Father which ceaselessly bathes your soul, and your soul should dwell under this gaze constantly, just as the Israelites journeyed under the light of the column of fire which guided them.

It was explained above what it means to live in this way; and the intimate experience which was communicated to you teaches you better than any explanations.

Perhaps what is the sensible side of this experience will be extinguished by the ups and downs of your life, and above all, by the ashes of the immolation which God prepares for you. Yet, your faith must find the beauty of this gaze in the shadows when what is sensible disappears.

Another intimate gaze of your soul corresponds, as has already been explained, to this divine gaze, which will sometimes let you penetrate the mysteries of God with marvelous clarity but it will sometimes be veiled by darkness; however, even through this darkness this gaze will give you a profound understanding of divine things.

This constant, mutual, profound and holy gaze will constitute the life of your understanding.

Constantly open yourself to receive the light of this divine gaze. Live from your intimate gaze, and look upon everything through it, and do not look upon anything outside of it. This way of gazing, as I have already told you, is a foretaste of the manner of seeing in heaven, where *God is all in all.*

Love

Your love should spring from your heart under the impulse of the Holy Spirit, for this is the love of souls that have received the mystical incarnation.

This love, like all charity, has two goals: God and souls.

Your divine love should have three characteristics. It should be motherly love, third love,[307] and perfect love, according to the divine mode which the Holy Spirit imprints on it.

Offer yourself without reserve to this love without allowing anything to stop you, neither love's loftiness nor the experience of your own misery.

It is now time that your spiritual modesty should color this love with a gentle lucidity, but you already know that this very delicate sentiment – which in my judgment is what Jesus wants to remain of what we have called your "overdone" humility – neither extinguishes the fire of your motherly tenderness nor diminishes it; rather, it exalts it and gives it a new charm.

So go to Jesus with unlimited confidence, childlike simplicity and loving boldness; go to Him as a very tender mother approaches her adored little son, and love Him in a divine way, as you have learned in the divine school, as the Holy Spirit teaches you with His victorious impulses.

Love for souls should have the same three characteristics, because it is the same love.

Conchita's Reflections on a Retreat

Do not block the inmost impulses of your heart, the bursts of tenderness which the Holy Spirit produces in your soul, either out of humility or out of shame. Love souls with motherly tenderness, with the simplicity of a child, with heavenly purity. Love them as Jesus loves them, as the Father loves them, as the Holy Spirit inspires; and love Jesus in them, since loving them in this way, you will love them as you love Jesus.

Your Activity

By this I mean not only your words and apostolic works, but also your ordinary actions, even though they may seem common. You should have one goal: the glory of God; one essence: love; one seal: the divine, which is the effect of the movement of the Holy Spirit.

There is no need to tell you more about *the glory of God*, given that He has infused in you light, love, the vivid and anointed longings to seek Him in all things in the course of this retreat.

The glory of God, clearly *understood, passionately loved, enthusiastically* and *diligently sought*, must be the single, lofty and pure goal of all your actions.

All other goals should be subordinated to it, and this lofty goal should fill your life with its heavenly aroma, just as it filled the earthly life of Jesus with its exquisite fragrance.

Love should be the essence of your activity, so that it transforms all the acts of your life into love, and fills all moments of your life with true love, fleeting but precious links of your Chain of Love.[308]

Do nothing except to love. Love equally when near the Tabernacle or close to souls, in your relations with others or in the silence of your ordinary life.

May love be your prayer, your work and your rest.

May love be your relation with others.

And above all, may love be your constant immolation.

UNDER THE GAZE OF THE FATHER

Mode of activity

The mode of your activity must be always divine. Do not forget that because of the mystical incarnation the Holy Spirit moves you almost constantly, not only in actions which seem important, but in all actions, even in ordinary and small ones. Are there perhaps common actions for souls that the Holy Spirit possesses and moves? Even though you are unaware of it, your divine Spouse constantly moves your soul, and places His divine seal on your activity.

This activity should be especially exercised with regard to the Works of the Cross. Do not think that your influence, care, or responsibility for the Works of the Cross has ceased simply because they are already founded, and legitimately guided.

Although the children have grown up, the mother who gave them birth still needs to take care of them and perfect them, because the fact of giving life also confers the right and obligation of *bringing to perfection*. The shining ray of light requires a source of light from which it radiates. So the Works of the Cross to which you have given life expect their growth and development from you; and even in heaven – especially there – you will continue to exercise your influence on them with divine efficacy.

Undoubtedly with discretion, but with holy freedom and sound loving judgment, you should shore up what is weak in these beloved Works, heal what is sick, straighten what goes crooked, seek after what goes astray, hold on to what is useful and valuable with care, according to the words of Scripture which refer to the obligations of the Shepherd.

Sacrifice

Regarding sacrifice there is nothing I can tell you, since it is very familiar to you; there is no need to remind you of what you were told about the perfection which souls who have received the mystical incarnation should have. But I will underscore some very important points related to it.

Two sacrifices which are intimately linked, even more, which constitute only one sacrifice, should fill your life, the sacrifice of Jesus and yours.

With regard to the first one, you should not forget how much God taught you in the previous retreat, and in this He reminded you of the sublime and painful obligation to sacrifice Jesus for the glory of the Father and on behalf of souls.

You should constantly fulfill this commitment of loving Jesus as the Father loved Him, as Mary loved Him, and loving souls as they loved them.

Neither the beauty of the gaze of the Father, nor the longing for the glory of God, should stop you from this painful offering; rather, this gaze which increases the divine reflection in your soul, and this longing which is the reflection of the longing of the Father, should form the powerful and irresistible incentive which prompts you to offer the divine Son to be sacrificed.

With regard to the second sacrifice, bravely keep on with your cruel mortifications and accept the burden of human suffering which God's hand imposes on you daily. Yet, your own, most fruitful sacrifice, that which Jesus prefers, because it gives more glory to God and obtains more graces for souls, is the intimate suffering which participates in the ineffable suffering of the Heart of Jesus.

Thanks be to God, you will never lack this cruel and precious bitterness while you live; cruel, because it exceeds human sufferings, and precious, because it is Jesus' bitterness. Accept it lovingly; permeate all other sufferings with it in order to make them divine. Suffer this bitterness, experience perfect joy in giving glory to God and graces for souls.

The treasure of suffering possesses two jewels to which you should pay attention, because God has signaled them especially.

1. To renounce the consolations of the sensible presence of Jesus.
2. To bear the sins which the Crusade atones for.

You know by experience that the first of the jewels is as valuable as it is crucifying. Now you have a new strength, or rather two very powerful ones, enabling you to endure this martyrdom: the glory which you give to God through this and the love for souls which you satisfy with it.

What will you not suffer now for the glory of God?

And if you understand that what is most painful, above all, when it is intimate and has the divine nuance, gives immense glory to God, then the sensible absence of Jesus will become for you a most intimate union, even though hidden, and true consolation for His Heart.

Love for souls has grown in you amazingly in these days, especially love for priests. Will your motherly generosity not gladly renounce the consolations of Jesus with more heroism than ever so that priests may enjoy them?

With regard to the sins which the Crusade atones for, Jesus has placed them in your heart in the same way that He carried them in His.

Is it not enough to receive this beloved Cross with joy?

But you have other motivations: the good you will do in families in this way – this is your favorite virtue – and especially the glory of God which emerges from this atonement.

In closing, your spiritual life is outlined in this summary, which in reality is a program which has its source in the mystical incarnation.

If you would like to see what I have just said in a simplified outline and concise form as resolutions of the retreat, I will simplify all your spiritual life in a *unique* resolution, and I will draw out of it some points of your spiritual program as practical consequences.

The unique resolution

You must live the grace of the mystical incarnation intensely and cooperate with all your strength in its full development and happy consummation.

In order to achieve this:

Conchita's Reflections on a Retreat

1. Try to study the grace in depth and get accustomed to look at it directly and with your eyes wide open.
2. Try to make the mystical incarnation your spiritual program as it was outlined in the summary, which includes the following points:

Light

1. Live under the gaze of the Father, and correspond to this intimate gaze, by which "God should be all in all" for you.

Love

2. Offer yourself fully to Jesus' love with the three characteristics which were indicated: motherly love, third love, and with the perfection of the divine mode.
3. Love souls with this same love embellished by these three characteristics.

Activity

4. Seek the glory of God in all things with very pure love.
5. Turn your life into love.
6. Act always under the impulse of the Holy Spirit.
7. Care for the Works of the Cross with motherly and discreet solicitude.

Sacrifice

8. Sacrifice Jesus constantly, according to the teaching of the previous retreat.
9. Accept inward sufferings with perfect joy.
10. Renounce the consolation of the presence of Jesus on behalf of priests.
11. Bear the sins which the Crusade atones for.

Your spiritual program is vast, sublime and holy, since it corresponds to the richness of the graces you have received.

In order to put this program into practice, remember that you have the ever-Virgin Mary as model, help and Mother.

The grace which you have received is a reflection of the unique grace of Mary, and she knew how to live it with inimitable purity, exquisite perfection and royal fullness.

Run after the heavenly fragrance of Mary and learn the secret of how to love with heroic and perfect fidelity from her.

It is her responsibility – by the omnipotence of her prayers and the inexhaustible abundance of her graces – to help souls especially like yours which have received the reflection of her mission and prerogatives more than other souls.

Being mother for Jesus and for souls, you also have a great need of a Mother, since your motherly duties are arduous, delicate and torturing.

You need as well – and more than other souls – a loving and welcoming lap in which your agonizing soul can find rest and consolation.

Who better than Mary can understand you, she who bore in her immense and purest soul the heart-rending burden of Jesus and souls, even much more than you bear it?

Who better than she can fuse your heart with hers, filled with inimitable love and great suffering?

Cast yourself into her motherly lap, dwell on it, especially in the bitter hours of unspeakable abandonment and great desolation.

Do not forget that you have a Mother who loves you tenderly, caresses you lovingly, who listens to your intimate confidences and fills you with consolations, with the ineffable consolations of the Paraclete.

Concluding, I wish to condense in one sacred and unfathomable formula all that God asks of you, and all that I wish for you from the bottom of my heart, because this expression condenses the teachings of these days and embraces, in its simplicity, your future spiritual program:

"May God be all in all for you." Amen.

Conchita's Reflections on a Retreat

Personal Reflection of Conchita
THIRTY-SIXTH DAY

The Fruit of the Retreat
Peace.
Abandonment.
Simplification.
The gaze of the Father.
Expanding the soul.
Suffering all for the glory of the Father.
Giving Him glory in all actions.
Enjoying the lack of consolations and the sensible presence of Jesus for the sake of priests.
Motherly love for Jesus and souls, with the characteristics of the third love.
The Crusade and bearing the sins which it atones for.

Reforms
Being mother with the characteristics of the third love, overcoming myself.
Writing to different Houses of the Cross each day of the week.
Visiting the Mother General[309] once a week.
Writing to Fr. Angel M. Oñate once a month.
Visiting Fr. Felix, Fr. Treviño and the Church of St. Philip.[310]
Two fixed hours of prayer.
Confession once a week.
Spiritual reading of the meditations of this retreat.
A monthly retreat.
Visiting the Sisters of the Cross when the Mother Superior invites me.
Mortification.
Letting the Father's gaze permeate me.
All for the glory of God.

CHART OF RETREATS OF CONCEPCIÓN CABRERA DE ARMIDA WITH BISHOP LUIS M. MARTÍNEZ 1925-1936

DATE	PLACE	WRITINGS	THEME AND GRACES OF THE RETREATS
July 1-10, 1925	General House of the Sisters of the Cross of the Sacred Heart of Jesus	AC 45, 183-475; SE[311] 3, 215-216; 227-241	"Your Life in God" (cf. AC 45, 187; SE 3, 228). CCA makes a summary of the graces received from the Lord during her life (cf. AC 45, 217f). She starts her spiritual direction with Bishop Luis M. Martínez (cf. AC 45, 375).
July 16-25, 1926	Morelia, Mexico, Archbishop's residence	AC 47, 1-148	"Loving with the Holy Spirit" (cf. AC 47, 6). CCA is unified in love, loving with the Holy Spirit (cf. AC 47, 32).
September 9-17, 1927	Morelia, Mexico, Archbishop's residence	AC 48, 241-397	"To Be Mother" (cf. AC 48, 259). The Lord makes CCA an echo of His love and suffering (cf. AC 48, 248-250).
November 22-30, 1928	Morelia, Mexico, Archbishop's residence	AC 52, 296-400; AC 53, 1-63; 87-89	"To Be Jesus Crucified" (cf. AC 52, 297). CCA becomes aware of belonging to the Church and being a spiritual mother of priests (cf. AC 53, 13-41).
November 14-30, 1929	Morelia, Mexico, Archbishop's residence	AC 53, 338-401; AC 54, 1-347	"The Interior of the Heart of Jesus" (cf. AC 53, 346). The Lord conferred priestly graces on CCA to be communicated to others (cf. AC 54, 160; 245).
December 11-25, 1930	Morelia, Mexico, Archbishop's residence	AC 56, 15-281	"The Consummation in the Unity of the Holy Trinity" (cf. AC 56, 234). The Lord makes CCA a fire to burn vices and enkindle charity (cf. AC 56, 256).
December 25, 1931- January 14, 1932	Morelia, Mexico Archbishop's residence	AC 57, 283-400; AC 58, 1-400	"The Third Love" (cf. AC 58, 169). CCA lives the third love (cf. AC 57, 301). Together with the Blessed Virgin, she is present at Mass (cf. AC 58, 95).
March 6-25, 1933	Morelia, Mexico, Archbishop's residence	AC 59, 205-400; AC 60, 71-373; SE 4, 1-228	"The Reposes of Jesus" (cf. AC 59, 207). CCA receives light on the divinity of Jesus (cf. AC 59, 212). She should be light (cf. AC 59, 219).

July 28- August 21, 1934	Morelia, Mexico, Archbishop's residence	AC 61, 226-399 AC 62, 1-65; 70-358 SE 4, 230-451	"To Offer Jesus to Be Crucified" (cf. AC 62,97). CCA should crucify Jesus and crucify herself in union with Him in order to give Him to priests (cf. AC 62, 253-324).
October 14- November 18, 1935	Morelia, Mexico, Archbishop's residence	AC 63, 203-371 AC 64, 1-192 AC 65, 5-28	"The Mystical Incarnation" (cf. AC 64, 14). All for the glory of the Father (cf. AC 64, 39-40). Crusade on behalf of Families (cf. AC 63, 344).
October 3- November 2, 1936	Morelia, Mexico, Archbishop's residence	AC 65, 162-398 AC 66, 1-175 SE 4, 495-516	"The Perfect Joy" (cf. AC 65, 214). CCA participated in the interior Cross of Jesus (cf. AC 65, 216). She sensed that it was the last time in her life she would make her retreat (cf. AC 65, 327; 66, 29).

ENDNOTES

1. Her published works are forty-six; some of them are very brief, written at the request of other persons as an aid for meditation and prayer. They amount to approximately nine thousand pages, but these are only an eighth part of her total output. Her unpublished works are more numerous. These include the 6,227 letters addressed to her spiritual directors which have been preserved, and which are marked by a high spirituality. Her account of conscience (*Cuenta de Conciencia*, see note 89) runs to sixty-six volumes (22,500 pages) and it was written for her various directors. Additionally, there are various other writings, which amount to 15,500 pages.
2. *Vida* [Life], Vol. I, (Private edition), p. 112.
3. *Autobiografía* [Autobiography], Vol. I, (Private edition), p. 40.
4. *Apuntes Espirituales* [Spiritual Notes], Vol. I, p. 158. Conchita was privileged to have visions of Christ, mystical experiences about the Holy Trinity, God's love for humanity, and other spiritual illuminations.
5. *Autobiografía* [Autobiography], Vol. I, p. 51.
6. The Works of the Cross consist of five associations: (1) the Apostolate of the Cross, founded on May 3, 1895; (2) the Sisters of the Cross of the Sacred Heart of Jesus, founded on May 3, 1897, as an institute of contemplative women of perpetual adoration who offer their lives especially for the sanctification of priests; (3) the Covenant of Love with the Sacred Heart of Jesus, founded on November 30, 1909, which gathers together lay people who commit themselves to seek perfection within their lay vocations according to the Spirituality of the Cross; (4) the Fraternity of Christ the Priest which was founded on January 19, 1912, for bishops and priests; (5) the Missionaries of the Holy Spirit, founded by Fr. Felix Rougier on December 25, 1914, as a clerical religious congregation dedicated to priestly ministries and to the spiritual direction of souls.
7. Cf. Second Vatican Council's Dogmatic Constitution, *Lumen Gentium*, chapter 5.
8. Archbishop Luis María Martínez (1881-1956) directed Conchita for her last 14 years. Throughout the period of religious persecution Bishop Martínez held various responsible positions in the Church, such as Rector of the Seminary in Morelia, Apostolic Administrator of Chilapa, Auxiliary Bishop in Morelia, Archbishop of Mexico City and Primate of Mexico, member of the Mexican Academy of Languages. His spiritual writings exhibit sound doctrine, great personal holiness, serenity and optimism to such an extent that he was called the "Archbishop Peacemaker." A man of profound spirituality, he was spiritual director not only to the Venerable Conchita Armida, but also to Blessed Rafael Guízar y Valencia, and the Servant of God Mother Angélica Álvarez Icaza. Archbishop Martínez' reputation for holiness of life gave impulse to the opening of the process for his beatification in 1985.
9. The Archbishop of Morelia, Leopoldo Ruiz y Flores, insisted in his letters that Conchita should seek spiritual direction from his Auxiliary Bishop (from September 30, 1923), L.M. Martínez, because he felt that Bishop Martínez would be the right spiritual director for Conchita.
10. *Account of Conscience* [hereinafter *AC*], 44, 135. See note 89.
11. The letters of Concepción Cabrera de Armida to Archbishop Martínez (about 895 letters) and of Archbishop Martínez to Conchita (about 361 letters) were published in a private edition in Spanish.

12 Conchita read with interest his articles published by Fr. José G. Treviño, M.Sp.S., in the review "La Cruz," founded by Father Felix de Jesús Rougier, founder of the Missionaries of the Holy Spirit, in 1921.
13 See note 55.
14 Cf. *AC* 45, 186: July 1, 1925.
15 Cf. *AC* 45, 217: July 3, 1925.
16 Cf. *Catechism of the Catholic Church* n. 537; 2565.
17 Cf. Concepción Cabrera de Armida, *Under the Gaze of the Father*, Retreat Directed by Archbishop Luis M. Martínez on the Grace of the Mystical Incarnation, October 19, 1935 (cf. *AC* 63, 262-266).
18 Cf. *AC* 22, 299-306: April 30, 1906.
19 Cf. *AC* 35, 81-94: February 21, 1911.
20 Cf. *AC* 48, 148-150: May 31, 1927.
21 Cf. *AC* 47, 122: July 23, 1926.
22 *AC* 45, 435-439: July 8, 1925.
23 Juan Gutiérrez, M.Sp.S., *Concepción Cabrera de Armida, Cruz de Jesús, Vida mística e itinerario espiritual*, Vol. I, Editorial de la Cruz, p. 477.
24 After having relentlessly begged her spiritual director, Conchita received permission to physically brand the name of Jesus (JHS) on her chest to mark her symbolically as the possession of Christ and thus inaugurate her divinely given apostolate. From the moment she made this symbolic act on the feast of the Holy Name of Jesus on January 3, 1894, she became single-heartedly zealous for the salvation of souls (cf. *AC* 1, 264).
25 *AC* 1, 407-412: 1894.
26 *AC* 9, 33-34: February 17, 1897.
27 *AC* 9, 55-56: February 22, 1897.
28 *AC* 22, 167-177: March 24-25, 1906.
29 At this time, she had been a widow since 1901 and had been allowed to make private religious vows.
30 At this time, it was customary to receive Communion before Mass.
31 At the words of the Creed, "and became man" (*et incarnatus est*).
32 *Memento* means *remember*. The Roman Canon or the First Eucharistic Prayer has two *mementos*: the first *memento* is a prayer for the living and the second one, after the consecration, for the deceased.
33 Cf. *AC* 22, 167-177: March 25, 1906.
34 "The Eucharist is the perpetual incarnation in the souls, another sort of incarnation which concludes when the sacramental species conclude, leaving only the effects, but at the end, just the same, incarnation" *Vida* [Life] 5, 325: July 24, 1906.
35 Cf. *AC* 22, 167-191: March 25, 1906; *Vida* [Life] 5, 82: March 26, 1906.
36 Cf. *AC* 22, 328: May 3, 1906.
37 Cf. Retreat Directed by Archbishop Luis M. Martínez on the Grace of the Mystical Incarnation, *op. cit.*: October 20, 1935 (cf. *AC* 64, 43).
38 *Ibid.* November 6, 1935 (cf. *AC* 64, 136). Cf. Eph 3.
39 *Ibid.* October 16, 1935 (cf. *AC* 64, 14-15). Cf. *AC* 23, 84-89; *AC* 25, 189-190; cf. *AC* 46, 188-190.

Endnotes

[40] Retreat Directed by Archbishop Luis M. Martínez on the Grace of the Mystical Incarnation, *loc. cit.*, November 7, 1935 (cf. *AC* 64, 141-142).
[41] *Ibid.* November 9, 1935 (cf. *AC* 64, 149-151).
[42] Cf. Concepción Cabrera de Armida, *Ser Jesús Crucificado* [To Be Jesus Crucified], Retreat of 1928, Ediciones Cimiento, p. 30.
[43] *AC* 48, 149-150: May 31, 1927.
[44] Cf. *AC* 22, 408-416: July 21, 1906.
[45] *AC* 41, 270: June 16, 1917.
[46] Cf. *AC* 25, 175-179: February 6, 1907.
[47] Cf. *AC* 28, 63-64: October 19, 1907.
[48] Cf. *AC* 28, 129-134: October 22, 1907.
[49] "You are My altar and you will also be My victim; in union with Me offer yourself constantly to the Eternal Father with the noble purpose of saving souls and of giving Him glory" (*AC* 22, 408-416: July 21, 1906).
[50] "You have to carry out the priestly office, but sacrificing yourself at the same time. That is the true priesthood, be a victim with the Victim, as I am, assimilating Me to it in all its parts" (*AC* 12, 89-91: July 17, 1906).
[51] Cf. St. Thomas, *Summa Theol.* III q. 63, a. 3; III q. 65, a 3. According to St. Thomas Aquinas, by the baptismal character, we receive the capacity of offering Christ and of offering ourselves in union with Him, but it is by means of the Eucharist that the Christian is fully transformed into Christ and brings to fulfillment His priestly offering.
[52] *Lumen Gentium* n. 10: "Though they differ from one another in essence and not only in degree, the common priesthood of the faithful and the ministerial, or hierarchical priesthood, are nonetheless interrelated: each of them, in its own special way, is a participation in the one priesthood of Christ. The ministerial priest, by the sacred power he enjoys, teaches and rules the priestly people; acting in the person of Christ, he makes present the Eucharistic sacrifice, and offers it to God in the name of all the people. But the faithful, in virtue of their royal priesthood, join in the offering of the Eucharist. They likewise exercise that priesthood in receiving the sacraments, in prayer and thanksgiving, in the witness of a holy life, and by self-denial and active charity."
[53] *AC* 41, 270: June 16, 1917.
[54] Cf. *AC* 40, 299: July 6, 1916.
[55] The doctrine on the grace called the "Chain of Love" (also called "Chain of Gold") should be understood in the light and under the influence of the grace of the mystical incarnation. Conchita, by virtue of this grace and, firstly, of the grace of baptism, was invited to be transformed into Christ Priest and Victim by the practice of the virtues, and to offer herself in union with Jesus to the Father for the salvation of mankind. In her writings we find very rich teaching on the practice of the virtues (e.g., *Virtues and Vices, The Treatise on the Virtues of the Perfect Consecrated Person, The Rainbow of the Perfect Virtues, The Seasons of the Soul, The Treatise on Spiritual Direction*). Every baptized person is also called to exercise his or her baptismal priesthood through receiving the sacraments and the practice of the virtues. The fourteen rules-virtues of the "Chain of Love" are: (1) humility, (2) purity, (3) prayer, (4) hiding oneself with perfect spiritual modesty, (5) poverty, (6) self-abandonment, (7) emptying the heart of all that is earthly, (8) love for the Virgin Mary (imitating her perfect obedience), (9) purity of intention through living in Jesus' presence, (10) tending to what is right and holy, (11) courage in suffering and love for the Cross, (12) disinterested love, (13) fidelity and correspondence to grace, (14) living only for Jesus (dying to everything that is opposed

to Him). These have countless degrees, conforming the soul to Jesus and enabling it to offer itself to the Father in union with Jesus.

56 *AC* 25, 220: February 8, 1907.
57 Retreat Directed by Archbishop Luis M. Martínez on the Grace of the Mystical Incarnation, *loc. cit.*, October 19, 1935 (cf. *AC* 64, 33a).
58 *AC* 26, 141-142: March 16, 1907.
59 *AC* 46, 85-88: October 20, 1925.
60 *AC* 41, 274: July 16, 1917; *AC* 42, 281-283: June 22, 1919.
61 Cf. *AC* 41, 274: July 16, 1917; *AC* 42, 281-282: June 22, 1919.
62 Cf. *AC* 41, 218-219: June 11, 1917.
63 Stage from the Ascension of Jesus to the Assumption of Mary to Heaven.
64 Cf. *AC* 41, 271-272: July 16, 1917; *AC* 42, 83-84: May 24, 1918; *AC* 42, 286-289: June 23, 1918.
65 Cf. *AC* 49, 54-55: September 26, 1927.
66 Cf. *AC* 25, 219-222: February 9, 1907.
67 *AC* 45, 207: July 3, 1925.
68 *AC* 45, 206-208: July 3, 1925.
69 Concepción Cabrera de Armida, *Loving with the Holy Spirit*, Retreat Directed by Bishop Luis M. Martínez, July 18, 1926, Editrice Vaticana, 2007.
70 Cf. *Dominum et Vivificantem*, p. 41.
71 *AC* 37, 67-72: August 6, 1912.
72 *AC* 32, 119-121: February 21, 1909.
73 Cf. *AC* 57, 199-203: October 8, 1931.
74 *AC* 66, 64-66: October 25, 1936.
75 Retreat Directed by Archbishop Luis M. Martínez on the Grace of the Mystical Incarnation, *loc. cit.*, October 23, 1935 (cf. *AC* 63, 304-305).
76 *AC* 48, 248-249: September 10, 1927.
77 Concepción Cabrera de Armida, *Sacerdotes de Cristo* (Priests of Christ), Editorial La Cruz, Mexico, 2004.
78 Conchita heard Jesus speak these words to her: "Offer yourself in sacrifice for My priests; unite yourself to My sacrifice so as to obtain graces for them. It is necessary that, united to the Eternal Priest, you carry out your priestly role, offering Me to the Father, and drawing down graces and mercy for the Church and its members. Do you not remember how many times I have asked you to offer yourself as a victim, in union with the Victim, for the beloved Church? Do you not see that you belong to her, because you are Mine, and you are Mine because you are hers? Then, by the special union that you have with My Church, you have the right to share in her sorrow and you have the sacred duty of consoling her, sacrificing yourself for her priests" (*AC* 49, 26-27: September 24, 1927).
79 Cf. *AC* 53, 33-40: November 29, 1928.
80 Cf. *AC* 53, 33-40; 49-52: November 29-30, 1928.
81 *AC* 53, 33-40: November 29, 1928.
82 Cf. *AC* 64, 182: November 16, 1935.
83 Cf. Retreat Directed by Archbishop Luis M. Martínez on the Grace of the Mystical Incarnation, *loc. cit.*, October 18, 1935 (cf. *AC* 64, 31-32a).

Endnotes

[84] *Ibid.* October 20, 1935 (cf. *AC* 64, 39-39a).
[85] *Ibid.* October 23, 1935 (cf. *AC* 64, 54-56).
[86] *Ibid.* October 18, 1935 (cf. *AC* 64, 33).
[87] *Ibid.* October 16, 1935 (*AC* 64, 21).
[88] St. Thomas Aquinas, *opusc* 57 in *festo Corp. Chr.* 1 in *Catechism of the Catholic Church*, n. 460.
[89] The writings we present in this volume of the Retreat are excerpts from the *Account of Conscience* [in Spanish *Cuenta de Conciencia*], from volume 63, 203-343; volume 64, 1-192, and volume 65, 5-28. The abbreviation *AC* is used herein to refer to this writing. Conchita arrived at Morelia on October 13, 1935, in the afternoon, as the train was late. Because of the religious persecution, the services were offered in private chapels. She found the Blessed Sacrament placed in a small room converted into a chapel and called it the "Little Cave," where the Beloved was hidden. The retreat took place from October 14 to 26. Conchita added to these texts many other meditations of the Archbishop on the mystical incarnation and the spiritual orientations she received from the Lord on the "Crusade of Victim Souls on Behalf of Families" during the days which followed.
[90] Every volume of Conchita's retreats with Archbishop Martínez has a characteristic style according to her interior states or needs at the time. Basically, all of these volumes are composed of the Archbishop's meditation and of Conchita's reflection. In some places, she casually intermingled parts of the Archbishop's meditations with her own responses, making her words and insights sometimes a bit difficult to present in a systematic way. In this volume, we present the Archbishop's meditation in the first section under each date and then Conchita's reflection following this in order to present the context with clarity even though sometimes we depart from the original style of her *Account of Conscience* according to the Spanish edition.
[91] Cf. Rm 8:26.
[92] Cf. *AC* 22, 207: February 8, 1907.
[93] Conchita was aware that the Holy Spirit had been her "spiritual director." She wrote in her *Account of Conscience* (1, 222-223; February 1894): "Alone, with evident graces of the Holy Spirit who, in reality, has guided me during the greater part of my life, I arrived at the point where I stagnated, stopped, until God permitted me to find a soul who could understand me and guide me. May He be blessed! Oh how can I thank the God of my heart enough for such a great benefit?"
[94] "The Dark Night," verse 8, in *The Collected Works of St. John of the Cross*, translated by Kieran Kavanaugh, OCD, and Otilio Rodriguez, OCD, revised edition, 1991.
[95] The days from October 14 to October 18 do not have consistent divisions in Conchita's writings and her reflections are written down in a different volume. Some of the meditations written by Archbishop Martínez were considered by Conchita on different days, not necessarily in chronological order. This does not, however, change their basic content. From October 19 onwards, the texts of the Archbishop's meditations and Conchita's reflections upon them correspond clearly.
[96] By virtue of the grace of the mystical incarnation, Conchita becomes "Jesus' mother" in a spiritual way.
[97] Absinthe is a bitter, yellowish-green, liquor which is made of wormwood and other aromatic ingredients. Here it is symbolic of the bitterness of Jesus' interior suffering.
[98] This term is very important in Archbishop Martínez' meditations on the mystical incarnation and so the following explanation is presented. The term δώξα, in general has

different meanings. The important one for us is *praise, honor, glory; magnificence, excellence, preeminence, dignity, grace, beauty; majesty* in the sense of absolute perfection of the Deity; a most glorious condition, a most exalted state. In the biblical sense, *glory* expresses the divine holiness and splendor manifested and communicated. Its presence in the midst of His people in the tabernacle in the desert (Ex 40:34-35), and in the temple (1 K 8:11) is a privilege of Israel (Rm 9:4). Sin had deprived Israel of this glory (Ezk 10:18-19). The new community will be established when the glory of God (Yahweh) returns to the temple (Ezk 43:2, 4, 5; 44:4). Besides its external sense, the word *glory* came to have an ethical significance, because, like the holiness with which it is associated in Is 6, it is related to Yahweh, who is viewed as an ethical being. As holiness gradually loses its physical sense of apartness, and comes to describe moral purity, so glory comes to have a moral sense. The term is applied to Christ to describe His royal majesty when He comes to set up His kingdom. In 1 Cor 2:8 Christ is "the Lord of glory." In 2 Cor 4:6, "the knowledge of the glory of God" we find "in the face of Jesus Christ," so that "the light of the good news of the glory of Christ, who is the image of God" may shine upon us. All people, because of sin, "are far from the glory of God" (Rm 3:23), so this glory is communicated to believers through Christ. All faithful followers of Jesus shall share in the glory of the Messianic kingdom. The term describes the essential nature, the perfection of the Deity, and is shared by others because they are made partakers of the divine nature.

99 Ph 4:13.

100 "The third love" was the theme of the retreat which Conchita made under the direction of Archbishop Luis M. Martínez in 1931. The term "the third love" means a kind of very high and close union, because the soul – transformed into Christ by the mystical incarnation – shares in the union of Jesus with the Father and the Holy Spirit. So the experience of Conchita is an effect and development of the grace of the mystical incarnation, which introduced her into the unity of God, and made her experience Trinitarian love. This term implies that there are two previous degrees of love. Both previous degrees are supernatural and divine in their origin and their goal. The first degree is still marked by the human way of loving, which is still under the domain of reason. The soul receives from God a way of loving which resembles earthly love, even though its origin is high and divine. Because of the divine invasion, the soul is called to let itself love God. The second degree of loving, rather, is passive, under the motion of the Holy Spirit, and the soul just lets itself be loved. This second degree of loving can grow in various stages, for love has no measure. When the soul arrives at that degree of loving in which it places no obstacles in the way of receiving God's love, God communicates love to the soul as fully as possible here on earth, according to His designs. This is spoken of as the third love. Aware of her smallness and poverty, Conchita learned to live within this unitive and loving dynamism of the Three Divine Persons. St. John of the Cross explains in his *Spiritual Canticle* XXXIX, 2, this ineffable mystery of God's love.

101 Gradually Conchita became aware of the central grace of her life, the mystical incarnation. On August 4, 1934, she wrote: "Oh, Jesus of my soul and of my life! With the help of Your grace, I promise You never to doubt Your eternal love. With what predilection You have always loved my poor soul. How could I doubt that a king had visited me if my hands are full of pearls?" (*AC* 59, 304-307).

102 Very frequently, Archbishop Martínez used to preach on "misery," so that he was called "the doctor of misery." This doctrine was not merely theory for him, as he had learned it at the "hard school of his own existence" (cf. J.G. Treviño, *Monseñor Martínez*, Biografía, Ed. México: Ed. La Cruz, 1986, pp. 96-100). The Archbishop expresses the

Endnotes

reason for which he loves misery: "I do not love forms of miseries because they are closely related to sin; I love them, because when exposed to the Divine Light, they become the brightness of Divine Truth, as they hide from all gazing, even from me, the treasure which dazzles; I love them, because they remind me of the loving veil which covered the Beloved in His mortal life, and which is retained in His Eucharistic life. I will try not to look at my wretchedness, so that I will see only Him" (cf. L.M. Martínez, *Notas íntimas* [*Intimate Notes*], México: Ed. La Cruz, 1971, p. 252).

[103] At the end of her life Conchita makes herself an echo of the Blessed Virgin Mary in her "Magnificat": "Everything which is good in me I received from Him... and my soul glorifies the Lord for He has done great and marvelous things in my poor soul" (*AC* 65, 275-276; October 10, 1936).

[104] Astonished by the insights of these daily meditations, Conchita copied parts of them in her reflections in order to assimilate them better. We have not repeated the texts as they are given in full in the Archbishop's meditations.

[105] Conchita's son, Manuel, entered the Society of Jesus, and her daughter, Concepción Armida Cabrera, made vows as a member of the Congregation of the Sisters of the Cross of the Sacred Heart of Jesus.

[106] Francisco, Carlos, Manuel, Ignacio, Pablo, Salvador, Concepción, Guadalupe and Pedro Armida Cabrera.

[107] In the *Spiritual Canticle*, stanza 14, 12-15, St. John of the Cross explains the mysterious voice of God: "The third property of which the soul is now conscious in the roaring torrents of the Beloved is a spiritual sound and voice overpowering all other sounds and voices in the world. But the voice is a spiritual voice, unattended by material sounds or the pain and torment of them, but rather with majesty, power, might, delight, and glory: it is, as it were, a voice, an infinite interior sound which endows the soul with power and might. The spiritual voice is the effect on the soul of the audible voice, as material sounds strike the ear, and impress the meaning of it on the mind. This voice is infinite, because, as I have said, it is God who communicates Himself, speaking in the soul; but He adapts Himself to each soul, uttering the voice of strength according to its capacity, in majesty and joy."

[108] The following part belongs to October 15, according to the Spanish edition.

[109] Conchita first perceived the grace of the Father's gaze in 1894, when, after receiving Communion in the Church of Our Lady of Mount Carmel in San Luis Potosí, she suddenly heard the Lord say to her, "The Father is gazing on you." As she recounted later, those words made her tremble with awe and filled her with love, though she told nobody at the time about it, and did not even know that it was Jesus who had spoken those words and caused her to understand that this divine gaze communicated to her the germ of the grace of the mystical incarnation (*AC* 64, 14-15; *AC* 23, 84-89; *AC* 25, 189-190; cf. *AC* 46, 188-190). From the first day of the retreat in 1926, Archbishop Martínez made Conchita conscious of the germ of grace contained in those words of the Lord to her. Again in 1935, toward the end of Conchita's life on earth, she meditated on that inexhaustible mystery of the Father's gaze, as she had done so fruitfully since that grace had been imparted.

[110] In the original Spanish Conchita used the expression *Conjunto-Unidad*.

[111] Addressing Archbishop Martínez.

[112] In Conchita's writings, we discover repeatedly what we could call "the limits of mystical expression." She feels unable to express what she wants to. Trying to express her experience of God's holiness, for example, she writes: "How beautiful is holiness, the thrice holy God... the most pure and immense source of charity, of true perfection!

[...] When Jesus communicates these things to me, what a breadth of ideas; my understanding embraces immensities. I cannot express them exactly, because even should I attempt to describe them further, I see them as so concrete and yet so pale, that I am sorry I cannot explain them to the extent and with the clarity with which I grasp them when I receive them" (AC 6, 168-169).

[113] The Lord makes Conchita understand that the Father is constantly at work: "The Father constantly generates the Word in Himself, and is at work in the mystery of the Trinity, because there is no past in Him, but everything is present and active. He eternally delights in Himself in the unity of the Trinity. He desires to attract everything towards this unity. For this reason, He established His one Church, where all souls should be united in the Word through the Holy Spirit. The mission of the priest is to bring souls to this unity" (AC 50, 87-88; December 29, 1927).

[114] She refers to the grace of the mystical incarnation.

[115] Archbishop's Martínez's quotations from Scripture are closely interwoven with his text and we have chosen for the translation the *New American Bible*, but when the meaning of the Spanish text is not reflected in this version, we use different translations to reflect more closely the Spanish text, and it is marked in the note. Psalm 2:7, *Revised Standard Version*, CD-Bible Works 6.

[116] This quotation is actually from the Archbishop's meditation prepared for October 16 according to the Spanish edition, but Conchita cites it on October 15 in her reflection. She probably received the text of the first meditations in one block.

[117] Col 1:17.

[118] Jn 3:16.

[119] Jn 8:29.

[120] From the texts we could have quoted referring to the Works of the Cross, we have chosen the one dated September 17, 1927, in which the Lord said to Conchita: "My Works of the Cross have been sent to the world most especially to glorify the Trinity. Its entire spirit, all its parts, if studied carefully, are directed to that end" (AC 48, 364-365). And one of 1909: "The Works of the Cross are given in order to renew the world, that is, to renew in all social classes the spirit of Jesus Christ, the Incarnate Word, sacrificed out of love; to renew the spirit of the Cross, which has been extinguished in hearts. For this reason, the Cross is presented to the world once more, symbolizing the suffering which purifies, sanctifies and saves, and it is safeguarded by the Holy Spirit who is love" (AC 33, 272).

[121] Jn 8:29; Lk 22:42.

[122] See note 89.

[123] See note 109.

[124] Cf. AC 8, 263: March 2, 1897. See note 31.

[125] Cf. AC 8, 269-274: January 29, 1897.

[126] Cf. AC 6, 261-267: November 16, 1895.

[127] He was referring to the feast of the Annunciation on March 25.

[128] Cf. AC 9, 33-34: February 17, 1897.

[129] Conchita was in the habit of imposing bodily mortifications on herself as an aid to her spiritual growth. One of these frequently repeated mortifications involved prostrating herself on a bed of thorny branches, which she called "roses." See, for example, AC 3, 46.

[130] The spousal symbolism is often found in the experience and language of the mystics,

Endnotes

and it expresses the reciprocal spiritual love between God and the soul. It is not uncommon for the mystics, who have been awakened to this spiritual fire, to speak of "betrothal" and "spiritual marriage." In the spiritual journey of Conchita, "spiritual marriage" occurred in the course of extraordinary bestowals of grace. Of course, this spiritual reality is present in germ at baptism, by which the person becomes, in truth, a spouse of Christ. But the promise of union she received in the betrothal reached a fruition as "spiritual marriage" in the soul of Conchita on February 9, 1897, when she became so transformed into Christ and so joined to Him as to have become His permanent and total possession. From that moment, she enjoyed habitual experiences of the Trinity and received many insights concerning the Incarnation, the Eucharist and the Church.

131 This little church, called Portiuncula (the "little portion"), was a favorite place where St. Francis (1182-1226) retired and spent much time in prayer. At that time it was abandoned and in poor condition; it was subsequently repaired by Francis in 1207. Here, while the saint was praying, Christ appeared to him in a vision (1221), and bade him go to the pope, who would grant a plenary indulgence to all sincere penitents who would devoutly visit that church. Pope Honorius III confirmed this by a bull dated November 29, 1221. The original indulgence obtained by St. Francis, was confined to the day itself, the 2nd of August and to the chapel. Now it is extended to all the chapels and churches of the Franciscan Order. The original little church, or the Portiuncula as it is called, is now in the center of the spacious church annexed to the large Franciscan friary.

132 Cf. AC 22, 154-156: March 23, 1906 and 171-172: March 25, 1906.

133 Fr. Maximino Ruiz y Flores (1875-1949) was ordained a priest on July 20, 1901, and became Bishop of Chiapas in 1914. In 1920 he renounced his office to take vows as a Missionary of the Holy Spirit. He was Conchita's spiritual director from 1905 until 1912 and also at that time a chaplain of the Sisters of the Cross in their community at Mirto Street, Colonia Santa María de la Ribera, Mexico City, familiarly called Oasis.

134 See note 55.

135 In 1909, Conchita received from the Lord a new aspect of the Spirituality of the Cross to be lived by the Sisters of the Cross of the Sacred Heart of Jesus and the Missionaries of the Holy Spirit. In general, all members of the Works of the Cross should be intimately united with Jesus, with His redemptive sacrifice, as if to be His Blood. As His Blood is poured forth on the altars, so their blood, together with His, should be offered on behalf of those in need. Through this intimate union they should be transformed into Christ and offer themselves in union with Him in perpetual oblation. In 1917, Conchita was also invited to imitate Mary in the mystery of her solitude.

136 The Covenant of Love with the Sacred Heart of Jesus, founded on November 30, 1909, joins lay people who commit themselves to seeking perfection within their lay vocations according to the Spirituality of the Cross.

137 The Fraternity of Christ the Priest, one of the five branches of the Works of the Cross, was founded on January 19, 1912, for bishops and priests who seek to live the Spirituality of the Cross.

138 The Venerable Servant of God Bishop Ramón Ibarra y González (1853-1917) was the first Archbishop of Puebla, and the spiritual director of Conchita from October of 1912 up to his death in February of 1917.

139 She went on pilgrimage to the Holy Land and Rome in 1913.

140 The founding of the Works of the Cross (five associations: for lay people, priests and consecrated persons who seek to live the Spirituality of the Cross) was marked by

many difficulties and problems, which Conchita managed to resolve with the help of many bishops.

[141] In 1913, during her pilgrimage to Rome, Conchita received new insights on the mystical incarnation in the Church of the "Gesù."

[142] The Congregation of the Missionaries of the Holy Spirit was founded by Fr. Felix Rougier on December 25, 1914, in Mexico City.

[143] *Confidences*, written in 1927-1930, contain the beautiful message of the Lord to priests, in which He urges them to holiness and transformation into Christ. Jesus explains the dignity of the priesthood and all the dangers which priests undergo.

[144] See note 100.

[145] *AC* 53, 49-52: 1928.

[146] From 1932 until 1937, Conchita lived "in intimate relation with the Father." It is the characteristic feature of the summit of her spiritual life to love Jesus, but only as the Father loves Him.

[147] The offering made on August 4, 1934 (*AC* 61, 304-307).

[148] Bishop Leopoldo Ruiz y Flores (1865-1941) held many important ecclesiastical positions as Bishop of León and Linares, Archbishop of Morelia and Apostolic Delegate during the Mexican persecution. He was the outstanding protector of the Works of the Cross and the counselor of Conchita. Fr. Tomás Ipiña, S.J., examined the spiritual graces of Conchita.

[149] She refers to Archbishop Luis M. Martínez Rodríguez.

[150] Cf. Jn 4:14.

[151] Conchita received the central grace of her life, the mystical incarnation, on March 25, 1906, the Solemnity of the Annunciation of Our Lord. A few days later, Conchita wrote: "I can see, touch and feel the dynamic words of Jesus by the increase of light and strength. Jesus, may my every breath say to You: 'Jesus, Savior of mankind, save them!' I cannot doubt the grace which I received when I feel You, touch You, when Your life is mine" (*AC* 22, 262-265).

[152] Conchita and the members of the Works of the Cross are called to contemplate and imitate the mystery of the solitude of the Mother of God. After the Ascension of Jesus, when the life of Mary attained its height and fullness, which were of benefit to the Church, her solitude was the most perfect association with the redemptive work of Christ. From 1917 until 1925, Conchita became acutely aware of belonging to the Church, of her life on behalf of the Church and priests. Participating in the mystery of Mother Church, she would become the spiritual mother of many (*AC* 41, 39-43).

[153] Two days after having received the grace of the mystical incarnation, on March 27, 1906, Conchita was invited by the Lord to penetrate the interior mystery of the Church, considered as God's priestly people: "From the moment of My Incarnation I acquired graces, and I want you, transformed into Me, that is, living from My life, to do nothing but what issues from this grace from now on" (*AC* 22, 203-205). There is only one priesthood, that of Christ, but all the baptized share in it, because the spiritual priesthood is the characteristic and charism of the ecclesial community. The ministerial priesthood perpetuates Christ's oblation in bringing about the Eucharist in *persona Christi* and in this manner renders possible for the whole Church the exercise of the spiritual priesthood. Conchita was invited to participate in the mystical priesthood of the baptized by the practice of the virtues and the offering of sacrifices for the sake of the Church.

[154] See note 100.

[155] In his letter to Conchita of March 18, 1934, Archbishop Martínez wrote: "How great is

Endnotes

the grace of March 25 when you are aware that it is not only for March 25, but for all eternity! The 25th of March has not passed, will never pass. At every moment, the Holy Spirit possesses the beloved soul and forms Jesus in it through the Father's fruitfulness and, at every moment, the gaze of this Divine Person sees in your soul the Son with whom He is eternally pleased. The joy, love and thanksgiving of that unforgettable day must be constant and eternal. Is it not true that it is worth nothing leaving the bliss and peace of this divine world, to go in search of the petty and fleeting vicissitudes of this life? Just as God does not cease to realize in your soul the mystery of the 25th of March, you must not stop loving Him as you loved Him: in the self-annihilation of humility, love and happiness" (*AC* 63, 111-113).

[156] *AC* 61, 33-34; 63, 69-70.

[157] Conchita copied in this reflection large sections of the Archbishop's meditation which we do not repeat here. Part of this quotation belongs to the Archbishop's meditation for October 18 in the Spanish edition. See note 104 (October 15).

[158] Addressing her spiritual director.

[159] Addressing Archbishop Martínez.

[160] Conchita was in the habit of imposing bodily mortifications upon herself as an aid to her spiritual growth. One of her repeated mortifications involved prostrating herself on a bed of thorny branches, which she called "roses."

[161] Cf. Mt 3:13-17; 17:1-8.

[162] 1 Jn 5:11.

[163] See note 55.

[164] 1 Cor 6:17.

[165] Sg 4:9.

[166] Cf. Concepción Cabrera de Armida, *Loving with the Holy Spirit*, Retreat Directed by Bishop Luis M. Martínez, 1926, Editrice Vaticana 2007.

[167] St. Thérèse of Lisieux, *The Story of a Soul*, TAN Books and Publishers, 1997, p. 153.

[168] Rm 8:14.

[169] Gal 2:20.

[170] See note 104.

[171] Referring to the Cross of the Apostolate.

[172] Heb 9:14.

[173] Ps 123:2.

[174] Mt 4:1.

[175] Cf. Lk 10:21.

[176] Heb 9:14.

[177] Rm 8:14.

[178] Referring to the members of the Works of the Cross.

[179] She is addressing Archbishop Martínez.

[180] Conchita is here reaching the limits of human language in trying to express the inexpressible with regard to the generation of the Word from the Father. Clearly, she is not denying that the Word is "begotten, not made" as we proclaim in the Creed.

[181] Francisco Armida García died on September 17, 1901, and Conchita received from the Lord the grace to talk to him.

¹⁸² Gal 2:20.
¹⁸³ Archbishop Martínez refers to the procession of the Divine Persons in the Trinity. See, e.g., St. Thomas Aquinas, *Summa Theologica* I, Question 27, Art. 1-5.
¹⁸⁴ Jn 19:30: "It is fulfilled."
¹⁸⁵ Cf. 1 Jn 5:7-8.
¹⁸⁶ Archbishop Martínez refers to the retreat of 1934, "To Offer Jesus to Be Crucified."
¹⁸⁷ Concepción Cabrera de Armida contemplated the Cross of the Apostolate in a vision (January of 1894). It is the symbol that sums up the Spirituality of the Cross, which animates and gives life to the Works of the Cross. Conchita described this vision: "I was in deep prayer when, suddenly, I saw an immense image of living light. Its center was brilliant. How strange – a white light! Above this immensity of light, with thousands of rays of what seemed to be gold and fire, I saw a dove with its wings extended, somehow covering that torrent of light. I saw everything very clearly, since it was light. Two or three days later, again I saw a white dove in the midst of the great fire, which had clear and very brilliant rays of light. In the center was the dove, again with wings extended, and below it, at the far end of the immense light, a very large Cross with a Heart at the center-point, between the extended arms" (*Vida* [Life] I, 211-214).
¹⁸⁸ Cf. *AC* 33, 270-273, November 12, 1909: "How beautiful is your mission and that of your spiritual children, My daughter, to be My blood on behalf of the Church, priests and the whole universe. It is not that I am lacking in charity and immolation, but rather I offer Myself in what I am to the Father on behalf of all men: those who love Me and those who hate Me."
¹⁸⁹ Cf. Heb 9:14.
¹⁹⁰ Jn 12:24.
¹⁹¹ Heb 5:1.
¹⁹² Gal 3:28.
¹⁹³ 1 Cor 15:28.
¹⁹⁴ Addressing Archbishop L.M. Martínez.
¹⁹⁵ Conchita frequently uses the Spanish word *corteza*, literally, the bark of a tree, to indicate external human limitations.
¹⁹⁶ On May 28, 1912, Conchita wrote in her *Account of Conscience* eight points on the mode of transformation into Christ which the Lord communicated to her: (1) I did not come to be served, but to serve… (2) Learn from Me, for I am meek and humble of heart… (3) My food is to do the will of My Father… (4) I humbled Myself, becoming obedient unto death, even death on a cross… (5) I spent nights in prayer and being in agony, I prayed all the more earnestly… (6) They picked up stones to stone Me, but I never flagged in the mission which My Father entrusted to Me… (7) I passed through the world doing good… (8) Come to Me, all you… unlimited charity… (*AC* 36, 106-108).
¹⁹⁷ Cf. Jn 8:26, 40.
¹⁹⁸ See notes 77 and 143.
¹⁹⁹ In the letter of April 4, 1929, Archbishop Martínez wrote to Conchita: "Neither you, nor I, nor anybody knows the treasure which your spiritual writings contain. Many prepared persons and many years will be necessary to exploit those treasures to the full" (cf. *AC* 54, 78-79).
²⁰⁰ Cf. 1 Cor 15:28.
²⁰¹ St. Thérèse of Lisieux, *The Story of a Soul*, p. 167.

Endnotes

202 Addressing Archbishop Martínez.
203 She refers to Mother Julia Navarrete Guerrero who wanted to establish one community of her Congregation in Mexico City.
204 Conchita copied here a part of the Archbishop's meditation (see notes 104, 157). We reproduce here only this section, which Conchita commented on in this reflection.
205 Members of the Works of the Cross.
206 It is the *Sanctus* hymn addressed to God as the thrice holy, e.g. the trisagion of Is 6:3; Rv 4:8.
207 Here Archbishop Martínez refers to the concept of holiness as applied to God in the ethical and moral sense: pure, sinless, upright. The notion of holiness is used in the Old Testament in two distinct senses. Firstly, in the more general sense of separation from all that is human and earthly. It thus denotes the absolute majesty, and awfulness of the Creator as distinct from His creatures. Secondly, it denotes man's holiness, which is a share and reflection of the holiness of God. The injunction, "Be holy, for I am holy" (Lv 11:44), plainly implies an ethical imperative. The distinctive feature of the New Testament idea of holiness is that the external, or ritual, aspect of it has almost entirely disappeared, and the ethical meaning has become supreme. Jesus brings to perfection the concept of religion and morality, according to which men are cleansed or defiled, not by anything outward, but by the thoughts of their hearts (Mt 15:17-20), and God is to be worshipped wherever men seek Him in spirit and in truth (Jn 4:21-24). The Christian Church, in succeeding to Israel's privileges, becomes a holy nation (1 P 2:9), and the Christian individual, as one of the elect people, becomes a holy man or woman (Col 3:12). In Paul's usage, all baptized persons are "saints," however far they may still be from the saintly character (1 Cor 1:2, 14 with 5:1ff). The Holy Spirit has taken up His abode in the heart of every baptized person and a work of positive sanctification is going on in those who cooperate with His grace.
208 1 Jn 1:5.
209 Ex 3:14: "I am who am."
210 Ws 7:26.
211 Rm 8:32. Latin quotation from *Latin Vulgate*.
212 The retreat ended on October 26, 1935. In any case, Conchita remained in Morelia, in the Archbishop's residence, continuing her meditations until November 18 and that is why all these meditations are included in this book. They continue to be deeply related to the grace of the mystical incarnation, even though, at times, they are specifically dedicated to the Crusade of Victim Souls on behalf of Families. After the retreat, Conchita visited the Missionaries of the Holy Spirit, the Madrigal Family, and stayed until the 28th of November in the community of the Sisters of the Cross, her spiritual daughters. On her way back to Mexico City, she also visited the community of the Sisters of the Cross in Leon.
213 Mk 7:37.
214 Cf. 2 Cor 4:10.
215 Lk 24:32.
216 Referring to the *Summa Theologica*: Questions on virtues and gifts of the Holy Spirit.
217 Referring to the Easter hymn: "Amor sacerdos immolat."
218 Sg 5:16.
219 Jacques Bénigne Bossuet (September 25, 1627 - April 12, 1704), the Bishop of Meaux,

was the most eloquent and influential preacher and spokesman for the rights of the French church. He is now chiefly remembered for his literary works. He was a devoted bishop who lived mostly among his flock, preaching, and busied himself with charitable organizations and directing his clergy. His excursions outside the diocese were in relation to the theological controversies of his time: Gallicanism, Protestantism, and Quietism.

220 Cf. Heb 4:12.
221 Sg 1:13.
222 Heb 12:2.
223 Jn 17:13.
224 Cf. Jn 17:19.
225 St. Thérèse of Lisieux, *The Story of a Soul*, p. 147.
226 This was typical of the ascetic spiritual practices of her times. She shows great evolution in that aspect later on, even though she was always very penitent.
227 St. Polycarp, 166 A.D., martyr and bishop of Smyrna, was one of the most illustrious of the apostolic Fathers. He embraced Christianity very young, about the year 80, and was a disciple of the Apostles, in particular of St. John the Evangelist, and was constituted by him bishop of Smyrna, probably before his banishment to Patmos in 96, so that he governed that important see seventy years. Cf. Butler's *Lives of the Saints*, on CD-Rom, Harmony Media, Inc.
228 A nuptial song or poem in honor or praise of a bride and bridegroom.
229 2 M 7:27-29.
230 Cf. The retreat of 1934.
231 2 Cor 11:29.
232 2 Cor 12:15.
233 St. Thérèse of Lisieux, *The Story of a Soul*, p. 171.
234 Sg 8:6.
235 Jn 10:10.
236 Mt 3:17; 17:5.
237 Ps 2:7.
238 Jn 12:28.
239 Jn 12:23.
240 Dom Paul Delatte, O.S.B. (1848-1937) was the third Abbot of Solesmes.
241 Cf. Gal 4:19.
242 Cf. Ph 4:1.
243 Cf. Ph 1:8.
244 1 Th 2:7.
245 St. Thérèse of Lisieux, *The Story of a Soul*, p. 167.
246 1 Cor 15:28.
247 Ps 30:12.
248 Jesus frequently called Conchita "mother," a grace flowing from the mystical incarnation.
249 Mt 19:21.
250 French spiritual writer who lived from 1801-1900.

Endnotes

[251] Retreat on the third love on December 25, 1931, until January 14, 1932. See also note 100.
[252] 1 Jn 4:18.
[253] Mt 23:9.
[254] 1 Cor 4:15.
[255] Cf. Eph 3:15.
[256] See notes 167 and 201.
[257] Cf. Eph 3:15.
[258] Lk 1:48.
[259] Cf. Ps 104:32.
[260] Gn 1:31.
[261] St. John of the Cross, *The Spiritual Canticle*, stanza 5.
[262] Ps 138:6, *The New Jerusalem Bible*, CD-Bible Works.
[263] Eph 3:17.
[264] Cf. Ps 110:3.
[265] Cf. Ws 7:26.
[266] Cf. St. John of the Cross, *Spiritual Canticle*, stanza 32.
[267] *Ibid.*, stanza 12.
[268] *Ibid.*, stanza 32.
[269] Sg 1:5.
[270] *Spiritual Canticle*, stanza 33.
[271] Gal 2:20.
[272] Conchita first perceived the grace of the Father's gaze in 1894. See note 109.
[273] 2 Cor 9:15.
[274] Cf. Heb 11:1.
[275] Jn 21:7.
[276] Cf. Est 5:2.
[277] Addressing Archbishop Martínez.
[278] Mrs. María Videgaray de Macouzet, Sara Iturbide de Laris Rubio, and Concepción Villaseñor de Alvarado.
[279] Jean-Baptiste-Henri Lacordaire (May 12, 1802-Nov. 21, 1861) was a Dominican priest and one of the leading ecclesiastics in the Roman Catholic revival in France following the Napoleonic period. His sermons appealed to Parisian intellectuals and in 1835 the Archbishop of Paris invited him to preach at Notre Dame, where his lectures became known.
[280] *Spiritual Canticle*, stanza 32.
[281] Mt 5:8, the *New Jerusalem Bible*.
[282] Cf. Eph 1:18.
[283] Ps 36:10.
[284] Conchita had always desired to enter the cloistered Sisters of the Cross of the Sacred Heart of Jesus, which she had founded and which the Lord referred to as the Oasis.
[285] Ws 8:16.
[286] Eph 3:18.

287 Eph 3:15, *The New Jerusalem Bible.*
288 Eph 3:19.
289 She is addressing Archbishop Martínez.
290 On May 4, 1913, the Lord said to Conchita: "The Works of the Cross are to unite the sacrifice of many souls in the one, only sacrifice of your Jesus; they are to unite all immolations in My one immolation, so that they may have the value of unity in God, thus becoming divinized. All devotions which do not unify by charity and are not simplified in unity will make noise, but will not have value for heaven. This is why the Holy Spirit, the principal Protector of the Works of the Cross, comes to shelter all hearts beneath His shadow, breath and life, making them one with Mine, and transforming them in unity in order thus to merit heaven. The Works of the Cross are works of love because their author is the Holy Spirit, whose aim is to unite souls in My Heart, nailed to the Cross, by voluntary sacrifice and to pass from My Heart to purest union with the Holy Spirit and, through Him, with the whole Trinity. These Works will glorify the whole Trinity, as I have told you, thus fulfilling their goal" (*AC* 38, 180-182).
291 Conchita refers to Fr. Felipe Torres Hurtado, M.Sp.S., imprisoned because of the religious persecution.
292 Ps 10:14.
293 She refers to Archbishop Martínez.
294 Cf. Mt 22:37.
295 Pope Pius XI.
296 Bishop Leopoldo Ruiz y Flores.
297 Fr. Félix of Jesus Rougier, Edmundo Iturbide, José Guadalupe Treviño, Tomás Fallon, Pablo Guzmán, Félix María Álvarez, Vicente Méndez, Manuel Hernández, Ángel Oñate, Missionaries of the Holy Spirit.
298 M. Manuela Cacho Ordozgoiti, M. Catalina García Martínez, M. Octavia Rivero Fernández, M. Concepción García González, M. Guadalupe Monterrubio Poza and M. Dolores Alcorta Pérez Palacios, Sisters of the Cross of the Sacred Heart of Jesus.
299 Fr. Primitivo Cabrera Arias, S.J.
300 Conchita's son Manuel Armida Cabrera, S.J.
301 See note 187.
302 The hymn of the Seraphim invoking God as the thrice holy in Is 6:3.
303 See note 98.
304 Jn 10:34; Ps 82:6.
305 1 Cor 15:28.
306 Archbishop Martínez.
307 See November 5 and note 100.
308 See note 55.
309 M. Manuela Cacho Ordozgoiti, Superior General of the Sisters of the Cross at that time.
310 Fr. Felix Rougier, the founder of the Missionaries of the Holy Spirit; Fr. José Guadalupe Treviño, M.Sp.S; San Felipe was a national shrine of reparation in Mexico City in the custody of the Missionaries of the Holy Spirit.
311 *Directed Retreats* of Concepción Cabrera de Armida, unpublished work of 4 volumes, which contain the 54 retreats made by Conchita during her life.

WORKS BY ARCHBISHOP LUIS M. MARTÍNEZ AND CONCEPCIÓN CABRERA DE ARMIDA

Luis M. Martínez, *Secrets of the Interior Life*. Sophia Institute Press, Manchester, 2003.

Luis M. Martínez, *True Devotion of the Holy Spirit* (former title: *The Sanctifier*). Sophia Institute Press, Manchester, 2000.

Luis M. Martínez, *When Jesus Sleeps*. Sophia Institute Press, Manchester, 2000.

Luis M. Martínez, *Only Jesus*. John Paul II Institute of Christian Spirituality, 2001.

Luis M. Martínez, *Spread your Wings*. Ediciones Cimiento, Modesto, CA, 2002.

Luis M. Martínez, *Meditations for Christmas: A Spiritual Retreat as a Preparation for Christmas*. Ediciones Cimiento, Modesto, CA, 2001.

Concepción Cabrera de Armida, *Before the Altar: A Hundred Visits to Jesus in the Blessed Sacrament*. CMJ Marian Publishers, 2001.

Concepción Cabrera de Armida, *I Am: Eucharistic Meditations on the Gospel*. Alba House, 2001.

Concepción Cabrera de Armida, *Irresistibly Drawn to the Eucharist*. Alba House, 2002.

Fr. M.M. Philipon, O.P., *Conchita: A Mother's Spiritual Diary*. Alba House, 1978.

You Belong to the Church. Concepción Cabrera de Armida, Pilgrimage to Rome 1913. Libreria Editrice Vaticana, 1999.

Concepción Cabrera de Armida, *Loving with the Holy Spirit*. Retreat Directed by Bishop Luis M. Martínez, 1926. Libreria Editrice Vaticana, 2007.

Concepción Cabrera de Armida, *A Mother's Letters: A Vision of Faith in Everyday Life*. Alba House, 2004.

Concepción Cabrera de Armida, *Seasons of the Soul*, Alba House, 2005.

Concepción Cabrera de Armida, *Holy Hours*. Alba House, 2006.

Concepción Cabrera de Armida, *Roses and Thorns*. Alba House, 2007.

Concepción Cabrera de Armida, *To My Priests*. Archangel Crusade of Love. Cleveland, 1996.

For Further Information

Religiose della Croce del Sacro Cuore di Gesù
Via Appia Nuova, 1468
00178 Roma, Italia
Tel/Fax: 06-7-934-0094
e-mail: relcroce@pcn.net

Religiosas de la Cruz del Sagrado Corazón de Jesús
Francisco Sosa, 105
Col. Coyoacán
04000 Mexico, D.F., Mexico
Tel: 554-0011; Fax: 554-0335
e-mail: cimientocoyo@hotmail.com

Sisters of the Cross of the Sacred Heart of Jesus
1320 Maze Blvd.
Modesto, CA 95351 USA
Tel/Fax: 1-209-526-3525

Missionaries of the Holy Spirit
Christ the Priest Vicariate
U. S. Headquarters
P.O. Box 956
Garden Grove, CA 92842-0956 USA
Tel. (714) 534-5476
Fax. (714) 534-5184